Two And A Half Deserters

and how the turmoil of war brought three combatants
from opposing sides to the bond of friendship

The Reverend Dr Andrew Sangster has degrees in Law, Theology
and History; he is the author of two biographies, two history books,
a school text book and two books of humour. He was ordained as
an Anglican priest in 1969, served in parishes here and overseas,
became a Headmaster, before returning to work in the Church.
While researching for his biography of Field-Marshal Kesselring,
he came upon this incredible account of how two English soldiers,
one time friends, had deserted and met again in Italy behind enemy
lines. There they met a Waffen-SS soldier, still a wanted war
criminal, and the circumstances that led to them forming a lifelong
friendship.

By the same Author –

Field Marshal Kesselring

From Nazi Thug To British Mayor

Diary of a Parish Priest

Tales Out of Church

Pathway To Establishment

Debating and Public Speaking

Two And A Half Deserters

and how the turmoil of war brought three combatants from opposing sides to the bond of friendship

Andrew Sangster

Arena Books

First published in 2015 by Arena Books

Arena Books
6 Southgate Green
Bury St. Edmunds
IP33 2BL

www.arenabooks.co.uk
Distributed in America by Ingram International, One Ingram Blvd., PO Box
3006, La Vergne, TN 37086-1985, USA.

Andrew Sangster
    Two And A Half Deserters and how the turmoil of war brought three
        Combatants from opposing sides to the bond of friendship

British Library cataloguing in Publication Data. A catalogue record for this
Book is available from the British Library.

ISBN-13   978-1-909421-60-8

BIC classifications:- BGH, BK, HBLW, HBW, HBWQ.

Printed and bound by Lightning Source UK

Cover design
by Jason Anscomb

Typeset in
Times New Roman

PREFACE

Whilst researching for my book on the *Reappraisal of Field Marshal Albert Kesselring*, I met some interesting people with some extraordinary lives. One a pilot who flew to a Yugoslavian island where he and his navigator buried gold and money for the partisans, they suspected it would never be collected. This pilot sailed to the same island postwar, and returned to the UK a few years later as a very wealthy man. This story should not be told for another hundred years. However, I had another meeting with an ex-serviceman which resulted in this three part biography of two English soldiers and a SS-Waffen soldier who had deserted during the Italian campaign. It is a true account, but as the book will reveal those involved must remain anonymous. One was AWOL all his life, one was a wanted war criminal, and one rose to ecclesiastical prominence. The first part of the book explores their early lives, Horace with a typical Public School background, Harry a lad from the working class, and Wolfgang, the German boy who came from a very different background. Their different social environments, during the 1920s and 1930s explain why their lives panned out for them in the way they did. Their backgrounds typify the lives of so many on both warring sides. It traces their life before and during the war when all three were wounded several times. In their different units they fought in France, Poland, the Balkans, North Africa and Italy. It was sheer coincidence that brought them together during the war, each with a very individual account as to how they appeared in the same part of war-racked Italy face to face. The book finishes with a similar coincidence when many decades after the war they re-discovered one another. Curiously, the conclusion of their account may explain the provenance of the long lost Fabergé egg which turned up mysteriously in America, and sold for twenty million pounds in 2014. Everything in this book happened, but the three main characters must and will remain anonymous.

The Revd Dr Andrew Sangster, February 2015

CONTENTS

HARRY, HORACE & WOLFGANG

I thought long and hard about the risk of having this book written because as a true story it involves illegality, someone technically absent without leave from the army and still in hiding, a war criminal whose current cover would shock the world, and a senior clergyman of the Church of England. I thought such a book could never be written because someone somewhere would recognise the details, and the press would have a field day. I had read a book called "From Nazi Thug to British Mayor," a story of a German POW who stayed in this country, and rose to be Mayor of his town without anyone knowing about his background; they all thought he was Polish. I was contacted by Andrew Sangster, the writer, and after a meeting we started to trust each other, and he explained the one major deceit he had employed to keep his subject anonymous. Because I had been thinking of this venture for a long time I had accumulated notes from the three main characters, a brief biography in the one case and two extensive ones, but I had to promise all three that I would never identify them.

This meant I had to keep my own identity secret because I am well known where I live, as was my father who has just died. My father, a respected clergyman in the Church of England, and I will not even name the position to which he was finally appointed, because even that may start too much speculation, had instructed me that he had to 'be with the Lord' before I thought of publishing. I may be asked why write the account if so much is at stake, but such is the nature of this story I believe it needs to be told. I am a professional man but not a writer, so I have handed the task over to Andrew Sangster, and even if it is not published there will be a record of these three men, a German SS officer, an English officer and an English NCO.

When I handed over the brief biographies, diaries and notes I asked Andrew not to use the real names, to keep as close to the truth as humanly possible, but ensure anonymity was retained. I had made a start, all three men had agreed to write their experiences down in short bursts and send them to one another. The idea was not that they could change the other's account, but understand each other's perspective. This sounded sensible, but did lead to some complications, and I was entirely lost on how to put the thing into a readable narrative.

Signed, M.D, Harry's son.

CHAPTER ONE

Childhood

HORACE 1915-1933

I never liked my name Horace from the moment I arrived at school. The schoolmaster said I would be a fine Latin scholar with a name like that, while most of the boys accused me of being a wimp because my name sounded pretty. It was a prep school by the River Dour in Dover, my home town. My father was a dentist, whom the boys called the town butcher. By the time I had settled in at prep school I was prepared to fight anyone who mocked my father or laughed at my name. The name my father or mother had thought to have me baptised with transpired, on looking back, to have been a brilliant choice. In the playground and elsewhere the name Horace taught me to use my fists and in my little world I became the fastest gun in the west. The bullying stopped, even older boys decided I was not worth the risk; with the benefit of hindsight, I recognise that sometimes I started to throw my weight around too much.

The Headmaster was not overly happy with me, and when I was thirteen my father decided that I would be better off as a boarder at Kings School, Canterbury. There was an immediate and similar reaction to my name, this time the fighting tended to be in the dormitories, and the Housemaster dealt with me using a cane in such a way that I became cautious of authority. The name Horace stopped being an issue when I was made captain of the 1st XV. At 16 years of age I was a big lad, dark haired and with far too much energy. In the holidays I enjoyed my home at St Margaret's Bay being left very much to my own devices. I was an only child, and my mother assisted my father in his surgery, and I was free to roam the cliffs and bays around my home: even now fifty years later, still with a bullet lodged in my head, and having never returned since the war, I can recall every nook and cranny on the beaches and cliffs between Dover and Deal. I had few friends, most of the boys in my area went to Dover County School and a few to a Roger Manwoods in Sandwich, and we simply did not mix.

It seems ludicrous now, but social divisions were prominent. Ironically, as it transpires I can recall meeting and getting to know Harry Fenton who was at Dover County School. It was an Easter break, probably 1930 or 1931 I was looking for gulls' eggs at a place called *Deadman's Gulch*[1] when I became stuck on a ledge some fifty feet above

---

[1] A Bay close to Dover Eastern Arm, only approachable by a risky cliff path.

the rocks. Harry climbed up to see if he could help only to find we were both stuck. A slight overhang was easy to climb up and over, but was too risky when descending. We were alone, and I was conscious he had come to help me and was stuck in the same predicament. We were of the same build, but whilst I was dark haired and dark eyed, Harry had fair hair and piercing blue eyes. We sat and talked as the angry herring gulls wheeled around our heads and kept looking down nervously at the beach below. It was probably fifty foot, and there were huge chalk rocks that would not react like trampolines.

It was Harry's idea. He asked me if I could swim, which I could. We had sat there for two hours and it was clear nobody was going to walk our way and organise help because the tide was coming in.

"We jump," he said, "we jump between the two rocks. When the tide has nearly covered the rocks we jump between them, and we can then swim back to the beach, if we time it right we should be safe."

We were lucky that it was a calm day and the waves were not hammering against the shore; that was usually the case. We sat together for another two hours, and I have to confess I was becoming more and more startled at the prospect of launching myself off the cliff face. I decided I would try and climb down, but if I could not make it I would throw myself out between the rocks; that would give me at least six to eight feet of water deep and twenty feet wide. Just as the water was washing over the last rock Harry stood up on the ledge and jumped. He made it look easy, and not to be outdone I jumped as well. The next thing I could remember was waking up in Victoria Hospital, Dover with a splitting headache. Apparently my aim had not been as good as Harry's and I caught my head a whacking blow on the side of one of the chalkie rocks. I had six stiches, and was told I was lucky to be alive on several counts. First the rock was made from chalk and not granite, secondly Harry had been strong enough to drag me to the shore line, and thirdly he had managed to run for help before the tide covered the rest of the beach.

After a few days I was allowed home where I faced a lecture from my father. He was angry that I had been climbing cliffs in the first place; he thought I was stupid for having a silly interest in bird's eggs, and, to my astonishment did not think much of my company.

"My company?" I asked, "Harry rescued me."

"Some rescue, you could have been killed. Anyway, I went round to where the boy lived and thanked him, and gave him a ten shilling note. His father's a dock labourer you know. I don't spend all that money to send you to a good public school to spend your time with such boys."

I could not reply, my father stood up and left the room, and I was a little stunned at his reaction to Harry. I was about fifteen or sixteen when this happened, and it was the first time I could recall my father being concerned about what he seemed to regard as social cast. It was however a feature of him which I would see more and more as I grew up. The Easter holidays drew to a rapid close and soon I was back at school where, academically, I was beginning to have a tough time. It was during a long hot afternoon of a Latin exam that my mind wandered back to Harry on the cliff ledge, and I reflected I had not seen him since that occasion. I had a few friends at Kings, but Harry was the first boy I had ever met from Dover.

Living up at St Margaret's nearly all the houses were, on reflection, expensive, detached, and many like mine with superb sea views. I knew one next door neighbour was a doctor and the other side was a retired Admiral, but I knew few others and guessed they were all well off or professional. Dover was essentially a working town with a few factories, railways, a local railway station and one serving the port. If I remember correctly one station was called Priory and the other known as the Marine Station. We had an exeat[2] from School on Whitsunday and I made a point of calling on Harry at his home, having found the address in my father's wastepaper bucket. At first I thought, as I cycled down Park Lane, that he lived in quite a respectable area, turned into Salisbury Road which also appeared socially good, but he lived in a small house in Albert Road which connected Salisbury and Masion Dieu Road. I shall never forget knocking on his door, up some steps, only to be told he lived downstairs.

It never occurred to me that in this really small house one family lived upstairs and Harry and his family lived in the basement. Standing there on that Saturday morning I can recall feeling the social chasm of those days. I was asked by a lady wearing rollers and a headscarf to wait on the steps while she went in and shouted for Harry. He did not recognise me at first, and when he did he invited me into what he called their front room. I do not think I was a snob, if I were it was because of my upbringing, and was certainly not intentional, but I was thunderstruck by the smallness of the room, and when Harry told me he had two sisters and a brother, I was equally startled when I heard they all slept in the same room. The room was tidy and clean, although the chairs looked faded and well worn, but it was the sheer size that caught my attention, it was like a doll's house except two adults and four growing children lived here. My bedroom alone was the size of their front room and back room put together, I was the only child and we had five bedrooms.

I spent the day with Harry; he did not have a bike so we walked around the area. He was an altar server in Charlton Church that surprised me; in fact he was the first person I met who went to church on his own volition. At King's Canterbury I had to go every day, but that was

---

[2] Public school language for time away from school; usually a long weekend.

obligatory and it bored me to tears, whereas Harry seemed keen on the Church. It was what they used to call a High Church, nearly Roman Catholic, and Harry was going to be thurifer[3] next day, Whitsunday, and seemed almost excited about the prospect. At the top of his road was a convent between Salisbury Road and Park Avenue, and Harry had a girlfriend who attended the convent school, I met her that day with Harry in Connaught Park and, from today's perspective, somewhat embarrassingly, I was immediately infatuated with her. There was simply something about Edna that was extraordinarily attractive. The Convent was St Ursula's and its entrance was 22 Park Avenue to a house called *Fair View* that I thought most appropriate for Edna.

My friendship with Harry started because he had come to my rescue, and continued because I was obsessed with his girlfriend Edna. We had little else in common, I was something of a loner at home who collected stamps and bird eggs, enjoyed sport at School, and lived in a posh house, or, as Harry described it, in a posh neck of the woods. Harry, when he did visit me at home was made very unwelcome by my mother, who looked him up and down as if checking him for scabies, and quietly warned me not to bring Harry home if my father was there.

If the size of Harry's house had stunned me so did his father who was simply a giant of a man. He must have weighed at least twenty stone and was nearly seven foot high. He was a foreman at the docks and spent most of his spare time at the Red Lion, a small pub just outside Harry's church in Charlton Green. I liked him instantly; he smiled with ease, shook my hand so I thought it would break, and ruffled my hair as if I were six years old again. He was one of those men easy to get along with, who obviously enjoyed life, but someone no one with any sense would pick a fight with unless they were intent on a visit to the hospital. I had a suspicion that Harry would be like him one day, but Harry was actually quite clever and confided in me he had plans to work his way up either in the Post Office or in Local Government. That's when it dawned on me that I had no plans at all apart from hoping to convince Edna to kiss me instead of Harry.

WOLFGANG 1914-1932

I was born in November 1914 in Marktsteft, a municipality in the district of Kitzingen in Bavaria. I gather I was born in Günterstraße, but my infancy was in Hauptstraße, and eventually, and all I can remember was Marktbreiten Straße, which is odd because the last two streets meet

---

[3] Thurifer swings the thurible which burns incense.

one another, and the first crosses them. Strangely the town's only claim to fame today was that it was the birthplace of Albert Kesselring who was to become a Field Marshal under whom, one day, I would serve. My father had been gassed in the Great War and returned home in 1917, but I can barely remember him because he died from the gas in 1920. I remember him in the room at the front of the house, coughing and spluttering, there was a bowl beside his bed that was always full of frothy blood and yellow sputum. I did not understand at the time why he had been gassed, or what gas was, but it was a most dreadful death.

Sometimes a few of his friends would come round and I would overhear them talking. I eventually gathered that the British, who I was told lived on an island in the Atlantic, had done this to my father. After my Dad's funeral, which I was not allowed to attend, my Mum was never happy again. She hated the British, but most especially the French and the Jews. I gathered from her they had caused the war and now we were being bled by them and starved to death. From seven years of age, the year of my father's death I have to confess that my upbringing was one of politics and poverty.

We lived with my Mum's parents in their house, but not altogether; Mum, Hugo, my brother and I lived downstairs, and my grandparents upstairs which they reached by an outdoor staircase they had put in especially. We were poor, really poor, and I can recall that for a time Hugo, a year younger than me, we had to share one pair of shoes, and we lost them one day when fishing by the River Main. I remember my Mum crying because there were no shoes for us. Eventually some of Dad's old soldier friends rallied and Hugo and I had a pair each. Food was a serious problem and Hugo and I would often sneak out and raid an orchard, and go farther afield and bring home some potatoes. My mother was always cross when we appeared with our stolen goods, but she always used them. My mother was a genuinely kind person, attended the local Catholic Church, though later I discovered that my grandparents went to the Lutheran Church. I think that Dad must have been a Roman Catholic and then Mum stayed one when he died.

We felt somewhat remote from the grandparents upstairs and I suspect, though I have never discovered the truth that this remoteness was something to do with Mum being a Catholic. On the other hand if they had not shared their home with us, and gave us the food and money they did we would have been in more serious trouble than we already were. Then, and I think it must have been about 1928 Hugo really managed to get himself into serious trouble. He had a friend called Enoch, not a popular boy being Jewish, but they were caught breaking into a food warehouse. This was not just raiding the local orchards or pinching the odd potatoes from some remote farm, this involved the police. Mum was distraught and once again called upon some of Dad's old friends to help us out. The old comrades convinced the police that if Hugo and I joined the Hitler Youth then there would be no need to take the matter further; the police agreed. I felt somewhat angry that somehow I was part of the bargain, but in fact from my first night in the Hitler Youth (*Hitlerjugend*)[4] I enjoyed the atmosphere. Hugo, strangely, the cause of the problem was not allowed to join because he was not yet fourteen, but had to join German Youth (*Deutsches Jungvolk*) which was a sort of junior section. I heard later that Enoch was badly beaten up in the police station, and a few years later he disappeared altogether.

Mum blamed Enoch for getting Hugo into trouble in the first place, but given Hugo's habits I am not sure Mum was right on that occasion. I remember being a little upset that Mum kept expressing surprise that Hugo had misbehaved, seeming to imply that she considered me the more likely candidate. The thing about the Hitler Youth was that for the first time adults treated us boys very seriously; they made us feel grown up, or growing up for a purpose. When I look back from my later years I realised this was one of the cleverest schemes the regime produced. It gave the next generation something close to veneration to the party, and an uncontrolled self-importance.

I would like to make one thing clear before I progress in this account any further. I am writing this at the turn of the century, over sixty plus years later and I am well aware of what happened in Germany and during the war, I am no longer a member of the NSDAP,[5] and I am acutely aware of the evils this period of German history spawned, and even more aware of how I was caught up in all that happened. Like many Germans of my age I can try and explain how we got caught up in the events, but I am not seeking forgiveness, and am fed up with expecting any understanding. Nor am I one of those Germans who expiates the past by making us appear as the victims and not the perpetrators.

Members of my generation were victims of the Great War and depression, but we became conveyors of brutal evil, and then became criminal and sometimes victims again. I pause to note this on two accounts. The first is to remind the reader and my two English comrades, as we agreed to tell the absolute truth, as we saw it at the time, and to pull no punches. Not how we would like to have seen it as from today, not as we wished we had seen it, but simply as we saw it. I shall therefore be describing events that any civilized person will find revolting, and which I do too, but not at the time they were committed. I shall write as I saw and felt then, not as of today. I feel compelled to add a second note. The

---

[4] Nazi Party –NSDAP – paramilitary organisation from 1922-1945.
[5] National Socialist German Workers Party – proper name for the more usual Nazi.

three of us agreed to write our pieces, section by section, and then read one another's accounts. I have just finished Horace's first section, and pause to reflect how different our lives were. He was wondering how to kiss Edna, and I was getting genuine pleasure in a paramilitary organization. He was bemused by the smallness of Harry's house, we were starving; he and Harry were stuck up a cliff bird nesting, Hugo and I spent a night in the cells because Hugo was stealing food.

In 1928 I was learning to understand why my Dad had been gassed by the British, how the French started the war, but how the whole business was orchestrated by the Jews, especially the Treaty of Versailles. We went camping, map reading, target shooting, and every outdoor skill imaginable. For the first time in my life we were taken out of Marktsteft, and just after I had joined we were taken by lorry to Bayreuth where for the first time I saw Adolf Hitler parade through the streets.[6] I could hardly wait to tell Hugo and Mum, and was feeling pleased that Hugo had been caught. Later our Hitler Youth Leader read the Führer's speech in Munich in which he attacked the French.[7] We were especially proud when one of our members, a boy called Heinrich, denounced one of our teachers as a communist, and the man lost his job. Communists, we were informed were as dangerous as the Jews, as deceptive as the French, and even more ice-cold than the British.

School, which I never enjoyed, did not seem so important because it was apparent to me that my life was going to be given to Germany's future under Adolf Hitler. We really did think he was someone very special, Mum believed he was sent from God, boys of my age just saw him as our great leader, the Führer whom we would always obey. There was a considerable amount of unemployment in the town, but the growing activity was the Brown Shirts we all admired so much. They sometimes left the town in force and we felt very important when we were told where they were going. I can still remember how they all left to go to Nuremberg for a rally of strength, and then one day to Würzburg and later Bamberg in order to get rid of the communists or oppose their disgusting rallies. Communists and Jews were the focal point of our corporate energy of hatred; it was instilled in us how destructive they were to true Germans, how they tainted our blood line.

It was especially dangerous when the Jew was a communist, and we would be given personal addresses to make their lives uncomfortable. We would pelt their doors with dog excrement, daub the walls of their houses and shout insults at them in the streets. There were not that many in

---

[6] 14th April 1928 Hitler speaks in Bayreuth.

[7] 17th April in Munich Hitler denounced Stresemann's policy of reconciliation with France as madness.

Marktsteft, but those who did live there we made them know they were bitterly resented. I never had any doubt whatsoever that what we were doing was right. The Jews had all the money, they supported communism, lurked in places of power in America, France and even Britain. They were the cause of the last war and the reason why Germany surrendered, and they obligated us to sign the Versailles Treaty. We were reliably informed they were not human like us Aryans; they were *untermensch*, sub-human.[8] I believed this; it was taught me by my superiors, who I considered educated, knowledgeable and above all patriotic Germans. Hugo did not always believe what our leaders said, and seemed to have a mind of his own. He joined in with the rest of us denouncing the Jew, but I had a suspicion he had warned Enoch's parents that we were going to pay them a visit.

Two days later I discovered he had done just that, and I was furious. I decided I would denounce him, but rather than bring shame on myself and my mother I took matters into my own hands. I took him out to the banks of the Main where we used to fish, and I thrashed him. It was a thorough beating, which included a broken nose and a broken rib. My mother was in a state of distress, but neither Hugo nor I said what had happened, because, I warned him that as I had rightfully denounced him it could have been far more serious. When I look back on this incident it appals me beyond words, but the promise to write what we thought and did at the time means I shall tell the truth as it happened; otherwise there's no point in this exercise to which we have committed ourselves. At the time I felt no remorse, but rather justification and felt my mother would understand in years to come.

When I reached my 18th birthday there was no work, but I became a member of the *Sturmabteilung,* the SA[9] and that kept me in uniform, food, drink and companionship, and there was plenty to do. It was unusual for a boy of my age to be allowed to join because in Marktsteft, members were nearly all old soldiers, but they had all been my Dad's friends. I was the youngest one by a long way, but they knew I was handy with my fists, nothing seemed to frighten me. I travelled with them in two

---

[8] Although usually considered to have been coined by the Nazis, the term *under man* was first used by American author Lothrop Stoddard in the title of his 1922 pamphlet *The Revolt Against Civilization.Untermensch* was used by Rosenberg and became the central theme of the genocide provoked by the NSDAP against Jewish people, Communists and others from the Slavic East. In a speech in 1927 to the Bavarian regional parliament the Nazi propagandist Julius Streicher, publisher of *Der Stürmer*, used the term *Untermensch* referring to the communists of the German Bavarian Soviet Republic.

[9] *Sturmabteilung*, the Brownshirts, partly uniformed supporters recruited in Munich by Röhm in 1921to protect NSDAP public speakers, mainly tough ex-soldiers.

lorries and a coach; the lorries were better sprung than the coach, but no one let on to the senior men who preferred the coach. We would attend meetings where some NSDAP speakers would give an address, and if any heckling started we would wade in and throw them out. More often than not it was communists and they were ready for a fight. On one occasion in Würzburg I realized how strong I was when I hit a man with my fist and he dropped like a stone. One of my seniors came by and pulled the man round the corner while I was still nursing my fist. Two policemen who had been standing over the road came across to the scene, but my comrades spoke to them and they just walked back and out of sight. It was an enormous sense of power that the policemen, of whom I had once been very wary and careful to avoid, they now avoided us. I plunged back into the hall to see what else was happening and managed to get caught up in another fracas.

I was conscious that some of the older men were talking about me, but I was too caught up in the business of throwing communists out to wonder what was happening. When we returned to Marktsteft, Kurt, our leader for the evening took me aside and said I had killed that man; he told me not to worry, there was one communist less and the police would not take it any further. I said I had only hit him once, but Kurt said he saw the punch and knew I had broken the man's neck. I did not feel any remorse or fear because we knew that communists and Jews were undermining the German nation. As Kurt said, it was my duty and a duty well done. There had been talk of disbanding the Hitler Youth[10] to stop widespread political violence, but it was the *Sturmabteilung* which had to be feared, and I felt proud to belong to them. My standing amongst my comrades rose considerably, but no one actually mentioned the incident, apart from Kurt referring to me as an Aryan superman.

Food continued to be a problem, and it was in 1932 that both my grandparents died. This meant we now had the whole house, but Mum rented out the top half and instead of rent took in groceries. In addition to that Kurt ensured that there was a supply of food always available. My Grandparents had once been rich but money meant nothing, but food shelter and employment were the critical features of survival. Mum liked Kurt, but I detected that she was becoming a little worried if not suspicious about the street violence; I was always returning home battered and bruised. Hugo barely spoke to me after the thrashing I gave him, a dull greeting when our paths crossed, and since I knew he was not so ardent in passion for a new Germany I also kept my distance, though

---

[10] In April 1932, the Hitler Youth was banned by Chancellor Heinrich Brüning in an attempt to stop widespread political violence, but the ban was lifted by his successor Franz von Papen to appease Hitler.

occasionally I looked back to the days when we had fished together on the banks of the Main. I was busy with the *Sturmabteilung* but Hugo found himself a job working as a post boy, running or cycling messages all around town. When he brought home his pay Mum spent it at once in case next day it was worthless. I remember feeling hurt one day when I was going out through the yard, and I saw Mum give Hugo a hug and tell him he was just like his father.

HARRY 1915-33

As usual I am the last one to get down to the writing, but at least I have had an opportunity to see some of the things that Horace and Wolfgang have written. I have to confess that I am shocked by what I have read, by both of them, and somewhat hesitant to write down my own feelings as a consequence. Nevertheless, we promised we would do this however painful, and so much water has passed under the bridge for all of us, it will help put our present lives into perspective. I was irritated when I read how Horace always hankered after Edna, I had no idea then, and I was also bemused at his observations where I lived. I thought he lived in a palace and I found his Mum and Dad quite simply horrible, they were snobs and that was apparent to me even in those days. All this seems so very trivial when I read what Wolfgang was doing.

Horace was well fed, I sometimes felt hungry but was never lacking food or shoes, I considered the Boy Scouts too military for me, and the thought that Wolfgang beat up his own brother and killed a man out of political ideology when I was only interested in birds' eggs leaves me speechless, even now. Horace and I may have been socially poles apart, but both our life styles in the late 1920s and early 1930s were far removed from Wolfgang in Bavaria; there is simply no comparison. I look at Wolfgang now and I cannot begin to conceive that what he does now for a living somehow arose from the road he travelled. I could say the same about Horace, and just possibly myself, and I must take care not to pass any judgments, but I wonder what would have happened to the three of us had we been born after the war. It was the times and places that made us what we were, and have now become, I think.

As Horace noted I met him on the cliffs at Deadman's Gulch just outside the eastern arm of Dover harbour. I was bird nesting, looking for gull's eggs and saw Horace stuck on the ledge, and foolishly climbed up and became stuck with him. After he jumped I was sure he was dead, and as I dragged him to the nearby beach I was convinced I was just recovering a corpse. I can recall his father giving me a ten bob note, and, while standing on our doorstep, telling me that I was a fool to go climbing cliffs. He never mentioned Horace's rescue, or the fact that Horace had climbed up in the first place, in fact, by the time he left I was made to feel the whole dreadful incident was entirely my fault. Ten shillings was a great deal of money in those days, and I stood there watching him drive away in his car, and saw the neighbour's curtains twitch because we seldom saw a car in Albert Road. Mum had been standing in the corridor, and I gave her the ten bob note that, to my disappointment, she took.

Later that evening my Dad quizzed me on the whole incident for the second time, and explained to me that he rarely earned ten shillings for a day's hard work; then he grinned and gave me half a crown, gave Mum half a crown, put the same in his pocket, then gave Mum the same again for housekeeping. That was so typical of my father, and when he rolled home at ten that evening he brought Mum a small bottle of brown ale and me a packet of crisps, and the same for my two sisters and Eddie my brother. I have to say that despite the fact we lived under cramped conditions we had a very happy family life. Dad had fought in the Great War although he rarely spoke about his experience. He had served in the Buffs,[11] the local regiment, and often mentioned he had once met the Colonel, a General Sir Arthur Paget, but Dad never explained how. He fought from 1914 until 1916, and then, when in the 8th Battalion, he was wounded at Delville Wood. He still reckoned he weighed a stone more than he should because of all the shrapnel in him. I once saw his back when Mum was giving him a bath in the scullery; he was a mass of scars and gullies and looked ghastly. I sometimes tried to get him to talk, but he brushed it aside every time by suggesting I was being nosey.

I did hear him one day telling Mum he did not like Germans, but they were more trustworthy than the French, and if he got stuck in a trench with a foreigner, he would prefer a German to anyone else, even the Welsh. My Dad was huge, and I guess if there were fisticuffs at work I would rather have him on my side, but he was a man who enjoyed laughter, could tell a great joke, and people seemed to like him. When he met Horace he was bemused by the way Horace spoke, as if he had a *plum in his mouth*, Mum said. Horace certainly sounded posh, went to a posh school, and, on the whole, I liked him. We were chalk and cheese socially, but we went bird nesting together, and enjoyed one another's company. When I asked Horace what his Dad did in the war he told me he pulled out teeth; that was when I realised that Horace's Dad was the dentist with a reputation of being the local butcher; I did not mention that to Horace.

---

[11] Buffs, Royal East Kent Regiment; one of the oldest in the British Army, 1572-1961, its lineage is now within the Princess of Wales's Royal Regiment.

Horace was getting a public school education, and I was at Dover County School,[12] which I enjoyed. Looking back I realise it was quite a good school and I certainly made many friends there. The schoolmaster, who taught us Religious Knowledge, as it was then called, had fallen ill and a Father Harold had taken his place for a brief time. Father H, as we called him had large ears, and the right ear was in two parts with a long red scar that went from his mouth to his ear right across his cheek. It was, he told us, a German bayonet. From that moment on us boys were putty in his hands, and when he offered me sixpence to cut his lawn each week I jumped. His Rectory was up a small avenue called St Alphege Rd by his church, and the lawn was extensive, but well worth sixpence. Today it is lost under a large ugly parish hall.

Three lawns later and he had taught me to serve at the altar. My Mum started to come to church and thought it was Roman Catholic because of all the candles and incense. Father H told me he burned as many candles as he could in memory of Father Sidney[13] who had gone to gaol for the right to put candles on the altar. I always thought Father H was exaggerating, but later in life discovered there was some truth in this story. I was confirmed a year later and so was my brother Eddie, and even Dad came to that service; I was supposed to be confirmed by the Bishop of Dover, but the Archbishop[14] turned up and Father H said Eddie and I were unbelievably blessed. It transpired the Bishop of Dover was ill. I enjoyed being a member of the church, Father H was brilliant, and occasionally I managed a ride in his car. Apart from Horace's Dad, Father H was the only other person I knew who owned a car. I used to serve at 7.30 am on Tuesdays and Wednesdays, before school, and on Sundays I would serve, or be the crucifer,[15] or be thurifer. I loved the ceremony and the dressing up, and loved being told what to do by Father H; many years later it dawned on me that slowly some of the words that droned past my head most days, were beginning to take root. I think because of Father H's influence I developed a great sympathy for the Christian way of life as I saw it in him, the man. My Mum became a regular at the church and joined in nearly all the services and activities. Occasionally she would encourage Dad to come, but he preferred the Red Lion, the other side of the church graveyard, and that still survives. Eddie also became a server, but there was nothing Mum could do to persuade my sisters, who were more taken with the Methodist Church in London Road, mainly because

---

[12] Now Dover Grammar School.

[13] Refers to the Reverend Sidney Faithorn-Green who spent 20 months in prison, because he refused to accept the right of the Privy Council to interfere in church matters.

[14] Randall Davidson.

[15] Carried the processional cross.

it had a good youth club. My sisters were younger than me and I tended to ignore them and what they were doing, or what interested them. I can recall on one occasion a boy at school expressing interest in Jane, two years younger than me. At first I thought it was the right thing to do to threaten him, but he was a nice chap and I can recall saying 'good luck.' He looked so surprised I think he thought I was going to get all defensive. As regards my own girlfriend, Edna, she was at the convent school at the top of my road. She lived in Frith Road opposite my church, but she was Roman Catholic and we always met in secret. Her parents thought I was not only the wrong faith but was, as we say today, too "down market." Despite these problems, and my own Mum never knew I had a girlfriend so young, we would walk together in Connaught Park,[16] and sometimes down the seafront and along the Prince of Wales Pier, and when we were alone we would snuggle together, and the occasional kiss. That was about as serious it ever was, and in those days considered quite daring.

I wanted to do something important in life but quite what or how I had no idea, and I left school at fourteen, though closer to fifteen. Father H had all kinds of ideas, but Dad and Mum made it clear that they could not afford for me to do anything else but go out and earn my living. In the end they reached an agreement, Dad got me a job down at the docks, but Father H paid for me to attend Night School, and gave me lessons himself; he did this for many years. I was given a job in the shipbreaking and Salvage Company[17] that worked in the eastern docks. It was hard work but I enjoyed the challenge. I started as what they called a brass monkey, making the tea and running messages, and then moved onto lugging heavy chunks of metal to the right cages. I developed quite powerful muscles, and I started to enjoy a point of mild or even bitter, but I kept that from home. The chaps I worked with always pulled my leg because I was the youngest, but when I fell from an old destroyer's gunnery platform into the sea, two of my chief tormentors jumped in to save me, and everyone made a fuss of me. I learned then that in the workplace some terrible jibes may take place, but they were really my friends. I did not earn much as a boy and I gave it all to my Mum, who then gave me back two shillings which was my weekly allowance.

It was down at the docks I saw my first death. We were having a tea break and three of us were sitting in the sun rather than the caddy, the name for our rest room, when there was a shriek, it was not a cry but a soul rending long sharp shriek that made us all look up the cliff above us.

---

[16] First park established in Dover, opened by R.H. Duchess of Connaught on 14th July 1883.
[17] Stanlee Shipbreaking and salvage Co Ltd took over the Admiralty's dismantling of warships in 1920, and also invested in general scrap. Continued until 1964 when it gave way to new ferry port.

My first impression was that a large sack was falling down towards us, but then I realised it was a person, and as he fell the arms and legs became more prominent, he appeared to pick up speed, and then bounced against a small outcrop, and in a small arc fell in micro-seconds on the path the other side of our caddy with a distinctive thump, a sound I have not forgotten sixty years later. For a moment the three of us seemed to freeze then we jumped to our feet and rushed around the hut.

The sight, like the sound, is now part of me. I had not realised how much blood there is in a human being, the stomach had split open and the back of the head had opened up, and there were brains on the concrete path. I felt faint and nauseous, and Henry, one of the old boys took me by the arm and led me away. I think I was about seventeen when this happened, but it shook me a great deal, and for the few years I had to walk along that path I always walked around the spot. It transpired that the man had committed suicide, and I gathered from Father H that as such he could not be buried in consecrated ground, or have a Christian service. It was one of Father H's parishioners and I knew he was vexed by what had happened. On the Friday night he surprised me and all the family by turning up on the doorstep wanting to speak to Mum, Dad and me. It all sounded very conspiratorial, and so it was. Father H said he did not want to break Church Law, but he did not want Giles somebody or other, I cannot remember the surname, who had fought gallantly in the Great War, to be buried in some cow field without any Christian recognition. Mum and Dad agreed to be congregation and I was to be crucifer.

Father H had made arrangements with the undertakers in Beaconsfield Avenue that Gile's coffin would be brought to the Charlton cemetery on the Old Charlton Road at 10.00 the next morning. I carried the processional cross and my cassock and stood at the head of a grave which had been dug the other side of what is known as suicide's hedge, and Mum and Dad and few other like-minded members of the congregation stood around as Father H read the funeral service, and after the blessing we all trooped off, duty done. I could hardly take my eyes off the coffin wondering what he looked like now. I think Father H knew what was in my mind, because in the vestry he pulled out a silver flask and I had a swig of the first mouthful of whisky ever; it burned my mouth, throat and brought tears to my eyes, but it made me feel like a man being offered this special drink. In the years to come I would see many more dead men, and I would kill a great many, but this man Giles always stays with me. I studied maths at Night School; Father H taught me English Literature and Latin. I recall Horace being horrified that my Latin was so much better than his when I helped him with some Ovid he was trying to translate. By the time I was eighteen I was probably the best-educated person working in the Salvage yards, still looking for birds' eggs with Horace, and still in love with Edna. Horace was still at school, Edna was training to be a nurse, and Father H was trying to get me an administrative post with the Dover Harbour Board.

Apart from witnessing Giles's death my early life was a pleasurable experience. My family was solid and full of love and laughter, Eddie and my sisters had their own lives, but we rarely quarrelled even though we lived in bunk beds and only had one lavatory. Sometimes we could have eaten more but we never starved, there was unemployment but most of us found work in the end. I owed much to Father H because he took an interest in me, and why he did I shall never understand. He was not odd in any way, happily married, he had children of his own, could talk to my father man to man, my mother adored him, and in all my time I never heard a bad work spoken about him. I think he saw something in me, but I shall touch upon that later in my account. My life was not, and is not extraordinary in any way, and on reflection, I was happy to be learning in the evenings and scrapping metal in the day, Horace was still labouring at school, but Wolfgang had already killed his first person.

CHAPTER TWO

Early Manhood

HORACE 1933-8

I wrote my contribution first and thought I was late. I wondered whether to mention Edna, but since we have all decided to tell the truth, however painful, and in the war years it became seriously painful, then teenage flirtations seemed trivial. We all know now there was far worse to come and if, as was suggested, this can be a cleansing of the past, so be it. Like Harry, I was struck by Wolfgang's background that could not have been more different from mine or Harry's. There is a tendency to look back with rose coloured glasses, if only to hope there is some chance of redemption.

There are a myriad of reasons that may explain why we become what we eventually become. It could be that someone was badly brought up, or spoilt, or their family were suffering from starvation, or had a happy or unhappy home, and for some the past may hold redemptive powers, and this may well be true with Wolfgang, though I do not think he agrees with me. It may be true for Harry but to a lesser extent, but there are no redemptive features in my past. My mother and father did not spoil me, but I had everything I needed, my parents were materially good to me, I went to a good public school, I was healthy, I was popular at school if lonely at home, and I was indescribably lazy. My school work was a disaster, and even Harry knew this; he worked as a manual labourer in the docks and helped me with my Latin. My father was unhappy about my lack of progress as he had been anticipating that I might make it into Oxford.

He was a dentist with an LDS[1] and had made plenty of money from his rich pained-patients. For some reason he had pretensions of me of becoming a scholar, preferably in the sciences. I knew, as did my schoolmasters, that this was simply laughable. I wrote a few essays, and sat a few exam papers, but it was clear to everyone that I was not going to make Oxford, Cambridge or any of what father called the red-bricks. I had developed a penchant for girls, and although Edna was the love of my life, I made no effort to approach her because of Harry. I did approach others, including Patricia, my housemaster's daughter who was two years younger than me. We flirted, held hands, and then one day it nearly went too far. We were both behind the garden shed in the old man's garden, when suddenly I was wrenched off her by one very angry housemaster. I

---

[1] Licentiate in Dental Surgery.

never knew what happened to Patricia, but I was sent straight home in ignominy, embarrassed to look at my Mum or father, and that was the end of my school days. I had no university place, I had no idea what I wanted to do with my life; if I were asked for an honest appraisal I would like to sit in the sun all day, play tennis, read, smoke my pipe and chase girls; not that my parents knew I had a pipe.

Father gave me the summer holidays of July and August and asked me to try and work out how I saw my future, and he would want an answer in September. Harry was at work, and Edna was in London training to be nurse at, if I recall, Barts.[2] I knew Edna lived in Frith Road in a large house, but I was cautious because I genuinely did not want to trespass on Harry's friendship. I played tennis with a couple of neighbours, read Trollope's *Barchester Towers*, went out with Harry for a swim on Saturdays, and generally did absolutely nothing worthwhile. About mid-August my mother's gardener died, and finding no one else willing to start work that month I volunteered. I cut the lawn, trimmed the hedges, did the weeding, even planted some shrubs, and I have to confess I thoroughly enjoyed myself. I did not totally ignore my father's request, and even went to Dover Library to browse around the books to find any ideas which might attract me; none, absolutely none. 1933 was a great summer, blue skies, tennis courts, and I was even feeling an interest in a lady across the road with whom I played tennis on several occasions.

She seemed to show an interest in me, and several times our conversation was, for those days, daring and suggestive, and had my mother not been so perceptive I could well have landed up in trouble. However, my mother was observant and took me aside; when she had finished I felt like a silly ten year old boy. She was right, the lady liked young men, and a few months later she was involved in an embarrassing scandal. I wanted to discuss it with Harry, but he had seen that person die on the cliffs, and simply muttered that there were more important issues in life than my sexual fantasies. September came and my father decided to have his man to man talk with me. To my astonishment he started with the proverbial birds and bees, and decided that I had to accept that if I went off the rails with some wayward women, it would kill my mother and he would disown me. It was probably a timely threat because at that age, and with nothing to occupy my mind the fairer sex was almost becoming obsessive. I had a whole hour of this, and even though I nodded my head as submissively as possible Father kept going until I nearly fell asleep. When he asked me how I saw my future I somewhat fatuously said I would do Mum's garden in return for pocket money.

---

[2] One of the best London training hospitals at the time.

It is the nearest I saw my father explode in temper, but even as he was dressing me down for not taking life seriously, I realised that I was totally without any ambition whatsoever. It seems odd to say this now, but I have always lacked ambition, always looked for an easy way, and the most comfortable. I should be embarrassed saying this, but the truth first. I am ashamed to confess that I never tried to see the situation from my father's perspective; he had spent money on my education, had hoped I would be a scholar, and all I could offer was cut the family lawn. He stood up, pulled himself straight and told me I had one more week to think, and then he would tell me what I would be doing. The sad thing is I could think of nothing, absolutely nothing and Harry's suggestion I should join the navy or army seemed so ludicrous I did not ask him again. Edna was home that weekend, looking as glorious as ever, and as I walked along the Admiralty pier with her and Harry, the happy gooseberry, she suggested I should follow my father into his dental practice. My father, when I aired this suddenly looked very positive and said I should attend his practice and help his nurse, and he would look into possible training.

Thus in late September I reported to work with my father and was given a white coat to wear. I was thoroughly disappointed with the dental nurse; she was not as good looking as Edna or a pleasant person, and she had the most dreadful spots all over her face. It struck me that all the people who came to father's surgery were frightened of him and what he did, and it occurred to me he did little to put them at their ease. I thought if I became a dentist I would try and be kinder and less authoritarian than he was. My first job was to watch and learn what the instruments were called, and I would operate the pedal that turned the drill when there was the occasional filling. Drillings and fillings were for rich patients; it was cheaper to have a tooth pulled. I did this for two weeks and then father said he and I were going to look at a placement for me in a new but excellent dental school at King's London. I looked it up in the library and saw the site was in the Strand, right in the centre of London, but I was disappointed on the day we went, the dental part of the college was in the sticks at Denmark Hill, south London.[3] It was all very clinical and I felt like a little boy again, because my father knew the university doctor, they were old friends, and all my failures at Kings Canterbury were discussed as if I were not there. The upshot was I was promised a place in the dental school the following year in 1934. Edna was pleased and, I was glad to note impressed; Harry kept his thoughts to himself.

---

[3] King's Dental School started in November 1923 and a new building erected in 1935 with 35 dental chairs, but not completed until 1939.

My time as a dentist-to-be did not last long; I never made it to King's despite my father's efforts. It would have been early 1934 I knew I was not cut out to be a dentist. My father had sent me from the surgery when he was doing major extractions, I used to go and sterilise the instruments. He then asked me to stay when his nurse had gone down with a cold. The first two were fine, two young boys with milk teeth problems, and they succumbed to the gas very quickly, and the teeth emerged without any blood. I was just beginning to think this was an easy job for the money when the next patient entered. She was a young pregnant woman, and I was immediately struck by how pretty her face was. She had a toothache at the rear of the lower jaw, and my father spent some time prodding and poking about making her quite agitated.

He explained to her that it was not just one tooth but several, and there was serious decay the other side of the mouth. His suggestion was that she had all her teeth pulled in two sessions, and have false teeth fitted. I shuddered at the very thought, but apparently this often happened. The only thought that crossed my mind was that my father deserved the infamous accolade of being the town butcher. To my utter astonishment she agreed without a question. My job was to use cotton wool and a suction pipe to suck out the blood so she did not choke. I could barely cope, but did so for the woman's sake. In reality I wanted to pass out, the blood was copious to say the least, and it took all my effort to keep her mouth clear. When she came to she was in pain, and although father gave her some painkillers they had little effect. She had to hold a towel to her mouth constantly, and shuddered with the pain. She came back nearly a fortnight later to have the rest removed. Thank goodness the regular nurse was back, but I saw her come into the surgery, she was no longer the radiant beauty she had been.

Her face was drawn, her cheeks sunk in, her eyes had lost their sparkle and she now looked like an ageing hag not far from her grave. I challenged father on why he pulled so many teeth, and healthy teeth at that, from such a young beautiful woman. He explained that it was more out of charity; to save the teeth would cost her a fortune, not only now, but for the rest of her life she who would be paying dentists. She came from a working class background where they ate the wrong food, were unaware of oral hygiene, and so for a bit of momentary pain she would be free of dental problems for the rest of her life. I wondered if Harry's Mum had all her teeth, and two weeks later when I saw the young woman return, haggard and weary I knew I was not going to be a dentist. I used to think highly of my father, but he was pompous, looked down his nose at people, at moments he was arrogant with people who were frightened. I did not want this life style and told him so directly. He accused me of being scared of blood, and anything to keep him happy I agreed. If he were to see me a few years later in the midst of the Italian war, he would know that blood was not the issue, nor, I later realised, was it the suffering. I simply did not like the way people treated one another.

There seemed to be a cruelty inherent in the so-called British class system; a sneering, a disregard in believing that others lack sensitivity, that people by their birth, where they live, how they have money dictates how they should be treated. Later in life I met an aristocrat who agreed with me, and another Eton bred landed gent who told me dentists were just tradespeople. I think, when I look back, that although my father and mother would have me believe I should be superior, and the public school education in Canterbury should put the seal on this fact, it was Harry who inadvertently made me think otherwise. Harry, the breaker's yard tea boy and muscle man was better educated than me, he felt free to laugh at me, and was completely oblivious to the fact that we were socially poles apart. Harry was clever, he was genuine, and as the years passed I realised he was my closest friend. At the time Harry influenced me in a way I never recognised, nor would he have known this, but I was drifting away from the ideals my parents had anticipated, and I was beginning to question the nature of the social order.

My father, fearing I was going to become what he called a left wing socialist or even a communist took a harder disposition towards me. I was informed I had to earn a living, and he had arranged for me to become some sort of junior administration officer for the Dover Harbour Board. I wore a suit to work, but all I did was take papers from one office to another, collect and carry men's wages, distribute forms, put notices on noticeboards, and after two years I was allowed my own typewriter to answer straightforward enquires from the general public or from the work force. It was not the sort of job that my father and even I had anticipated I would do for life. I was well aware that to my parents I was a bitter disappointment, but in a strange way I was very happy. I did less work than Harry, yet received more money, and whereas Harry had to give his wage packet over to his mother, I kept my salary. I was rarely questioned by my seniors, and I am sure if I disappeared for a week no one would notice. I frequently slipped out of work to go and play tennis up at Connaught Park or out at Kearsany Abbey.[4] If Harry slipped out of work he would be sacked. Harry played tennis but not often; he seemed obsessed with the local church and having lessons with the strange old priest there who had a slit ear.

In March 1938 I was given three week's early annual holiday in order that my seniors could have the summer months. I astonished myself and family by deciding to take a short break abroad. I had saved up sufficient

---

[4] Not an Abbey but grounds of a large house.

funds to take a Cook's tour[5] and soon found myself wandering around Vienna, a simply beautiful city. Apart from a visit to Calais it was the first time I had been out of the country, and after a week it dawned on me how much fun travelling could be. It was a pipe dream because even this short break cost me nearly all my funds, and speaking no foreign language was something of a hindrance. I promised myself that I would learn German, I had some schoolboy French and it was bound to be easier than Latin. I had arrived a few days after the *Anschluss*[6] and was at first bemused by all the excitement that pervaded the area; it certainly made my chosen holiday destination more exciting.

I had read about Adolf Hitler in the press, but had not paid much attention to the German leader. Nor did I see him in Vienna where he had passed through in some cavalcade that I missed. The night before I was due home I witnessed a scene that made me fill ill. There was a disturbance outside a large shop, and a group of people, some dressed in brown uniforms were making some elderly men and women lick the pavements with their tongues. When one of the elderly men looked up one of what I assumed to be policemen, kicked him in the side of the face; I could see instantly that the old man lost some teeth with this blow, and probably had a broken jaw. I stepped forward to make a protest, but a strong arm jerked me backwards with such a force I could not resist. I looked to who held me and it was huge fellow who spoke to me in English with what I now know to be an American dialect. He told me that the minute I said anything I would suffer the same fate. When I protested that I did not care, he pulled me further away and asked me if I wanted simply to disappear, because that happened to foreigners who were difficult. His name was Ernie, a decent man, and we sat and had a coffee together. He was surprised I was there on my own even though I was twenty two coming on twenty three.

We spent an hour in that café and he gave me a complete rundown on the nature of the Nazis and of Hitler in particular. He was a journalist who had travelled extensively, and when I look back over the vast distance of time I feel a great deal of gratitude towards this American.[7] He not only saved my skin, but he helped me grow up by explaining the nature of the politics, and on mature reflection I realise now how very accurate he was in his condemnation of what was happening. When I left Vienna the next day I was grateful to be returning to England now very aware that in England I was cocooned in safety and comfort. That trip politicised me, I felt strongly anti-fascist and intended at the first

---

[5] Thomas Cook, often simply known in those days as Cook's Tours.

[6] 1938 March German encapsulates Austria.

[7] I have wondered whether this might be the famous American journalist Ernie Pyle.

opportunity to oppose the black shirts growing under Oswald Mosley. I
had been aware of the BUF[8] and knew they were anti-Semitic but, in my
usual lazy way had not given it much thought. Vienna and the American
journalist Ernie changed my mind, he changed me.

When I spoke to Harry about the situation he seemed to know more
than I did, and it transpired that his father was much more political than I
thought, and had actually gone up to London to join in some protests
against the fascists. When I told Harry about the Jewish people being
beaten into licking the pavement, Harry got me to come with him and
describe what I had seen both to his father and to the priest. Harry's
father listened and told me the American had been right in all he had said.
I was a little stunned by my perception of Harry's father; I thought he
only went to work and down the Red Lion, and I was very wrong with my
usual assumptions. I was also wrong about the priest with the slit ear; he
was an extremely charming man and down to earth. He was convinced
that war would be the outcome. He said that he had fought the products of
the Wilhelmine period,[9] and that along with the Kaiser it was all
dangerously dysfunctional, and Hitler was worse. I clearly remember that
conversation because it was the first time I heard the word
'dysfunctional' used. As I cycled home that night I made up my mind that
I should join the army; I thought at last I had found my profession.

WOLFGANG 1932-39

Having read both Harry and Horace I wonder if I would have been like
them if I had not been born in Germany. They say there is little
distinction between nature and nurture, between what we are born with
and the environment into which we are born. If Harry had been born here
instead of England would he have become anti-Semitic and politically
minded, or would he have found comfort and resource in one of the local
churches; we had a Lutheran church but many of the people were
Catholic so he would have had a choice. I can honestly say that I did not
know any of my generation who went to church, apart from some
younger ones taken by their parents. Once I suspected Hugo of going to
the Lutheran church, but I learned later it was because he fancied the
minister's daughter. My Mum went, though she said she had once been a
more regular attender at mass, but the Great War destroyed some of her
faith. I note Horace never went to church, and he was bemused by

---

[8] British Union of Fascists.
[9] Period of Kaiser Wilhelm, a time of intense militarism.

Harry's loyal attendance, so the three of us, who became so intimately interwoven later, were all different in personality as well as background.

I finished my last section by observing that I was hurt when my Mum seemed to think Hugo was more like my Dad. I even made a point of telling Mum that Dad's old comrades had said how proud Dad would have been of me. Mum did not appear that certain, and I started to feel a slight gulf come between us, as there had between Hugo and me. I did not mean this to happen, and when I look back it is now apparent it was all my doing. Mum and Hugo were both supporters of the Führer but I now realise, with the benefit of hindsight that I was something of a young fanatic, and prone to violence. As youngsters we had been imbued with a virulent distrust of communists, and even more potent hatred of Jews, the ultimate *untermensch*. In 1933 the party organised an official boycott of Jewish shops[10] and professional Jews such as doctors, dentists and lawyers. We had a few in Marktsteft and I had a real sense of power when, with two others we were put on duty outside a Jewish jewellers. The Jews did not resist our presence as we painted *Juden* across their windows, and people doing their shopping made no effort to come near the shop until late morning, when the Catholic priest stopped to look in the window.

My comrade asked him why he was interested in Jewish tinsel as it was overpriced and he could not afford it anyway. He replied the shop always had the best in town, and we were right he could not afford it, but that or our presence would not stop him admiring the pieces. This felt like a direct challenge to our authority, and I pointed out to him that they were the same Jews who had crucified Christ. I thought that was a clever remark, and felt quite proud of my sharp intellect until he spun on me and pointed out that Christ was Jew, the saviour of mankind had been born a Jew. I think he sneered as he said it, looking at me with sheer contempt in his eyes so I pushed him against the window, and Heinrich tripped him over and kicked him in the ribs. Someone from over the road shouted 'thugs' but when we looked up it was difficult to see who, and the old priest was stumbling way as fast as he could. People simply did not understand we had to take a hard line against the enemy.

At the end of that day I was further exhilarated to be given the job of travelling with Heinrich and two others in a lorry to Munich. We were to accompany three well-known communists who were going to be put into a special camp just opened outside Munich at Dachau.[11] It was a long journey and we had some fun taunting the communists about their future. They were a miserable looking bunch and would only reply when we

---

[10] 1933 April the first official boycott.
[11] Dachau started life as an SA camp in march 1933.

insisted. The camp was impressive and I could see that it would reform those who had gone off the rails. I would remind the reader that I am stating things as I saw them in those early days. Nor am I going to make the fallacious claim that I had no idea what concentration camps were going to be like in later years. Then, in 1933, as far as I was concerned Dachau was a reforming prison camp for enemies of the state. Years later I would hear about the extermination camps, and how people also died in ordinary camps, and I really could not understand why people objected to culling sub-humans; Jews were even shaped differently. That is what I believed. I thought about asking if I could be detailed to work in Dachau, but Heinrich said that I would need more experience on the streets first; it was, he said, the duty of all would be leaders to serve time in the trenches, in our case that was the streets of wherever we were sent. Our chief was Röhm, not that I ever saw him, but I gathered he was a close friend of the Führer, that they were on first name terms. It was just after I returned from Dachau that I heard the SA had come under the authority of the Ministry of War,[12] I felt quite proud. This did not last long because soon rumours were circulating that the Führer had used the officers of the SS to eliminate Röhm and other senior SA leaders.[13] I have to confess that I found this confusing, but Heinrich and a few others said Röhm had grown too big for his boots; I found it curious that the SS seemed more important than the SA, although we never discussed this.

In 1936/7 I was astonished to find that Hugo had joined the Wehrmacht, and although Mum knew, she did not share this with me. Then and there I decided I would better Hugo and filled in the necessary forms to join the *Schutzstaffel,*[14] better known as the SS. At first I thought I would have to join the Wehrmacht, but there was a special recruiting drive for the '*right sort.*' It was not such a long process; I had to report to a training college in Brunswick where I was tested intellectually and physically. While I was doing all this they were checking my ancestry to ensure no Jews had tainted our blood. The genealogical tests took the longest, and then they measured everything about me, including my ears and nose, I was tall, they checked the colour of my hair, which was very fair, and my sharp blue eyes made me their traditional Aryan. I was suddenly in the SS, but not to be trained at Brunswick but at Bad Tölz, which was south of Munich and closer to home. On my way back from Brunswick I made a point of calling into Magdeburg where my Uncle Heinz lived, my Dad's brother. He looked just like my Dad in the

---

[12] The SA, SS and Stahhelm were all placed under Ministry of War in the hope that the SA would be swamped: instead it increased Röhm's power.

[13] Night of the Long Knives, between 30th June and 2nd July 1934.

[14] Defence Unit, originally the personal guard for Hitler but transformed by Himmler into a state within a state and an army within the army.

mantelpiece photograph Mum kept, and lived alone in a small apartment in, if I remember correctly, the *Bahnhofstraße*, opposite hundreds of railway lines and rail yards where he worked. He was very kind and gentle and was pleased to see me, but looked a little bemused when I was rattling on about being trained in the SS.

On reflection I took it for granted that he was a party supporter, I never stopped to think my uncle might have been of a different mind. He dropped a hint that his brother, my Dad, was proud to be a German soldier, and that the Wehrmacht would have made me welcome. It struck me that my Uncle Heinz was poorer than we were in Marktsteft, but we had some excellent sausage and then we went out for a drink. As I travelled home I reflected that every time we met one of his friends that evening, and he had quite a few, he always introduced me as his nephew about to join the SS. At first I thought he was boasting about his young nephew, but on the train home it suddenly occurred to me that he was warning them. I asked Mum if my uncle was left wing because I did not want any taint in the family. I never found out, I never saw him again; he was killed by bombs at the very end of the war.

I was excited about arriving at the SS training camp in Bad Tölz, and was very impressed with the site they were preparing for the school; it was massive. I was amongst the first, and we had to start our training while living in some basic huts.[15] It was very tough, they took us all, nearly two hundred if I recall, down to the River Isar at about five in the morning, it was barely light, and they instructed us to swim across. The river was flowing rapidly, but I thought do or die and made sure I was the first to plunge in; after all I had done the same with Hugo in the River Main at home. It was icy cold and the pull of the current was challenging; about halfway over I wondered if I had been silly, and thought if I did not reach the opposite shore soon I would start failing. I looked back and saw with relief that some boats had appeared out of nowhere, I raised myself up and looked around me; there were only a few of us. As I swam on I wondered whether the others had drowned or been picked up. I eventually made it between an old wharf and a mud bank. I swam to the wharf because I spotted a ladder to climb out; as I pulled myself up the ladder I felt totally exhausted.

It transpired that only fifteen of us made it across, twenty others were rescued and the rest did not get in the water. We were assembled on the great square and divided into three groups, the first, my group who had successfully managed the crossing, the second about twenty who tried and failed, and then the rest stood looking rather shamefaced. The *SS-*

---

[15] The *Junkerschule* was not ready until 1937; this was a preparatory effort probably early 1937.

Hauptscharführer[16] then talked to us about what had happened. It was nothing to do with swimming or our ability to swim, but about responding to orders without hesitation. Six of us, including me, were summoned forward and he shook our hands and made us group leaders, *SS-Unterscharführer* which would be acknowledged in three weeks if we persisted in doing well. Apparently we were the first six to dive in without hesitation. The rest were told they had to swim over the river within five weeks otherwise they were being sent home via a labour battalion. I do not want to go into details about the various often obscure ranks and titles used in the SS, but it was clear that I was being trained by Waffen-SS for the Waffen-SS, that is in layman's language the fighting wing. I have often felt that built into the human psyche is a self-belief that we have a purpose or a destiny in life. In those early days I felt this impulse very strongly, and it was not until I was older that I questioned the truth of such feelings. In the SS training school I was out to win at all costs, to out-perform my comrades, to impress my superiors, and to be counted worthy of serving the Führer.

I heard later that legends circulated in the Wehrmacht about the toughness of our training that included such nonsense as balancing unexploded and exposed grenades on our helmets. This was downright silly, but our training was tough, so tough nearly a third of the original number dropped out, and several died, one from exhaustion and others by accident as our training was realistically demanding. Another group went to another training facility to train as guards, or at least that was the rumour at the time; we were not told what was happening, simply what to do and when to do it. We were instructed that if we were told to jump we jumped, and the only permitted question was how high. We were run into the ground, made to go hungry, and then we had the platform walk; that lost two who I regarded as friends. They placed a long plank on the floor, it was an ordinary builder's plank and we were told to walk along it two or three times, and then do it with a blindfold on, but with instructions from someone if we stopped. Quite why the instructions were necessary, it was a matter of placing one foot in front of another. It was so easy we felt they must be playing with us or having a joke. It was no joke; they then placed the same plank high on some scaffolding, at least fifteen metres off the ground that was unforgiving concrete.

We were told that we had to wear our packs and walk across the plank and back again and without hesitation. I was the first to climb up the scaffolding and when I neared the top I realised that from my position it was considerably higher than it looked from the ground, I also worked out before I arrived that the plank would bend this time and I must not

---

[16] Chief Squad leader.

look down. When I arrived at the plank I was pleased to see it was firmly held in place by giant clamps. The instructor opposite shouted to me as I approached the plank not to hesitate and I did not, I pretended it was still on the ground and walk over at once. As anticipated the plank did bend beneath my weight and I confess I was grateful I was the first and had it done. We all passed that test, and were hoping that we could soon go for some food when we were told we were only half way through the exercise; we now had to do it blindfolded as we had on the ground.

Again I was the first to climb and this time my heart was in my mouth; I worked out that four good strides in a straight line and all would be well. This time there was no warning about hesitation and an instructor put the blind over my eyes in such a way I had no hope of looking down. He lead me to the plank and I put my foot on it so I knew it was in the centre, then walked straight across. I would not do it now if you paid me a fortune, but my determination to come through meant I was stupid enough to risk my life and, on hindsight, the instructors were stupid enough to risk our lives. One comrade fell but caught hold of some scaffolding, heaven knows how, and three refused despite pleas from those below; they were gone the next day. The training was dangerously brutal and ruthless, and when I look back I realised they were turning us into dedicated automatons who would never question authority or disobey an order.

We were given plenty of classroom instruction, ranging from lectures on purity of race, to etiquette, posture and political, that is NSDAP philosophy. Some lessons were optional and I started to learn English. I had never been anything at school but now I was learning quickly. In the main hall, outside the commandant's office was a huge picture of the Führer, and over a table with a brass swastika was a picture of Himmler in his uniform smiling through what looked like several layers of chins; not that I made such an observation in those days. Himmler actually visited one day when I was there. We knew something was up because parade ground drilling was continuous, and we marched and marched, back and forth left and right that I even dreamed I was marching. I saw him from a distance, and even then with all the atmosphere and reverence of the day I could not help observing the sheer sycophancy of the senior officers when Himmler appeared, and I also noted that he looked feeble, double chinned, and would hardly have been allowed into the SS at the lowest rank. It was the only time I ever saw Himmler, and I never really came to understand the reverence he was held in, or the fear many felt.

Had it been the Fuhrer I would have understood; all these thoughts and questions crossed my mind, but I never mentioned them to anyone and never heard a criticism from others. We seemed to be bound together by some bond of obedience. The authority of an institution carries its own power and can last for a long time. This was true of Germany at that time; as individuals many of us had become incarcerated by the system of blind obedience, and made to feel good by the sense of loyalty and comradeship. I think what I am trying to say that if my comrades felt like me then we felt like cogs in a giant machine, but pleased and proud to be part of that machine. Any sense of individuality we retained, we sacrificed voluntarily, and took pride in our subservience to the greater good of the Reich.

I was soon a fully trained SS soldier, and told that as potential officer material I had to serve in the ranks for at least six months, and was given the rank of SS-Schutze[17] and attached to SS *Verfügungstruppe*.[18] Many of my lesser comrades who had survived but with poor marks joined the SS-*Totenkopfverbände* that administered the concentration camps. I was pleased to be joining the fighting wing and even more pleased when my unit was attached to the *Leibstandarte SS Adolf Hitler* whose top man was Sepp Dietrich. Later we were referred to as the Waffen-SS, but the fighting wing was by 1937/8 a very proud and disciplined army in its own right. I found the groups and titles very confusing, and looking back after all these years it is still just as confusing. Most of my early duties were attending parades and forming a guard of honour; we were paid well but had next to no leave. Time and time again we had to practice parades and we suffered inspection after inspection.

When I look back on this written contribution I seemed to have spent an inordinate amount of time describing how I went through the initial training. It was my choice, coloured by what was happening in Germany during the formative parts of my youth. You, that is Harry in particular, wanted to know how it was I landed up in the SS, and what it was like; I hope I have answered some of your curiosity. After the war started we did not necessarily stay with our original posting, after my spells in hospitals I was sent to join different regiments and units, all depending on what was happening. I know in the years to come the SS would be condemned by international agreement as a criminal organisation, and deservedly so. I also know that they were often used as an alibi for the rest of the nation. There were members of the Wehrmacht and other officers of the state who committed atrocities in the name of the Führer, millions in fact, but it suited the majority to use the SS as the culprit that helped exonerate the greater majority. This is not the place to discuss this issue, and I am certainly not offering any form of apologia for the organisation or for myself; all I need state at the moment is that in the summer I was given

---

[17] Grenadier or rifleman.
[18] Dispositional troops at the personal disposal of the Führer.

the junior officer rank of SS-*Scharführer,* which for the SS was rapid promotion. This had been my projected ranking at Bad Tölz and it was now confirmed. That summer I enjoyed Berlin, it would be the last summer I would ever enjoy.

HARRY 1933 – 39

I have read Wolfgang's account with considerable attention, Horace's too, but I had a good idea about Horace in those days, or at least I was familiar with the territory. Wolfgang's contribution comes as something of a shock. Not about him being an SS officer, we knew that from when we met in Italy during the war, nor how hated the SS were, and feared, but his analysis of being trapped in a system. I suppose we are all products of our background, our environment and where we are born happens by sheer chance. I was born into what we now call a liberal democracy, but knew from our poverty that it was not an ideal society. There were those who struggled for a living and those who had everything, meeting Horace made me sharply aware of this fact.

However, compared to what was happening in Germany I, and especially Horace, lived in a very different world. I know Horace had been horrified by what he had seen in Germany when he travelled there, I read the papers, my Dad and Father H frequently spoke about the dangers of dictators, but it was all so very far away. Horace played tennis, I spent time being educated by Father H and saving money from my work when I was able. I noted that Wolfgang realised how stupid the plank walking test was, but I would have described that as criminal. I do not mean criminal in the exercise, which I think it was, but criminal making young men do that because they knew they were training unthinking automatons who would blindly follow instructions and commands, however criminal they were.

The SS, especially the Waffen-SS were fighting soldiers of high quality, but they were brutal, ruthless and, in my opinion, downright evil. I know circumstances brought Wolfgang and me together in strange conditions, I owe my life to Wolfgang, Horace owes his life to me, and Wolfgang owes his life to us both. This must come later in our unusual story, but I raise it now because I look forward to hearing from Wolfgang how he eventually broke the mould in which he had been cast. Most people stay bound to the system in which they are raised, that would be true for me, but how Wolfgang challenged what they had made him is difficult to imagine, especially knowing what sort of person he eventually became.

I must stop this commenting on Wolfgang because part of the agreement was that we would say what was happening to us; compared with Wolfgang's commitments I was doing very little. I actually enjoyed dismantling old ships as a labourer for a scrap metal-merchant. I worked with men whose company I enjoyed; they were a pretty tough lot, some of them were too fond of their beer, one or two seemed to get into occasional scraps and appeared on Monday with black eyes or swollen knuckles. When I started they used to pull my leg, but in fact as the years rolled by I realised they were good natured and led pretty tough lives. Bert, who lived down Peter Street, near where I lived, was lucky to earn two pounds a week with nine children to raise. When he broke an arm it was his fault and there was no compensation. Following a suggestion from Father H, I suggested a whip round, and for three weeks we managed to slip Bert enough groceries to keep him going. I was pleased that it worked, and only embarrassed that someone told Bert it was all my idea. There were about twenty of us working there with various sub-contractors coming and going, but we regulars knew who we were, and so did our bosses.

I was not political, but can remember the debate that took place at the Oxford Union Society whether they would be prepared to fight for King and Country.[19] Father H was furious with the result, and I remember thinking that was because he had fought in the Great War, and then later that year he drew my attention to the fact that Winston Churchill was warning of the dangers of German rearmament.[20] Apart from that 1933 was a time of working hard, walking out with Edna whenever she was home. It had taken a long time but I eventually declared my true love for her after kissing her one day on Shakespeare Cliff; unfortunately it was not a long kiss because some urchins nearby started to clap and cheer, and we were both embarrassed. I think after that we were sort of unofficially engaged, but knew we would have to wait until her training was well and truly finished and I was firmly established in a good job.

Father H was ambitious for me and I was reading history under his guidance; he would give me a reading list, which we would then discuss before preparing an essay for him. I have never really fathomed out why he gave me so much attention, it was not as if he did not have his own family, and although I attended all the services I was able, and served and assisted whenever I could, Father H gave me more time than I did to him. It was almost as if he had adopted me intellectually, and my parents thought he was wonderful. Father H even gave me books to keep so I built up a formidable library, sometimes books hot off the press such as

---

[19] Oxford Union Debate February 9th 1933.
[20] August 12th 1933, Churchill's first speech on this subject.

Graves's *I Claudius.*[21] I put shelves up in my room, but as there was no space for a desk I used to work in the library, on my lap or at the kitchen table. There was more room in the house now because both of my sisters married young, one to a chap I liked very much and who lived in Folkestone. He worked on one of the cross channel ferries and was good fun and obviously cared for my sister. My Dad also liked him unlike my other brother-in-law who lived up Tower Hamlets;[22] of whom we were all suspicious, and Mum had to convince Dad to say nothing when a baby was born six months after the wedding at St Bartholomew's. His name was Ted, and he had been a coalminer at the East Kent Colliery, Tilmanstone[23] but now assisted a coal merchant called Blacks or Blackmans, I cannot remember. What I do recall is that I felt he was not trustworthy, and I heard Dad saying to Mum that if he laid a finger on Edith my sister, he would break every bone in his body. I suspect he knew how we felt because we rarely saw him, although Mum stayed in constant touch with Edith and the new baby called Frank.

Dad was late home one evening, and when he did fall through the door I could see he had not been revelling in the Red Lion, but he had two black eyes and a split lip. Mum sat him down and washed him while I made the proverbial cup of tea. I wanted to ask if Ted were still alive but decided that it was best to wait until Dad was ready to speak. To my astonishment it was nothing to do with Ted or anyone else in Dover, but Dad had gone up to London with a group of mates to jeer at Mosley's British Union of Fascists, and not unexpectedly had been caught up in some fighting with the black shirts.[24] He told me more about it later in the week, but that evening he was in no real mood to be his usual cheery self. When I told Father H he smiled, and said the world would be a safer place with men like my father. Father H went up to London himself just after, but that was to watch Fred Perry and Dorothy Round win both the singles finals at Wimbledon.[25] I can recall the occasion quite vividly because Horace was as equally wound up about the tennis whereas I could not muster the slightest interest.

I was old enough now to appreciate Father H much more than I did as a youngster, a remarkable man who helped me for no other reason than the fact that he thought I was worth more than a scrap metal worker in the dockyards. He was, to my mind quite holy and devout, yet any mention of Germany would make him look angry, he disliked politicians, loved

---

[21] Robert Graves, published 1934.

[22] Not the famous district in London, but an area in Dover.

[23] Kent had four small coalfields of which Tilmanstone was one; it started in 1906 and although uneconomic survived until 1986.

[24] Probably June 8th 1934 when Mosley held a massive BUF at Olympia, London.

[25] July 7th 1934.

tennis, cricket and rugby, but detested soccer. He became angry when the government imposed a speed limit of 30 mph[26] on traffic in Dover and other built up areas. When I pointed out that he rarely went over twenty he replied that it was the principle that the government should not interfere too much with personal liberty, especially since they seem prepared to give Mosely total freedom. Father H became really upset when the newspapers reported that England and Germany had struck some deal regarding their navies,[27] but pleased when it was announced that 90% of people were in favour of multilateral disarmament. Dad said Father H was right to be pleased, but if 90% of British people were in favour he reckoned only 10% of Germans were in favour, as they watched the 90% prepare for the next war.[28] Meanwhile I was studying the nature of the English Civil War.

I was happy but they were not the idyllic days which is always a temptation when looking back to one's youth. Mum was not well, and although Dad called the doctor that was always an expensive affair, and at times we were all deeply concerned about her health. I guessed she smoked a good deal when she could afford to, her coughing was persistent and I now recognise that this was the onset of lung cancer; it took a while for us to realise how serious her situation was. During 1936 we all had to take a drop in wages and food went up along with most things. Dad was angry about the situation, and there was much talk in the household and the docks about the all the men who marched down from Jarrow as a protest against their unemployment.[29] There was also more trouble with Mosley's BUF in London, but Dad did not go with his mates because he was worried about Mum's deteriorating health.[30]

Father H visited Mum and brought her communion, but when he started coming once a week it dawned on me how serious the situation was becoming. To complicate matters my sister Edith's husband Ted was in trouble with the police, which transpired to be quite serious, and the next thing we knew Ted had disappeared from sight, the police searched our house, and Edith and her child Frank moved back in to Albert Road. This was not easy because Mum was so ill, and Dad moved her into a

---

[26] 30 mph imposed on urban areas in 1935, March 12th.

[27] June 7th 1935, Anglo-German Naval Treaty signed; Germany allowed a navy up to the size of 35% the size of the British.

[28] I think this refers to a peace ballot by the League of Nations on 26 or 27th June 1935.

[29] Jarrow March, October 1936 – their protest supported by their MP, Ellen Wilkinson.

[30] 1936 October 11th Battle of Cable Street, provocative march into Whitechapel by Mosley's BUF halted by anti-fascists.

makeshift bed in the front room. On the other hand Edith was able to help because Dad and I still had to go to work every day.

I state all this because I want the readers, be they just my two friends to understand that I am not wearing rose-coloured glasses as I look back to my youth. I was busy at work, engrossed with my studies, happy to be with Edna, but deeply distressed for my Mum and Dad. I lived in my own world and paid little interest to the rest of the world. When the King abdicated I think I was the last person to hear, because that was the day my Mum died.[31] Life was upside down. It was the first time I saw my Dad shed tears; we all cried but we were expected to. Quite why I did not expect my Dad to cry I did not understand. He was a big chap, he was tough, but because he was manly I suppose this did not make him insensitive. Father H held a Requiem Mass and I was staggered how many people turned up. The whole of Albert Road seemed to be in attendance, all the wider family, and the congregation who over the past few years had viewed Mum as one of them. Two of my workmates turned up and even Horace came.

There was no wake, there was no parish hall, but Father H opened up his lawn, and some of the ladies of the parish served tea and biscuits. Mum was buried up Chalkie Lane in Charlton cemetery and had it not been for Father H putting his arm around my shoulder and taking Dad and me away I think we would have stood there for days. Even as we walked down the hill I looked back and saw two men starting to fill in the grave which more than anything else seemed to be the final goodbye. They call it closure these days, but that was a terminology not in vogue then. For the first time ever I went with Dad down the Red Lion that evening and sat with him in his corner. His usual mates kept sending over drinks but kept a respectful distance. It was there in the Red Lion it suddenly dawned on me how important other people are; this may seem a rather stupid self-evident truism, but it hit me almost forcibly that day of Mum's funeral.

The people turning up to the funeral, my mates from the scrapyard who never met Mum, Father H's friendly arm guiding us home, the congregation like a huge family helping with the teas, the men in the Red Lion speaking in subdued voices out of respect, people I did not recognise and of course, Horace, my posh public school friend; the church was packed and this gave me some sort of strength. Later in life, on the battlefields, I would stand by the graves of good friends, having buried them, said prayers for them, having been the sole mourner.

---

[31] Dec 10th 1936 Edward VIII abdicates in favour of the Duke of York who accedes as George VI.

The end of 1936 and beginning of 1937 did not bode well. I think Dad would have gone and fought the fascists in Spain[32] had Father H not reminded him that he was responsible for a family, even if we were all grown up. Dad and Father H became a strange pair of friends. Father H certainly did not go to the Red Lion, and Dad came to a Sunday service about once a month, but I found them talking together either in Albert Road or walking along the promenade together. It was their shared views of fascism and world politics that brought them together. Later that year I turned up at the Rectory for my usual history discussion to find Dad waving to Father H as he walked down the road. My initial self-centred thought was they had been discussing me, but they had been sharing a drink together to celebrate that Mosley had been knocked senseless in Liverpool.[33] However, I was also right in so far that later I discovered that Father H had asked my Dad's permission to find me a place in a university. Father H said he would find the necessary money and search for any grants; to my surprise Dad agreed.

To my utter astonishment the whole future before me seemed to be changing, and Father H thought any matriculation would be easy, and he was aiming for me to enter King's College, Cambridge since he knew several important people there, and it had been his university college. The last time Father H had visited his old college one of the undergraduates had shot his tutor and then a police officer,[34] but he said it was improving! The end of 1937, the whole of 1938 and start of 1939 became one huge academic grindstone as Father H put me through my paces. I have to confess that I had a deep love and fascination with history, but I had to pass in Latin and a modern language. Latin was no problem, but Father H decided my language should be German, mainly because he was able to speak that language fluently. This did not go down well with Dad, but he was essentially a kind and thoughtful person and he said little more than 'ghastly guttural language.' I wondered if he were associating the word guttural with gutter, but there was more to my Dad than met the eye; he may have been a mere dock worker, but he was a reader of many types of books. As it happened I enjoyed German and took to it like a duck to water.

It was in late 1938 I went up to London with Father H and then onto Cambridge. Father H decided he would enjoy a few days roaming around whilst I sat some examinations and was interviewed. Most of the people I met were extremely friendly, all sounded like Father H or Horace and by

---

[32] Spanish Civil War.

[33] 1937 October 10th Mosley knocked unconscious at a BUF rally in Liverpool.

[34] 1930 this incident occurred - Cambridgeshire Constabulary - National Police Officers Roll of Honour and Remembrance In Memory of British Police Officers who lost their lives in the Line of Duty. Police Roll of Honour Trust.

the time I was back on the train to London I felt that I had done as well as I could. Father H told me that his old friends were impressed by my history and amazed my Latin was so good. I received a letter a day later; they were offering me a place in the Michaelmas term of 1939. I was wild with delight, so was Father H and Dad. I think everyone was delighted for me, Edna and even my mates at the scrapyard, who started pulling my leg by calling me either 'sir' or 'boffin.' Horace wrote and congratulated me, and Edna, who knew Horace's father, told me that he could hardly believe the news. I never made it to Cambridge for that Michaelmas term. Even as we had travelled up to Cambridge the newspapers were full of Chamberlain meeting Hitler to discuss the Sudetenland,[35] and the talk was all war or peace. Even Father H said he was surprised that conscription had not been re-introduced because war was inevitable.[36]

Dad felt the same and when I heard my brother was joining the army I felt this overwhelming desire not to let him go alone. Father H shook his head when I explained but said he understood. He looked very sad, I swear his eyes became watery, and he later confessed that he felt bitter that the 'war to end all wars' had failed, and that people like me were going to get caught up in the same maelstrom as his generation had endured. It was easy enough to sign on and we both joined Dad's old regiment, the East Kent, better known as the Buffs. Father H told me to mention my place at King's Cambridge, my matriculation and go for officer training, but Eddie had no chance, and to Father H's horror and Dad's delight I joined the ranks with my brother. That was the end of my youth, and my dreams.

---

[35] September 22nd 1938 Hitler receives Chamberlain at Bad Godesberg demanding the immediate cession of all the Sudetenland.

[36] Conscription was applied on April 29th 1939 for men aged 20 for 6 months.

CHAPTER THREE

Early War Years

HORACE 1938-1940

Once I knew I was going into the army my Father stepped up his usual overbearing influence. It happened that he had worked on the teeth of a Major-General Sir John Kennedy[1] who just happened to be the Colonel of the East Kent Regiment. The only thing I knew about the Buffs was that Harry's Dad had been with them in the Great War and they were fairly local, often garrisoned in Dover, and well known for causing problems in the many pubs in Snargate Street.[2] I was sent to the Royal Military College, Sandhurst[3] for several months which I found gruelling, until I read Wolfgang's account. Now I realise we were treated like gentlemen, expected to behave like gentlemen, and if I am being honest, apart from far too many senseless drills it was, on reflection a pleasant time; similar to a Public School.

It was tough, but our lives were not put at risk by balancing blindfold whilst walking the plank, and we were not instructed to swim the Thames. I played a good deal of sport especially rugby since it was mainly during the winter months I was there. We all knew war was a distinct possibility, and at least I had seen something of what the Nazis were capable of, but none of us thought the war would be another major world war. Most of my friends were hoping for time in the Indian army and an opportunity to see the world while they were paid, fed and sheltered. For once in my life I was more realistic, and listened more attentively to the news, and read the foreign correspondence with more care than I had done hitherto. Nevertheless, I did not change that much. I did not do brilliantly at the college; I enjoyed sport too much and still enjoyed the pursuit of beautiful maidens. The lifestyle suited me, my companions were good fun.

Most of them were like me, from good prep and public schools and no high-flyers, otherwise as one joked, we would not be in the army. That remark which was passed around the bar one night tended to haunt me later. In a few years, in France, North Africa and Italy I would realise that

---

[1] 1937-1943.

[2] Had a legendry number of Public Houses but many lost in the shelling from France.

[3] Not the current Royal Military Academy Sandhurst which was founded on the merger of the Royal Military College and the Royal Military Academy, Woolwich in 1947.

our officers were not up to the standard of those in the German military. It is difficult and embarrassing but I will, now it is just history, admit the German soldiers and their officers were far better trained than we were, better organised, and better fighters. They were better all round in nearly every aspect of military life, their equipment was superior, but it did not make them right.

The Buffs were expanding rapidly, almost with a sense of urgency reflecting the dilemma the government faced; three new battalions were raised in 1939 alone.[4] I was attached to the 2nd Battalion as a 2nd Lieutenant, I felt terribly junior and nervous, but also felt inept. I had passed out at the near bottom of the heap, but such was the demand for manpower no one seemed to mind. I was sorry I was not sent to one of the new Battalions being raised because the 2nd Battalion was equipped with experienced officers, NCOs and all ranks had considerably more experience of life than I had. The 2nd Buffs to which I was now attached had just returned from Palestine,[5] and the East Kent Regiment was now honoured with the title of Royal. The major administrative offices were mainly based in Canterbury,[6] and by the time I joined most of the 2nd Battalion was in Borden Surrey, but I was attached to a small remnant at Shorncliffe, near Folkestone. We were in effect all over the place; the 1st Buffs had been in India, then Burma, and during my time more and more Battalions were being raised, pioneers, territorials and many others.[7]

I always found it slightly galling that some of the NCOs and men seemed to smile quietly every time I appeared. Apart from my sport there was one aspect of my new life in which I appeared to excel, and that was target shooting. There was a small range down beyond Hythe and I used a new 4 Mk 1 Lee-Enfield with a 3.5 telescopic sight[8] in which I was constantly able to outshoot anyone. My firing was so accurate that Major Hopper, a formidable giant of a man, paused in the Mess to congratulate me. This with my sport gave me a little more credence with the men, but I always felt uncertain in their presence.

One morning in early July I was instructed to take myself off in the company of a Redcap[9] to Hastings police station where one of our corporals was in trouble. The ride across Romney Marsh with its long

---

[4] 4th and 5th (Territorial Army) Battalions (1939-1947) and 6th (Home Defence) Battalion 1939-1941.

[5] Sent there in 1936 to quell a rebellion

[6] A new depot was built in Canterbury in 1938.

[7] By 1938 11 Battalions were formed and raised.

[8] Lee Enfield Rifle No 4 Mk 1 was not issued until 1939, and the telescopic sight a year later so this must have been part of the experiment in trying to mass-produce more sophisticated models.

[9] Military policeman.

twisting roads took time, but it was beautiful especially watching all the Peewits[10] rising and falling. We travelled in an old Morris and our conversation was limited to the weather. The corporal had been AWOL[11] for a week and had landed up in the police station because of a fight near the seaside pier. The police were only too happy to hand him over to us, and when my military policeman wanted to put cuffs on him I suggested that would not be necessary, and I would sit in the back with him. The policeman was considerably older and more experienced than me, and it was his business more than mine, but young as I was, I was the officer and there was no argument. This enabled me to speak to the soldier who would have been in his mid-twenties. He was reluctant at first until the military policemen, who was driving us towards Rye asked if it 'were women problems or drink?' I thought that, at least, was directly to the point and the soldier, called Aitkens, said his wife had run off with a grocer's boy. He had discovered they had 'holed up' in Hastings and that explained his departure. He had found the wife's lover working on the pier in the entertainment's section, dragged him outside and had 'given him a going over.'

The next day I had to appear with Corporal Aitkens in front of Major Hopper and present his case. I was astonished at being given this quasi-legal job, but apparently the Major always insisted that an officer represent his own men. It was not until then I realised that Aitkens was my corporal. I know it sounds incredible now, but I had only been there five weeks, for two of them Aitkens had been absent, and a man in uniform looks very different to a man in civvies. Aitkens was marched in at the double, a process that struck me as a mix between absurd comedy and cruel behaviour. He was asked if he were guilty or not to which he seemed to bellow at the top of his voice, 'Yes Sah.' I then described precisely what Aitkens had told me about his wife, the sense of anger and humiliation he had felt, and what I called the moderately inflicted punishment upon the adulterer.

Major Hopper sitting at his desk with his arms folded looked quite antagonistic, and then asked me for any recommendations. I had no idea what to say so I spoke honestly and suggested that Aitkens be given leave to sort out his domestic issues. I can recall to this day Aitkens looking at me from the side of his eyes as if I were stark-staring mad. The military policemen attending in the corner could hardly keep the smirk off his face. Major Hopper looked at me, and told me the army was a disciplined force and men could not take leave as when they wanted, not even on the death of their parents. He then sat down and glared at Aitkens as if he

---

[10] Green Plovers, Lapwings, common in that area until quite recently.

[11] Absent without leave.

were the devil incarnate. The next two minutes was a total silence as Major Hopper sat and looked at Aitkens and then me. "Soon," he said, "we may be going to war, and Aitkens you are an experienced and generally good soldier. I am going to remove your stripes for two weeks. I am giving you two days in the cold,[12] and the two days you go, with your officer here, to Hastings, and without causing the police to be brought in you can try and sort out your problem; dismissed." I do not know who felt the most shell shocked, Aitkens, the military policeman whose mouth seemed to have stuck wide open, or me at this incredible generosity from an officer known for his ferocity. Major Hopper said nothing further to me apart from instructing me to take the staff car. I stood out on the parade ground and watched another recalcitrant being marched up and down as I lit a cigarette; I still could not believe what had happened. The other three 2nd Lieutenants I shared my billet with also found the verdict unbelievable, and so out of character was the Major, they thought for a time I was spinning a yarn.

After Aitken's incarceration I went back with him to Hastings. In those days it was difficult to speak man to man with a soldier who saw officers, albeit young and junior, as belonging almost to another cast, but by the time we had driven through Winchelsea I was making progress. Aitkens was grateful to me for my defence, and I read him my version of the riot act telling him not to hit his wife's lover again. It was not a successful visit because the wife had now run off with someone else. It transpired that Aitkens had only been married six months, and it was not the first time this had happened. On the way back to barracks I tried to convince him that the marriage was hardly worth hanging onto as she seemed so wayward. Whether I succeeded or not I never discovered. Aitkens lived in a small village outside Maidstone, Aylesford, and had met his wayward wife in the local pub; I recall it was called the Chequers, but she lived in Chatham and Aitkens' whirlwind romance precluded him from finding out much about her background.

Normally one waits for two years before anticipating promotion, but by the time war was declared in 1939 I was made Lieutenant and given special duties on the firing range at Shorncliffe. I really enjoyed this aspect of my military life; I had found the start of life in the Battalion somewhat shaky, but thanks to my natural aptitude to aim accurately I gained a degree of respect and felt more at home. You can imagine my shock when Harry and his brother Eddie turned up for training. I had no idea Harry was joining up, the last I heard was that he was down for Cambridge, my father's one-time ambition for me. It was all very formal, I gave him a quick wink, and then later in the day, on the pretence of

---

[12] Local expression for the army gaol.

looking at his rifle, we managed a quick chat. As a new man I guessed he would be going into one of the newly raised Battalions, but his marks were understandably outstanding and he was brought into the 2nd Battalion. His brother Eddie was also good but was snatched as a replacement for the 1st Battalion and was shipped out to Egypt to join them as one of forty odd replacements. Harry was unhappy about being parted, but I managed to point out that we had little say in such matters. I shall never understand Harry's reluctance to accept the offer of officer training, but it was no surprise to me that he soon had corporal stripes on his shoulders. Harry also proved to be excellent with sharp-shooting, and I noted that he was very popular with not only the other new recruits, but even the older hands, which was unusual.

I can recall the sheer expectancy of September 1939; we waited for the bombers and the orders day after day, but the news was mainly naval and Poland. I was given a few days' leave that I spent at home. My father seemed unduly worried, but then he had been through the first war. He was talking about moving to Wales or Scotland on the grounds that if the Germans invaded they would do so across the English Channel which we overlooked. I was staggered by him taking such a pessimistic view because most of us felt fairly upbeat about winning; he seemed to assume we would lose. There is no fathoming what goes on in the minds of other people; even one's own family. Mum was totally against any movement, but only because she had spent so much time and effort in her garden of all things. Now when I look back I can recall a couple of officer friends who were treating the possible conflict as a potential sporting encounter, and even some people in the ranks felt very confident. I can also recall, at least in two cases, where the over-confidence was really a cover because when the bullets started flying one broke down, and another disappeared. I had started to get to know Corporal Aitkens and he was far from happy, not with the long discarded family situation, but claimed that war was dangerous and nothing to be pleased about; I tended to agree with Aitkens. I am ashamed to say I did very little personal preparation, and apart from a general schoolboy attitude had little idea about the French and Belgium borders where we were supposed to be heading.[13] In a very childish way I started thinking of it as a holiday, but sleeping under canvas with limited and primitive facilities soon made me hanker for the barracks.

I was approached by a captain from another regiment who had been told I was something of an expert on guns. I explained that I had a reputation as a marksman but little else. Nevertheless, he persuaded me to help him, and a few others, to look at some new anti-tanks guns which

---

[13] The British Expeditionary Force (BEF) started crossing to France on September 9th.

had arrived, as none of the platoons, who were supposed to be experts in anti-tank warfare, had ever seen them before. It seemed incredulous that an army going off to war was sent guns that no one had seen before.[14] It was a strange looking weapon and even loading it was difficult, but when I looked in one of the packing cases out fell a manual. After that we found more manuals and about an hour later we had learned all we could about the new weapon. I was somewhat feted because I had had the sense to look in the packing cases for the instructions. We really were just a bunch of amateurs, at least most of us officers were. We had few cars, many of them civilian, a few lorries, weapons we had not seen, radio sets which would not work, and maps that were hopelessly out of date; that is how we set off from Calais. Our greatest confidence was in the French Army, supposed to be the largest and best equipped in the world; I also hoped they were better trained than we were.[15] We had a French army on our flank, but we noted with some consternation, that as amateur as we felt, we still sent patrols out on a regular basis, but the French never bothered.[16]

We were all called to attention one day when the Secretary of State for War suddenly turned up.[17] He looked a very jovial sort of chap, but he passed by at high speed, obviously intent on meeting more important people. We soon had another contingent for our Battalion, if I recall correctly they had been training in Wales as pioneers. At my level I had no idea what was happening in terms of the war, we seemed to know more what was happening on the high seas with the Graf Spee[18] than what was happening in front of us. I suppose on hindsight this is always the case for foot soldiers and their junior officers. We exercised, marched, cleaned our weapons, and too often held parades if only for something to do. Had I not had the foresight to bring several books I think the sheer boredom would have driven me mad. It was impossible to get hold of reliable news, and the decent newspapers, when they did appear, often arrived a week late. The temperature of the corporate psyche rose when we heard from above (senior officers) that we were actually fighting the Germans in Norway.[19] I was just beginning to wonder whether the Germans were frightened of facing the massive French army, when news

---

[14] This must be referring to the new 25mm Hotchkiss gun produced at this time.

[15] It was only in February 1939 politicians agreed to increase the size of the army. By the time the Germans attacked there were ten more or less complete British Infantry Divisions in France; some were not well trained.

[16] General Alan Brooke was uneasy about the state of the French Army.

[17] Nov 1939 Leslie Hore-Belisha visited BEF following a row known as the Pillbox Affair.

[18] Graf Spee scuttled in River Plate estuary 17th Dec 1939.

[19] April 15th 1940 British units fighting in south Norway.

came that the Germans were attacking through Belgium into northern France. We were suddenly on the move and I think it fair to say none of us were feeling very exalted at the idea of imminent combat. My only prayer was that I would not be a quitter; I had succeeded at little else, but I did not want to be a coward.

Because of what happened to me a few years later I cannot remember all the historical details, and my memory is one more of impressions and scenes than a serious connected thread. The Royal Lancers[20] led the way and we followed; I moved with my platoon behind some tanks and smoked heavily to take away the smell of their ghastly fumes and calm my nerves. It was still a few days later before I heard guns firing but we were soon in the thick of a local tank battle. To this day I have no idea where we were except somewhere in Belgium, and the scene of devastation and panic was upon us and enveloped us so quickly, I felt as if I had entered another world. We came upon some French tanks which had been totally destroyed, and there was smoke pouring from one nearest me, which even as I studied it burst into flames. To my horror a man emerged from beneath the tank covered in flames and came running towards us. Someone standing behind me shot him dead. "He wasn't a Jerry" I screamed.

The Corporal on my left replied that the shot was an act of mercy. Before I could reply I was suddenly conscious of what felt like angry bees around my head and some distinct clanging on the tank; it took several seconds and a soldier on my right falling down before I realised we were actually being fired at. I dropped down at once, but then realised the soldier who had got down just before me had done so because he was dead. His face had simply disappeared, no eyes, no nose, the lower lip was in place and a tongue was hanging out, but the rest was a pool of unrecognisable blood and flesh. To be completely honest I was nearly sick. I looked up over the bank but the Corporal pulled me back. It was none other than Aitkens, the man who lost his wife. It was he who shot the poor burning devil staggering from the tank. Aitkens pulled me down just on time because no sooner had he done so than a storm of wasps buzzed above us and dirt kicked up on the bank where my head had been one second earlier. "Thanks" was all I could bring myself to say as I squirmed down the bank and tried to bury myself in the dirt.

There were about a dozen of us caught behind the bank and it transpired I was the senior man there. That sounded absurd then, when it dawned on me and just as absurd now when I look back. The only time I had fired a gun was on the tranquil ranges of Shorncliffe, and I had never been under fire in my life. It was a near state of panic. I looked to Aitkens

---

[20] His history is correct here; the Royal Lancers were the BUF Spearhead.

for help but could say nothing. I think he understood me because he said that we were probably best keeping our heads down for an hour until it became dark. As we lay there listening to some intermittent shooting and the occasional explosion, it dawned on me how totally insignificant I was. Someone somewhere had directed that troops be sent to France then Belgium, then someone, still far above me, had directed us to walk in this direction, and now we were being shot at; there were no directions. No one had said find the enemy and shoot at them; that was what the Germans were doing to us and most effectively. To shoot back meant putting one's head over the bank to see what was happening, and that brought a hail of deadly lead.

My war here was not some grand design, not some act of military genius, not a tactical display of a greater strategy; it was a few men nearly sick with fear trying to stay alive by hiding in a damp smelly ditch. We had covered the dead soldier's face, but already the flies were gathering around him, and there was a vile smell of excreta wherever I turned. Life had suddenly become horrific, terrifying, and in the so-called great scheme of things I felt like a flea who was trying to survive on an elephant's back, having no idea of what was going on. When I did try to move I realised that without knowing it I had messed my pants; such was the fear I had not been conscious of this embarrassment, and my hands were shaking uncontrollably. It was the shame of my personal situation that suddenly drove me into action. Instead of looking at Aitkens for instructions I said we were going to move back towards the farmhouse, and we would do so in twos and threes. While two crawled back on their bellies the rest waited in case the enemy crept closer. I insisted that I would be the last person; it was not bravery, but gave me a chance to give myself some sort of clean up.

As I worked my way back a German machine gun[21] opened up; bullets were blowing puffs of dirt and twinging small stones all around me. I was stuck in the field about a hundred yards from the farm house, this time not so much paralysed by fear, but by circumstance, I was in a small hollow and I simply could not get out. Every time I moved bullets started up, I was, as in the old cowboy films I used to love so much on a Saturday morning 'pinned down.' I nearly fell asleep but a voice woke me with a sudden jar, it was Harry of all people, pulling me by my coat.

"Are you hurt?" "

"No, but how did you get here?"

Apparently he had crawled, thinking I was wounded. I gathered that it was now or never because the Germans were working their way forward

---

[21] Possibly an early Spandau.

and there had been reports of some German artillery being moved into our sector.

"In a minute I am going to yell, and the chaps will open up with everything they have from the farmhouse and those walls on our flanks, that's when we move as fast as we can."

He shouted and I stood up with him only to have my legs collapse under me. I was not wounded, I was not paralysed with fear but I had lain motionless for so long both legs were dead with cramp. Harry thought I had been wounded because he picked me up as if I were a large pet dog, and carried me to the farmhouse. Even to this day I can remember how immensely strong he was; I guessed it had been all those years working in the scrapyard. I barely had time to thank him and he was gone. Aitken knew Harry and told me he was attached to a post a mile to the west somewhere near a place called Oudenarde[22] under some officer called Ernest Edlman. That is all I can recall, a place called Oudenarde somewhere in Belgium.

I could not help reflecting that in our brief lives Harry had rescued me twice. Back on my feet and feeling better with a hot cup of tea, I realised that we were in a terrible predicament. We were in an isolated spot on the edge of our own salient being slowly surrounded by German infantry. Fortunately they did not appear to have any artillery or tank support, because we only had our rifles, two Bren guns and a concern about the amount of ammunition. Aitkens had explained that Harry had been sent by this Captain; at least I think that was his rank, Edlman to retreat when it was dusk. I remember Edlman's name because I had a man in my platoon with a similar name. It was dangerous to stand near an open window or doorway; we were met by a storm of bullets. We had quite a few wounded down in the cellar, some of them in a terrible state, and we had no medic. I crawled into a roof space with a 303[23] and watched and waited for movement in the long grass ahead of me. There was no movement, and this did not surprise me, the Germans had a reputation for excellent field craft.

What they could not conceal was the flash of their weapons. I recall this incident because it was my first, but having noted that a flash occurred between an old wall and a low hedge I fired into the gap two rapid shots. There was no mistaking the target who seemed to hover then fell backwards. I heard Aitken shout his praise because he had been watching through my binoculars looking for targets. I felt exhilarated at

---

[22] South of Oudenarde the Germans were trying to forge what is known as the (River) Escaut front; the 2nd Buffs were severely attacked at Petegem (two miles south-west of Oudenarde during the 20th-21st May. The Buffs suffered some 200 casualties during this engagement which involved both defence and counter-attack.

[23] Lee Enfield 303 rifle.

first, but then sad. It was a strange feeling and I can recall thinking I was not cut out to be a soldier; this man had been trying to kill me yet I felt terrible about killing him. I did not have time to think because my position in the roof was exposed, and I heard what I suspect was an anti-tank missile buzz by the roof. I scrambled down in time because the next one took the roof away, and the ceiling crumbled making us all look like ghosts. It dawned on me that by being in the house we were a focal point for their firing, and as the only officer I asked for any NCOs to report to me, but that was only Aitkens; there were two sergeants but both were below seriously wounded.

We decided one corporal and a junior officer, to start moving out as soon as possible. We would leave the seriously wounded in the hope the Germans would provide some medical care because we had nothing. It fell to me to explain this to the men and I was borne up by the way they took it as the most sensible thing to do; I had feared they may show resentment at being left. Again I decided that along with Aitkens and two others and one Bren gun, we would try and hold the enemy's attention while the others went south and west.[24]

At first we were lucky, and I cracked a joke about the Germans stopping for tea, but they must have heard me because there was a flurry of activity across the field, so we let rip with the Bren gun. It would be at least nine o'clock before it was dark, and it was now only about 7.00pm. I was just about to say something when a huge explosion rocked the house and the stairs collapsed. I called up the stairs but there was no answer from the two men at the Bren gun; I called again but even amongst other extraneous noises there was a deathly silence from upstairs. Aitkens and I gave one of the wounded a large white sheet to hang out the window once we were gone. I ran with the corporal beside me; we simply ran, not even trying to crouch, but ran towards a line of trees. We had just about reached it when I thought Aitkens had slapped me on the back, so hard I fell over in yet another ditch. It was Aitkens who pointed out to me as I struggled to my feet that I had been shot.

The bullet seemed to have lodged itself into my shoulder, and although the impact had not felt serious the pain started to overwhelm me. All I could think was that now I was going to be a prisoner as well. Aitkens had got my coat and tunic off and was inspecting my back; he had no medical material at all, and so he used my shirt to try and stem the flow of blood which was not too much, fortunately, but the pain was fast becoming excruciating. It was now nearly dark, but I think that was more to do with losing consciousness.

---

[24] There was considerable fighting round the Escaut and two Victoria Crosses were won by British Soldiers.

There are many things I could say about this experience of war on my inexperienced young mind. I do know in my mind that war is evil and disgusting; I know that I am not a natural soldier, and I know that I am only alive because of other people, the kind of people my father would not have appreciated. I came and went from consciousness for what seemed an eternity. In that time, I learned later, that Harry had come back a second time to find me, and helped Aitkens get me out under cover of darkness. Then Aitkens took personal charge of me in some private citizen's car and drove me through lines of refugees to a makeshift hospital nearer the coast, where some immediate medical attention relieved the pain. I could hardly thank Aitkens enough, but I was deeply saddened to hear from him that Harry was killed in the attempt. I now know that Aitkens was wrong, and that Harry in fact survived, but I was not to find out the truth until much later. Harry had come to my rescue three times and had paid the price. Because I had once stood up for Aitkens he had also saved me, and brought me to safety. Then I gathered he had tried to find our unit again, avoided being taken prisoner twice but sadly was killed in North Africa. I am sad and angry with myself that I took Aitkens for granted. I should have done the decent thing and written him a letter.

I was angry with my father, who, when I explained what Aitkens had done, retorted that the better working class man understood the notion of duty. My father's reaction was so bad my whole attitude towards him changed. His notion of class, the way he treated some of his patients were bad enough, but viewing Aitkens as merely doing his duty put my father way down the scales, as we used to say. My mother was pleased to see me during convalescence, but seemed more concerned that her garden would not be damaged by enemy action. I never discovered what happened to my mother, but I suspect I was seeing the start of some mental degeneration. As from that day when my father made that stupid remark I turned my back on him. Looking back I regret it now, I never saw him or my mother again, but I feel more angry that I did not write to Aitkens before he was killed, and I felt pathologically sad that Harry was dead. My wound was more serious than I thought, and my convalescence period meant I was put on home duties at Canterbury for some length of time.

I had written the sad news to Edna and we met and talked about Harry and I am ashamed to say that we made love. I think Edna with her eyes tightly closed was making love to Harry, not me. Afterwards I felt no pleasure; even though Harry was dead I felt guilty, and I told Edna how I felt, but that I had always loved her, and gave her my address in Canterbury. I promised I would not contact her again, but would respond at once if she wanted. For three weeks I waited to hear from her, and hope faded slowly; I never heard from her again. When I look back I seemed to be the epitome of failure, I failed school, failed my parents, stopped loving them even, failed in my first soldierly venture, failed Edna; I was twenty-years of age and felt miserable about the past and the future.

WOLFGANG 1939-40

All three of us when we discussed this project unanimously agreed that we would remain anonymous. Quite how we are going to achieve this I have no idea, but I know from the time I killed the man in a street brawl, and because of my attitude then, I must remain totally anonymous. Even after my death which cannot be too far distant I wish to remain anonymous because of my friends. How could they believe that I did such things? I note that Horace is very unhappy with himself, but the failures and mistakes he made incline me to think he led a saint's life compared to me. I know why Horace wishes to remain anonymous, but in my opinion his so-called misdeeds are not that serious; the moral ramifications of my actions still cause me deep anguish to this day. I reckon myself amongst those who go down to the pit, like one forsaken among the dead, and I feel God's wrath overwhelming me. The things I have done make me a thing of horror to my companions.[25] I really do need a reassurance that this enterprise never reveals who we are: I must remain untraceable.

As a member of the SS we were focused, and trained time and time again to refocus on loyalty to the Führer and Germany; nothing else counted. It never crossed my mind that we had no right to move into the Sudetenland, take over Czechoslovakia, roll into Poland as if it were ours by right. I, like all my comrades knew it was right, and we never questioned any orders. Looking back after all these years I find it difficult to understand why I, and thousands of others, could believe we had a divine right, or some mythological purpose as the Aryan race to be masters. This question rises like unwelcome nausea every time I see a product of that period, a photograph, a Holocaust memorial, a war memorial, a film, and even Harry's rise from his working class to make it to a university only to have to join the army as a soldier because of what we were doing. The nausea rises not simply because of the unbelievable evil we perpetrated, but the fact that we thought we were right; it is this I find difficult to live with even in my fading old age. In writing this all down I am not apologising, it is too late to apologise, I am not even seeking understanding, I just want to place on record what happened.

---

[25] Wolfgang is almost quoting Psalm 88 verses 3 to 8; certainly paraphrasing it.

By August 1939 life was pleasant but tense. It was enjoyable because a good deal of my time was in my barracks near Potsdam where I played *Skat*[26] with some like-minded comrades, and tense because we wanted to be relieved of the parade duties and be ready for the war we knew was coming. We had to be careful how we behaved because most of us were suspicious that we were listened to and reported on. Eaves-dropping had become part and parcel of life. I can recall Albert, a real Berliner with his usual *Galgenhumor*[27] that I suspect led him into trouble as not only was he dismissed, but we never heard of him again. Another chap was dismissed because he opened his mouth too wide to a girl he flirted with for an evening.

There was no shortage of girls who fell in love with our very smart uniforms, the *Narzisse*[28] surrounded us, but they would soon report a misdemeanour or drunken revelation. I was bored to tears with parades and marching for the big wigs, and could almost feel the first elements of cynicism creeping into me as I watched the party members taking the salute with puffed out chests. I heard a joke had done the rounds that the true Aryan was as eagle-eyed as the bespectacled Himmler, as sure footed as the club-footed Goebbels, as slim as the big-bellied Goering and as fair as the black-haired Hitler. I heard it from my brother Hugo on leave, but I also knew that men could be sent to Dachau for laughing at the joke. Hugo and I did enjoy one weekend together at home, but after my thrashing him we never restored the closeness we felt as young boys. I noted that my uniform drew admiring glances most of the time and from some a degree of nervousness. Hugo's Wehrmacht field colours tended to get him more beers than mine did, but Hugo was not happy wearing it at home.

Hugo was infantry and I knew that he would be in action in Poland, and I was desperate not to be on parade duty if war started. The LSSAH[29] had most of the parade and guard duties for the top men, but many of us were fighting men, true Waffen-SS and wanted to disappear from the parade ground. Our *Obergruppenführer* was Sepp Dietrich[30] and the rumour was that he was pushing very hard to ensure the LSSAH was allowed to fight. It was sometime in the summer[31] we heard that the Führer had placed us under control of the OKH, the Army High Command, and I confess it was with great delight that in September we were the first to roll into Poland.

---

[26] Popular German card game.
[27] Typical cynical humour of Berlin, comparable to Cockney.
[28] Daffodils – slang word for female Nazis.
[29] *Leibstandarte SS Adolf Hitler.*
[30] Josef "Sepp" Dietrich.
[31] August to be precise, because of Poland.

The fighting was not as easy or straightforward as some history books would have people believe. To my knowledge there were no death and glory attacks on tanks by Polish cavalry; that was as much a myth as the belief that their air-force was destroyed in one day. On our second day I found myself pinned down by some very sharp rifle fire. They had no tanks or heavy artillery in the area, but somehow we were unable to push forward. We soon received a message from our *Hauptsturmführer*[32] that we must move forward or else. This was a direct command so we ran forward seeking what cover we could. There had been about twenty of us pinned down by one sniper, and before we got to the base of the church tower he had killed two more and wounded the man on my right. My adrenalin was racing and I managed to run right up against the church wall. I edged around and found a door that was open. Inside the church was empty, but I could hear firing from above in the tower for which I could not find an entrance, until I pushed over what appeared to be a large wardrobe with all the priestly vestments.

For once in my life I took my boots off and walked up the winding staircase in stocking feet and caught the two snipers unawares. I used my *maschinenpistole*[33] and killed them both with one long blast; one of the bullets must have struck an artery as the man nearest to me fell forward there was a fountain of blood; I could feel all its warmth down my face and neck. I ducked back down the stairs to let them know all was safe; I was not going to do it from the tower window because I knew our own snipers would be watching for the tiniest movement. We were angry that in such a small village we were held up several times by well-placed snipers. The church was the only stone building, everything else was wood, thatch and tin and before we left we made sure that every building was burning well; there would be no place for snipers there anymore.

It was a hot September and the dust and dirt in our faces and mouths will always remain a memory. We set pace behind two tanks and made rapid progress, eventually halting in a town called Błonie.[34] It was a small town but much more substantial than the villages we had destroyed, and in places reminded me of a small German town, but lacking our tidiness, and there was a high degree of obvious poverty.

It was in Błonie that I think I started to have doubts about myself. We had settled in by a day or two and I was billeted in a house on the north side of the Market Square, exhausted and grateful to have a comfortable bed and some decent food. Various prisoners were being mustered

---

[32] SS-Chief Assault Leader.

[33] Sub-machine gun, probably the MP38 or MP40 often erroneously called Schmeissers although Hugo Schmeisser had nothing to do with their design.

[34] Then a population of about 9,000 in mid-Poland; since 1902 a railway station there on the important Warsaw-Kalisz line.

outside in the square, some Polish soldiers, not many, and quite a few Jews. The Polish soldiers looked dejected and resentful, and were marched off towards the railway station. The Jews were a mixed bunch, mainly family groups who huddled together looking frightened. They were there for at least three days and since no one bothered to feed or water them they began to look quite hollow.

There was no sanitation and they used the gutters, but being a dry and hot September the smell soon became unbearable. Just when I thought we were going to be moved out I was ordered with my group to march the Jews out of the square to some woods on the outskirts. They looked almost grateful that something was happening, and one of them, although Polish spoke in excellent German asking me where we were going. He may have been educated, but he was a Polish enemy and, more to the point not really human like us, so I ignored him totally. Many of the local Polish population had emerged and watched the sorry procession, and they jeered and shouted at the Jews that clearly indicated to me that it was not just us Germans who found Jews so demeaning to the human race. One Polish man offered one of the Jews some bread, but one of my comrades pushed him back over the pavement with the butt of his rifle. When we arrived at the wood, hardly out of town two of our lorries were parked, and the order came to group them together and open fire on command.

When they were tightly huddled the lorry flaps were dropped and two MG34s[35] opened up spitting torrents of bullets into the Jews. We stood to the side shooting any who tried to run; one of my comrades said it was excellent target practice, and another laughed shouting it was like working at the abattoir. The smell of cordite was strong, and the screaming of what we called the vermin is beyond description. We then walked amongst the corpses finishing off anyone who was still alive. A young girl started to lift herself up on her elbows, and even as I pulled the trigger she smiled at me. She fell back on the corpse beneath her, the smile frozen on her face. I was transfixed for a moment, but my attention was drawn by the figure of a priest in a cassock standing not far from me. He had tears running down his cheeks and looking straight at me telling me in broken German that God would not forget this day. My reaction was without feeling or thought; I raised my gun and shot him in the chest.[36]

---

[35] Considered to be the first general purpose machine gun which could fire for long periods of time. It was introduced into the German army in the 1930s and gave way later to the more popular Spandau.

[36] The *Leibstandarte* murdered over 50 Jews in Błonie, but in December 1940 the town confined remaining Jews into a ghetto; in February 1941 its some 2,000 inhabitants were sent to perish in the Warsaw Ghetto.

Later that night I drank quite a bit along with my comrades. Most of us had already become accustomed to killing, but it was the first time we had eliminated so many in one haul. We made jokes all evening, told funny stories, reasoned that the world would be better for a few more purges, and then collapsed into a deep sleep. During the night I kept dreaming of the girl smiling at me and her face transformed into that of my mother, and the priest was there too, but I kept getting him confused with Hugo my brother. When I was eventually woken in the early hours, our rest over, I was beginning to feel slightly distraught.

I cannot pretend that my involvement in this massacre, for which some of my old comrades were executed after the war, started to change my mind about what we were doing, but it sowed doubts. The girl's face and the priest still return to my mind even last night, that is, less than six hours ago as I now struggle to write this account more than half a century later. The killing of children we were told was necessary because they might grow up and retaliate, and they were not truly human anyway. The girl's smiling face was very human to me, and the priest had fair hair like mine. These were doubts, but I did not share them with anyone because everyone else seemed buoyed up with the experience. I think the thing that disturbed me most was the fact that I knew I would never be able tell my mother that I had been complicit in such a massacre.

It was outside Błonie that I had my first injury. We thought the fighting had finished apart from titbits in Warsaw; I had opted to walk and we were strolling towards a small village. It could have been a Sunday afternoon at home, the temperature was warm to cooling; there was some dust in the air churned up by our vehicles and a good deal of laughter and chatter. I felt the impact of the bullet before I heard any noise, I felt as if I had been kicked by a horse and immediately a searing pain shot up my back as my leg gave way. Heinz, a friend who had been walking beside me dragged me down into a ditch. There were several snipers both in the village and the flanks; we had chatted our way into a trap. The amount of blood seeping through my battle dress caused both Heinz and me some panic. The wound was high in my leg and there was nowhere to apply a tourniquet, and although I wanted to try and stand Heinz virtually sat on me for an hour until the opposition had been sorted or fled. The village was burnt to the ground, and we hanged about twenty men who seemed old enough to have fired at us. My loss of blood was causing concern to the medical orderly, and the next thing I knew was that with two others I was in a commandeered lorry being driven back to a nearby Wehrmacht hospital.

As it transpired all was well, the wound had done little damage but the danger had been the bleeding that they stopped, they told me, just on time. Had I arrived at the hospital an hour later it may have been too late.

I thanked Heinz for saving me by letter; I never saw him again, but read that he was executed for the Błonie massacre after the war. I deserved to be with him, but events unfolded very differently for me, as you will come to understand. I had a week in the hospital, most of the first part dozing and seeing the girl with the smiling face; I have to admit my conscience was not overly disturbed, but her constant presence and the image of the priest who looked like Hugo continue to haunt me. The officers and staff of the Wehrmacht hospital were very efficient, but I could not help but feel a degree of disdain from some of them. I think in the early days the Waffen-SS had a reputation as a bunch of upstarts, political thugs and amateurs, but we were soon recognised as a formidable fighting force by the Wehrmacht and the enemy. I wondered at first if the way we treated Jews and torched villages was the cause of their attitude, but I knew many Wehrmacht units had done the same.

I was given home leave that I felt exhilarated about; it seemed like an eternity since I had seen my mother. When I did knock on the front door I was surprised when Hugo opened it still in uniform, and with his gear still on his back. We had been on the same train without realising it; he too had been given home leave. I was astonished at his rank, it did not make sense. He had entered as a *soldat, grenadier*, I think that is Private in English terms, but now he wore the insignia of an *Obergefreiter*, which is best described as a senior corporal, normally given for six years' service, and Hugo had accomplished nothing of the sort. He explained that he and another soldier had accomplished a daring mission against a heavily armed farm house, and there had been talk of the award of the *EKII, Eisernes Kreuz 2 klasse*,[37] but a zealous senior officer had literally bribed the two with home leave and a rise in the ranks; they had grabbed this position simply because of more pay and being an *Obergefreiter* meant they were freed up from menial tasks. Such a thing could not have happened in the SS, and I confess I was surprised at it happening in the Wehrmacht, and wondered how he managed to swing the six years part. I was also astonished and amused that Hugo preferred rank and money to a medal; I knew men who lost their lives for the sake of just an *EKII*.

It was good to be home; there was considerable satisfaction that Poland was now in our control, pleasure that England and France had not attacked, and a slight curiosity as to why Stalin had been allowed to share the spoils of war in Poland. We had always been taught that the communists with the Jews were our fundamental eternal enemy, and yet we appeared to be fighting with and not against Stalin and his red communist empire. Hugo and Mum both raised this, but I stuck to my

---

[37] Iron Cross 2nd Class.

embedded loyalty and answered that the leaders knew what they were doing.

My relationship with Hugo still had that sense of distance ever since the beating, but we did go for some strolls along the River Main and chatted.

"Do you remember Enoch?" Hugo suddenly asked me as we sat smoking and watching a small boat work its way down river. I nodded, I would not forget that period of time when Hugo was betraying the national cause. "I got a letter from him a couple of years back, I didn't tell you because you were pretty mad with me." It transpired that Enoch had left Germany, travelled to France and was busy learning English because he thought that would be the safest country. I resisted any strong opinions or pronouncements; I wanted to get over that period of time with Hugo. I carried on smoking and watching the boat, but Hugo persisted, "he was just like us," he said, "Jew or no Jew he was German."

I restrained myself, pointing out that Jews being subhuman could not possibly be German; they only spoke the language as a means of gaining control. "I saw a massacre in Poland," Hugo continued, "where some of your mates had wiped out nearly twenty Jews, and as we walked by they looked exactly the same as you and me. If they didn't have that circumcision, which is some religious rite, there was no physical difference. You know in that massacre they had killed some women as well...and the women are certainly no different from any other woman." I did not answer for a moment, at first I wondered if Hugo were referring to Błonie, but we had killed many more than twenty, and as I looked at Hugo I saw the priest's face and shut my eyes, only to see the smiling girl. "You alright?" Hugo could see I was uncomfortable.

I took him by the arm and said that I did not mind him talking like this to me, but under no circumstances should he mention it to other people, or he could be in very serious trouble. He shrugged his shoulders in a way that was typically Hugo; I could tell that he was a good soldier, but he was not a true member of the party ideal.[38] I spent the rest of the afternoon talking about anything that would distract him from bringing up Poland and Jews.

The next day we went down town to do some shopping for Mum when we bumped into Kurt, my old leader in the SA. He was in civilian clothes and looked bloated beyond belief. I had never seen anyone run to seed so rapidly, and although it was mid-morning he stank of beer. I found it difficult to imagine a time when I had so admired him. He greeted us with considerable delight, even though he was uncertain who Hugo was, and wanted to take us for a drink. We declined, but we sat and had a coffee

---

[38] NSDAP, frequently referred to as the Nazi Party.

with him while he rambled on about how badly he had been treated. He suddenly turned nasty for no reason at all. He was besotted by my uniform but started to sneer that Hugo, who was wearing his Wehrmacht dress, had been obliged to save the *Leibstandarte* in Poland. I had no idea what he was talking about, but I quickly gathered that he felt the SA had been betrayed, and that the SS had taken their rightful place.[39]

I looked at Hugo and it was immediately clear that Hugo had switched off long ago, and was watching a rather young shop girl setting out a counter outside the shop opposite. I was polite, but decided it was time to go, but Kurt suddenly put his hand on my arm forcing me down stating he was not finished. Hugo came alive immediately, and threw coffee in Kurt's face. We both stood up and walked away only to have abuse thrown at us. The word 'cowards' made us both stop, and Hugo headed back to the furious Kurt and said something that made him sit down and shut up. I never did ask or hear what Hugo said but it worked since Kurt sat and looked suddenly very meek. I was genuinely sorry for Kurt; he had become a misfit, gone to seed, and was completely lost. When I look back on this event from this distance two things occur to me. The first was that Kurt was probably unstable as a person, but it took a bit of growth on my part to realise the truth of this fact. The second is that I have barely remembered Kurt, and it is only by writing this brief personal account as agreed, that such memories are re-emerging.

The human mind is a strange phenomenon, I frequently found myself recalling the girl who smiled and the priest I shot, but Kurt, two or three times in half a century. I think I only recalled him this time because I was ruminating on what a professional soldier Hugo had become, but I think, on reflection, his politics and philosophy were suspect by the standards of that day, but in a fire fight he would be a most welcome comrade. There was no question that I could not give him a beating now, and although we never spoke of that occasion it was always there. We talked and laughed together, but we were never as close as we had been when boys; the new Germany had driven a wedge between us, and I was to blame.

I also felt sad that my Mum seemed to adore Hugo with an affection that I suspected was greater than she felt for me. When Hugo had returned to his unit I tried to re-establish some of the old warmth, but while I knew she loved me, I had a distinct feeling there was a gap between us. One evening she mentioned that Hugo had mentioned the massacred Jews he had seen in Poland, asking me if I had seen the same. I could hardly tell her that not only had I seen the same, but that I had participated in a larger massacre. I tried to avoid the subject by pointing

---

[39] In fact the *Leibstandarte* had to be rescued by an army regiment at Pabianice, but Wolfgang may have forgotten this, or was not there.

out that the Jews were subhuman and were our enemy. "I agree," she said, "that the Jews let us down in the last war, they signed the Versailles Treaty, they hold all the wealth, but they are human and killing the women seems grotesque." I looked at her and for a moment saw the girl who smiled. What would my Mum have said had she known I killed not only women but children and babies? I did not answer and Mum said she hoped that Hugo and I were not involved. I lied, I nodded, and to escape her questions went for a smoke by the river. When I said goodbye to her a week later she gave me one of those looks that made me wonder if she knew the truth. I sometimes think mothers may not have a magical insight into their offspring, but they have a powerful instinct when things are not right. I thought my actions were right, I was good at obeying orders, but my mother's instinct seemed, on reflection, to penetrate to the moral depravity and evil to which we had all so readily adapted.

When I returned to my barracks I was attached as infantry to a new Motorised Artillery battalion. This was novel to me, but my role was more to do with infantry than guns, which still meant more training.[40] I had to stand in for parade duty for further injury recovery time in Potsdam, and enjoyed some pleasant moments in Berlin. The city felt vibrant, and we all knew the new emerging Germany was succeeding. There had been a fear that the French would attack, and that the British would be in support. Most of the older people could remember the last war and the possibility of a long war of attrition was for them inconceivable. Those of us who were younger did not have the same fear, and often when we spoke about it we felt encouraged that, unlike the last war, it would only be a war on one front, since the Russians, strange bedfellows that they were, now came to the party as our allies.

After a few parades and too many evenings wandering up and down the *Tiergarten*,[41] I joined my new unit that, for a time was detached from the Artillery battalion for special training. The early part of 1940 was complex with constant difficult training, and we were hardly given any spare time, frequently confined to barracks and ordered, if given any form of home release, not to mention the training. We all realised, though we were not formally told, that an attack was being planned, and we guessed it would be along the French border. All us pundits, as usual were wrong.

In May we suddenly received orders to move, and the *Leibstandarte* became part of a Wehrmacht Division[42] but, once again, I and many others were sent to a hastily set up training camp not far from the Dutch

---

[40] In March 1940 Hitler authorised creation of four motorised artillery battalions; the OKW were reluctant to supply the guns from its own arsenal but the *Leibstandarte* was soon up to strength.

[41] German for Animal Garden, a famous park in the centre of Berlin.

[42] Part of the Wehrmacht's 227th Infantry Division.

border. It was clear to most of us by then that we were avoiding the Maginot Line[43] of defence, and were going to attack through the Low Countries. There is no question that we were concerned, we may have been arrogant young men, but we believed that the French, backed by the British would be a formidable foe. It was well known that the French had the largest army, the British a formidable navy, and some quietly expressed the view we may be biting off more than we could chew. However, in the *Leibstandarte* we felt unbeatable which I put down to the arrogance of young people misled by politicians whom I now recognise, were not just fundamentally flawed, but downright evil: I did not think like that in 1940.

In early May[44] we were given new uniforms which we thought were demeaning because they were Dutch, and given precise instructions where to cross the border. My small group set off just north of Venlo, travelling down the *Dammerbrucher Staße* where there was a Dutch border post here the name changed to *Weselseweg*. Just before we came in sight of the border we traversed some fields and a small copse, passed a farmhouse and emerged in Holland without any incident. We then re-formed on the *Weselseweg* and marched back towards home; that is Germany. It was a clever ruse, the few border guards who were awake in the middle of the night assumed we were Dutch since we came from the Dutch side, and thought we were reinforcements since news of our build-up of forces must have been known.

Our only Dutch speaker was in front, but he was not naturally fluent and this concerned us, and as *Scharführer* I stood right behind him my MP38 ready to fire. We need not have worried too much, there were only about fifteen men there, though no doubt there were barracks somewhere nearby which our seniors would have detailed others to deal with. When an elderly Dutch officer spoke it became clear that our so-called Dutch speaker was not coping, and whilst this simply bemused the senior officer I noted that just behind him a young soldier was bringing his gun to the ready. I decided that hesitation was the last thing we needed so I shot him with a short burst and ordered them to drop their weapons. They understood German better than we did their Dutch, there was little delay and they were clearly outnumbered, outgunned and completely taken by surprise.

We sent a signal and within minutes the border crossing was dismantled and our troops travelled through in great numbers and at full speed. We jettisoned our Dutch uniforms as soon as possible, the last

---

[43] Named after André Maginot the minister who started the fortification; it worked well, the Italians failed to breach it but the Germans went round it eventually breached it at Saarbrücken.

[44] May 9th-10th.

thing we needed was to be shot by friendly fire. The next few days were so hectic I can hardly recall them. I remember a day later I was fighting on the outskirts of Rotterdam. Here we met some resistance, but they were not professional, and although we were outnumbered I could not help feeling that usual incredible sense of superiority and confidence that we would win. The victory was secured by the bombing of the resistance areas by the Luftwaffe,[45] and we were soon under new orders to head toward The Hague. The Dutch were folding up wherever we appeared, and most of the time we spent taking prisoners and removing their weapons.[46]

We were all exhilarated, and there is little question that the speed of our advance, our use of planes and tanks and planning had taken everyone by surprise. Later this was referred to as *Blitzkrieg*, but we never used that expression, it was for us just the efficient planning by our seniors and the use of surprise.[47] Apart from the exhilaration I can also recall the dejected looks of the Dutch soldiers as we rounded them up, but it was the occasional civilian who caught my eye when they looked not so much dejected as deeply resentful. "What right have you got to do this?" someone shouted. One of my men started to walk over to the elderly man whom we think had shouted this out in good German, but I called him back and ordered my men to ignore any taunts, we had work to do.

We had no time to catch our breath because after some non-combatant troops moved in with security forces all Waffen-SS were ordered to catch up with the fighting. We moved into France without a break[48] and became part of the XIX Panzer Corps under the command of General Heinz Guderian. As we travelled the amount of destruction we saw was unbelievable, and as we headed towards Dunkirk I could hardly believe the number of British vehicles that had been abandoned. There was the smell of death that we had experienced in Poland, mainly untended corpses but also cattle and horses probably killed by artillery fire. From the back of my lorry I saw a family huddled in the ditch, but it took a few seconds for me to realise they were all dead. Even as I looked at the pathetic huddle of bodies I saw the girl who smiled, and like a tune which

---

[45] This was Kesselring's *Luftflotte* wing; the bombing was supposed to be tactical, but because of the height lacked any precision and was therefore indiscriminate. Red flares had been fired from the ground to warn the pilots not to release their bombs because surrender had occurred, but the smoke obscured the flares for most of the pilots.

[46] The *Leibstandarte* reached The Hague on My 15th and took some 3,500 Dutch POWs.

[47] Seeckt who had helped rebuild Germany's military machine always insisted 'surprise' was critical.

[48] May 24th.

grips the mind the image would not go away as we trundled down the road to our new posting. We saw so many French prisoners it became something of a joke amongst us.

Later in the war we found a lot of support from the French though they would deny it today, and it was not just in Vichy France. There was even a Waffen-SS Charlemagne (1st French) and they would fight to the bitter end. Many French resented the British more than they did us, and I have heard more French died fighting for us than they did for our enemies. I know they developed a resistance towards the latter part of the war, but it was never as formidable and dangerous as it was in Eastern Europe, the Balkans and Italy. Since the end of the war I have read various history books of serious analysis, but to my knowledge there has never been an official French history of the second war.

It was at a point some fifteen miles south-west of Dunkirk that we took up a position along the line of the Aa Canal[49] and found ourselves mainly opposed by some very solid French soldiers. We could feel almost instantly that we were meeting a very different form of resistance. We were now a large force[50] and, if I recall rightly we were somewhere between Petit-Fort-Philippe and Gravelines which was close to the coast, and then down to Watten where I found myself. It was not going our way, we had driven the British into the sea, so we thought, but the French and a small British contingent were opposing us in a way we had not yet encountered, especially south of Watten where I found myself pinned down by murderous gun fire. It was here I experienced for the first time fighting the traditional enemy, the British Tommy, and with his back to the sea he made it clear he had nothing to lose. Down by a crossing there was a small cluster of houses, and I was ordered to take them as soon as our shelling stopped. The noise, smoke and stench were horrendous, and I was convinced that nobody would have survived in the ruins of those French houses. I was wrong. I lobbed a grenade into what had once been a dining room and expected no one to have survived.

Again I was wrong; even as I landed on my feet I was conscious of a soldier behind me as I turned. His battle dress was that strange khaki the British insist on, and he was quick. With his rifle he smashed me in the face causing me to fall back, and before I could bring my own weapon to fire he had stabbed me through the shoulder with his bayonet. His face was expressionless as he pulled out the bayonet; I faked death, but as he turned to go I raised my gun only to find it had jammed. The noise of the faulty mechanism caught his attention and I thought I was finished as he

---

[49] Aa is a Dutch word for water; the canal was 89 kilometres long.

[50] The LSSAH were with the *Grossdeutschland* regiment and both attached to the 1st PzD.

almost casually pointed his rifle at my face and pulled the trigger. I remember the instant pain then nothing. I found myself being carried by my own people on a stretcher and was puzzled as to why I was still alive. My face was swollen, my shoulder ached but I was very much alive. The casual way he had shot me came back; he had hit me but missed the skull. My right cheek was shot through as was my ear, and I was forever going to look a mess, but I survived.[51] I was being taken to a makeshift hospital once again, and allowed myself to doze as others took my body to safety. Even as I dozed I wondered about the expressionless look on that British Tommy, for some reason it unnerved me more than had he looked fierce or angry; it was like meeting a machine. When I did sleep the Tommy went and the girl who smiled returned with the Tommy's expressionless face in the background.

I was lucky at this stage to be removed, because some of my troop were involved in a massacre of some British and French POWs, and were hunted down after the war with a vengeance.[52] When I heard of the massacre I gather it was a reprisal for the way the enemy had fought; they had produced a resistance we had not met before. The rights and wrongs of it never touched me at the time, but they did a few years later. I have spoken to Harry many times about this incident for two reasons, the first because he told me he was at Watten, but I know he was not the one I met, but later, when I got to know Harry, as a soldier he was also ruthless and also had an impassive face. The second reason is that as a result of the rifle shot my face and ear was badly scarred like Harry's priest at home, and this was to save my life one day.

HARRY 1939-40

I saw Edna before I reported to Canterbury and I proposed, or rather suggested that if the war ended, and we were still together that perhaps she might consider marrying me. It was a strange thing to ask a girl, but I had this strange premonition that the war would be long, unpleasant and yet I felt it was sad asking someone to wait. I had no money to support her, and nursing, in those days, meant that marriage was frowned upon if not prohibited. It was a very different world then. To my delight she jumped and said 'of course.' I walked with a bounce and promised I would write to her as and when I could. She promised to wait for me as

---

[51] The Aa Canal Battle was mainly fought between May24th and 28th by French and a few British in this area south of Watten.

[52] This may refer to Wormhout where 2nd Battalion of the *Leibstandarte* murdered some 80 British and French prisoners.

long as I did my best to stay alive. That took a bounce out of my step for a few seconds; the idea of dying had not crossed my mind.

The next few months were a mixture of boredom, frustration and annoyance. I sincerely hope that training as a soldier has changed since the days when Eddie and I joined up. We spent nearly all our time square-bashing,[53] marching back and forth and being shouted at by the most obnoxious sergeant-majors possible to imagine in the worst nightmares. It struck me that they were unnecessarily insulting and tended to pick on the men who were likely to feel their venom the most. We had to behave like chorus girls, arms and legs in unison, and after weeks of this I really began to wonder what the purpose was. In later years I heard it argued that it was all part of a discipline, but looking back on the war we fought in France, North Africa and Italy I cannot for the life of me understand how square bashing helped. We were given physical training and some of the recruits needed this, but Eddie and I were both very fit, and the only thing I found useful was rifle training and target practice. It was whilst doing this that we met Horace smartly dressed, which we would expect of an officer. I paid him the due respect with a smart salute that he acknowledged but winked at me at the same time. I wondered whether Horace had found his niche in life at long last; he certainly seemed to fit the role, and he had a good reputation for his ability on the shooting-range.

As we write these agreed accounts it is strange the way our paths crossed. Some claim Charles Dickens relied too much on coincidence, but it happens that life is sometimes about these strange meetings. I met Horace on the cliffs, again in training, then in France, and later some of the strangest meetings; some would suggest that it is a coincidence too far, but these quirks brought the three of us together. I may have even have taken a pot-shot at Wolfgang because I can remember vividly the fighting in the small houses near Watten where Wolfgang was badly scarred. I have watched many war films over the years, and few of them convey the truth of the moment. There was little real heroism, but a great many frightened men, men hoping to survive by keeping their heads down, men who could not move for fear they would disgrace themselves, and sometimes it was only sheer anger that eventually drove us to fight. The fighting at Watten was like that, at times hand to hand, and I fully understand Wolfgang's note of the man with the impassive face, it is the sort of minor detail that stays in the recess of the memory and will not budge.

Before all this started I was suffering from another problem few people associate with being in the army, sheer insufferable boredom.

---

[53] Military drill performed repeatedly on barrack square.

Father H had spoilt me with his friendship and education, and although I mixed with my mates I really became tired of their need to go down to the traditional pubs and get 'blotto' as we used to say. I never alienated myself by being stand-offish, working in the scrapyard had taught me to value the friendship of those I worked with; because a man did not study Ovid and had no interest in history did not detract from his humanity. This was personified later that year as I would owe a great deal to a chap called Joe who was a dreadful womaniser, always gambled, drank too much, could barely read and write, but risked his life to save me, and lost his later helping another mate. Joe was not a bravado man, but quite coolly and calculatedly risked his own life to save his mates; he never received any medal or recognition that is why I mention Joe now. Having noted this I was not inclined to spend any valuable spare evening becoming saturated with him in the pub while he chatted up the barmaids. I would go for a quick drink but then slip away, and used the time to read my favourite author, Trollope, or study my German. This had served me well for my Cambridge entry examinations, and I intended to keep both my Latin and German alive.

Both Eddie and I did well on the ranges, and our skill was noted, but to our detriment. In a scheme to make sure there was a balance of skills and personnel, at least that is what I conjectured, we were split up. I was made up to a corporal, and Eddie was attached to the 1st Battalion that was going to be shipped off to Egypt almost immediately. We did not even have time to spend a weekend together before he disappeared somewhere down west.[54] It was the last time Dad and I saw him; in those days people did not hug one another, well I did not, I do not think we even shook hands; we just wished one another good luck and said cheerio. Dad did not even have the opportunity to say that to his son. Eddie was killed at a remote spot called *Sidi Suleiman* in June, 1941. I wish to God I could hug him now. I discovered long after the war that Eddie and his 1st Buffs joined with the 3rd Coldstream Guards and the 2nd Scots Guards and fought a tough battle known as the escarpment force. It was all part of a plan codenamed Operation Battleaxe, but it was one of the first times that we came up upon strong German forces organised by Rommel.[55] It was a long time before I heard of Eddie's death because of the hectic way our lives were unfolding.

I travelled to France with the 2nd Buffs and, as Harry has mentioned, met him at what we now call the battle or defence of Escaut. I will not

---

[54] 1st Buffs went to Pembroke Docks in 1939 before being shipped to Egypt. Many were trained as pioneers in Wales.

[55] It was the first time, however, that a significant German force fought on the defensive. The goal was the clearing of eastern Cyrenaica of Germans and Italians before lifting the siege of Tobruk.

dwell on this or Harry's account of how or whether I saved him. I dragged and carried him to safety, but then as I mentioned earlier the squaddie called Joe had pulled me to safety under severe gunfire, when I had been knocked senseless by the blast of a shell.

Warfare is a state of total disorder, confusion and at a personal level good and bad luck play a highly significant part. After Escaut it was a matter of disorderly retreat towards the coast with the sense that the Germans were on our heels all the way. It was not helped by the pitiless columns of fleeing refugees, and every now and then the Luftwaffe strafed the roads as we made our way. I have heard the various reasons and excuses for this Luftwaffe behaviour, but I clearly recall on one occasion a German fighter come down low over a column of fleeing French refugees, did it twice as if checking then flew off. On another occasion a fighter, preceded by a Stuka attack killed about fifty men women and children without looking to see if they were soldiers or civilians. As in all wars it depends on the morality of the person behind the weapon. I did not see the enemy as moral, even then we knew it was a corrupt regime, how deeply corrupt we were to discover later, but I had worked out that not all the enemy were by nature evil. It certainly increased our sense of anger to see such behaviour, and when we found some of our own comrades who had obviously been shot as POWs we all felt incensed with hatred. Had I been the one to shoot Wolfgang in the conflict he mentions, in those days I would not have missed.

In the rush to the coast we became separated from one another, and we lost sight of most of our officers. We met some French soldiers who were in a state of shock. We had been separated from our officers in the chaos, but some of the French officers, we were told later, had fled leaving their men, but not all. The French soldiers were in a greater sense of panic than us, but on hindsight, which is always easy, they were fighting on their own land. I always had the notion we would eventually cross the channel to the safety of home; they had no such hope. There was also a degree of antagonism expressed by some that we were betraying them by running for the coast and home. I heard this twice, but most of the time the discussions, when they took place were about staying alive, and avoiding the advancing enemy. I remember when we were trying to regroup at St Omer[56] I was sitting in a chicken house with three others, when one chap started to weep. I put it down to tiredness; we had hardly slept a wink for three days, and were simply exhausted wrecks.

It was not tiredness; he was weeping because he could not see how he would face his father who survived three years in the trenches. He had

---

[56] St Omer, La Bassée Canal, where it was hoped to prevent the Germans crossing from Watten to St Omer to La Bassée; this is where the remaining Buffs regrouped.

a point; in this war we were being literally chased off the continent, and I wondered how my Dad would view us. The idea was crossing my mind of the impossibility of getting so many men and their equipment back over the channel, but such high strategy was cast to the wind when we were rounded up, about twenty of us, and ordered to assist a group of Frenchmen guarding a bridge, a mile south-west of us. We found the bridge about six in the morning but no French soldiers. We scouted around cautiously in case it were a trap, but the place was empty, there were no buildings, just a small bridge and barren landscape; significantly the bridge was strong enough for transport and probably tanks.

We were in a complete and total mess, we had no digging tools between us, only our personal weapons and very limited ammunition, and we could not stop falling asleep. A sergeant arrived from nowhere and tried to take charge. He sent two men along the canal to see if they could find any tools and ammunition, and he and I sat on duty allowing the others to catch up with some sleep. It was so incredibly quiet for two hours, and had it not been for the sergeant's constant chatter about what was happening I could have dreamed I was out on a stroll, enjoying the sun on the outskirts of Hythe in south-east Kent. We sat on a small pile of rubble quietly smoking a few cigarettes watching the direction from which we anticipated the enemy; above us there was plenty of activity, noise of engines, trails of planes, but nothing in our sector; it was as if the war had stopped. We were suddenly disturbed by a motorcycle behind us, and a captain from another regiment who asked what was happening. I had to smile, because even he could see nothing was happening; the only noise at ground level was the rest of the chaps snoring away in a field the other side of the small track, even the officer's motorcycle had not made them stir. He cheered us up somewhat by saying we would soon be reinforced and that an armoured division was disembarking at Calais.[57] On that cheery note he rode off in a cloud of blue smoke and dust, leaving us with some hope, some new cigarettes, and the rest of the chaps never even woke up.

By mid-morning I was just about to suggest that peace must have been declared when a group of French soldiers arrived dragging a piece of heavy artillery by horse, under the command of an impressive French Colonel who barked out orders first in French and then in impeccable English. This time I had to wake the other chaps, because apart from one or two stirring they even slept through this noise. Hot on their heels arrived three British soldiers with a Bren gun, but there was no sign of the two chaps we had sent off looking for digging tools. Fortunately the

---

[57] He was probably referring to the 3rd Battalion Royal Tank Regiment, whose tanks were still deep in the ship's hold in Calais and never reached St Omer on time.

French had some, and so we set to digging small trenches and foxholes. It was hot sweaty work and the ground was not easy.

We all grumbled about the task, but the sergeant was right with his orders, I owe my life to him because when the shell landed amongst us I was deep in my foxhole retrieving my packet of cigarettes. I could feel the dirt and tufts of grassy mud thumping down on my back, and when I peered over the top the sergeant was literally in pieces, the French horses released from their weapon had bolted, and I was joined in my shelter by an equally terrified Frenchman. The noise had been so deafening I could not hear him, and there was a strange buzzing in my ears. I had barely stuck my head over the top when another shell landed and again the smell of smoke and cordite and someone screaming from what seemed a long way off will be a memory I shall never forget; it was a situation of sheer terror. There followed a lull and with great trepidation I crawled out of my hole to see what was happening.

The sergeant and two others were self-evidently dead, and the French who appeared unharmed were helping treat three others who had been wounded. I could not see any sign of the enemy, but kept a low profile because they could obviously see us. When I pointed to the apparently unharmed French piece of artillery, hoping that at least we could show some form of retaliation, a Frenchman waved his arms in despair; eventually I gathered the gun was fine, but they had been sent to help us with the wrong ammunition. Not only was I terrified, but this stupidity and lack of organisation by French and British cast a sense of gloom and despair amongst us. Our ammunition was short; I had enough for about thirty rounds and two hand grenades against an obviously well-armed enemy who could see us, but remained invisible to us. By mid-afternoon I was beginning to wonder whether the Germans had retreated again because it all fell silent. The French were a decent bunch of men, their artillery piece was useless but they stayed with us, and shared their food and produced some very welcome red wine. To be quite frank it was the first time I had drunk wine, and my initial reaction was one of disgust, but by the third mouthful I was not only enjoying it, but suddenly feeling very brave. We dug a hole in the field behind us and laid two men and the bits and pieces of our sergeant to rest with a wooden cross above them.

The sheer force of the shell's blast had stripped the clothing from the sergeant's torso, and I recall that he had a tattoo of the Buffs, a dragon with Buffs underneath on his chest. His arms, legs and head were missing and yet there was little blood. I lifted the torso with the help of another and the weight was incredible. By the time we put it down we had found the blood, it was all over our clothes, and a painful memory lodged deep in the mind. Whenever today I see builders stripped to the waist for some reason that memory returns. It is not as painful as Wolfgang's girl who smiled, but it always causes me to gulp for some reason. I said a few prayers and finished with the grace.

We were straining our eyes looking to see what was happening when again we were taken by surprise from behind by two Fusilier officers who had come to mine the bridge. They set to work right out in the open, and full of red wine I offered to assist. The red wine had a way of turning terror into nervousness. I was given the detonator and told that if I saw a white flare followed by a red flare the bridge had to be blown. I pointed out that I was a mere corporal, and that a French Colonel was standing near the path talking to his men, but they shook their heads and said they would trust me. I asked what happened if there were no flares and the Germans arrived. They gave me firm instructions that I had to wait for the last moment because some of our men would need these bridges, but after that it was over to me. A mere corporal, in the army only a few months, and I was standing in France responsible for blowing up what looked like an expensive bridge.

We never saw any more retreating troops, but ahead of us there was some sudden firing and the sounds of heavy machinery. I ordered my chaps back to their shelters, and I ensured I had the wires from the explosives disconnected from the plunger but safe with me in my hole. I noted the Frenchman had joined me, and I explained the detonator with half French half English and a good deal of finger pointing and hand waving. The Fusiliers may not have trusted the French Colonel, but I had no reason to distrust the Frenchman who had volunteered to stay; I had the feeling that had we met under different circumstances we would have been good friends. By about five that afternoon a yell from behind indicated that some Germans had been spotted nearing the bridge. I asked the Frenchmen whether his Colonel would give the orders but he indicated that the officer had gone, and I was in charge until he returned. It always struck me as odd that the Colonel never even acknowledged any of us; on mature reflection I think my French comrade was covering for his officer who had done a runner, as we used to say. I recalled a western movie I had once watched, and based solely on that experience I shouted out that no one fired until they were at the bridge. The water was too deep to cross, and the bridge, I thought, would narrow down the aim and save ammunition.

I had taken the precaution of putting some old sacking, which the French gun had been covered with, over my head, and trained my sights on the bridge, it was only about a hundred yards away. I bellowed at two in a slit trench behind me; they were both smoking pipes and it looked like a campfire. It was not a pleasant situation just waiting. There were sounds of gunfire all around us but our bridge did not seem part of the scheme of things. I closed my eyes for a brief moment, forcing myself to stay alert, but my French companion gave me an urgent nudge. I saw, with him the outline of two German helmets on the bank opposite.

One was studying the bridge with binoculars, obviously trying to see if it was mined. The danger were that he might see the wires so I aimed and fired; it was too close to miss and the man seemed to try and stand before he fell forward. His mate disappeared. After that the inevitable happened, from seemingly nowhere we were met by a hail of machine gun bullets and it took some time for us to pin point where they were. The Germans were excellent at their field-craft, but we were pinned down by sheer force of their numbers. Occasionally we managed to return fire but most of the time we ducked for cover. Twice the enemy tried to storm the bridge and twice we stopped them. I never had the opportunity to look, but there must have been at least six dead Germans on the bridge. Even then, when I hated them, I had to admire their professional skill and personal courage. One of them neatly camouflaged had crawled towards the bridge but he also died.

We were dug in and the bridge was more easily defended than attacked, and for once we were not being forced back. This momentary flash of pride did not last long, my French companion had propped himself up too high to get a better view and suddenly fell forward. I dragged him back into our trench, but he had a hole in the centre of his forehead; he would not have known a thing, one minute alive the next minute oblivion. I could not shift his weight, but managed to push him to one side so I could manoeuvre and reach the detonator. I managed this just in time because the evident sound of a heavy tank could be heard approaching. I remember the cold-blooded efficiency of that tank driver, moving towards the bridge and blasting shell after shell in our direction; when I dared peep up between blasts I saw that the tank was crushing the dead Germans we had shot. My hands were shaking but I tied the wires and worked on the plunger. It was no good shouting to the others what I intended to do, there was too much noise.

The bridge blew up without problems, the Fusiliers knew what they were doing, but I was surprised the wires had remained intact. Had I left it one more minute I may well have caught the tank, but covered in bridge debris it fired one more shot then reversed. There had been no red and white flares, we were very much on our own, but they had not crossed into our sector. The German infantry on the other side of the canal stayed and kept us pinned down. I watched to see if they had any other means to cross, but had already made up my mind that as soon as it was dark we were going to move out; our task was done.

When I woke up it was bright sunlight, and I was almost cuddling the dead Frenchman in my foxhole. He had changed colour, completely grey and there were flies gathering on his face and flying in and out of his open mouth. I had not slept for nearly four days and I had obviously collapsed. I pushed myself away from him in a sudden feeling of disgust, and tried to recall what had happened. I almost wondered if I had been knocked senseless, but I think it was sheer exhaustion. I looked cautiously over the top of the trench and there was total silence. I called out and there was no reply. Eventually I crawled out and looked around and it was clear that the Germans and all my mates had gone. I looked around with extreme caution, most of my fellow soldiers and the French were dead, but a few were missing. Much later I discovered that they had fled in the night and had assumed that since I was slumped across the body of the dead Frenchman I was dead as well. It was now mid-morning, I could not even recall the date I was so confused,[58] and apart from my rifle and a few rounds of ammunition I had nothing.

The red wine we had been drinking had now left me with a raging thirst, but I found one of the dead French soldiers had a water flask, it was tepid, but it helped. I decided to avoid the roads and headed what I hoped to be westward towards the coast. After just one field I came to sudden halt, barely two hundred yards in front of me was one of our Matilda tanks, but even as I took the picture in any hopes were suddenly dashed because the tank, apparently in good condition, was being inspected by a group of German soldiers. One of them turned and looked in my direction, but I froze behind the hedge through which I was peering and he looked away. I was now behind enemy lines.

I do not want to dwell on this part of my story too much, Horace and Wolfgang agreed we would write these notes primarily for ourselves and also for one another, and I do not think I have much to say about the few days I slowly and painfully negotiated my way towards Dunkirk. I ought to note that I became increasingly proficient at being covert, somewhat insensitive and hardened about searching corpses for food water or ammunition. As I moved cautiously across the landscape I kept coming upon little cameos of death, some like pictures from hell, corpses of humans and animals bloated. One that stands out in my memory is the sight of a Frenchman sitting on his chair outside his house. I approached him with care but could see no one else around, and his house, unlike others in the area looked intact. He simply sat there with a smile on his face, but I noted that the flies were once again flying around his face, and he was making no effort to brush them aside. He was dead, but from what I could see, there was no blood and short of pushing him from his set and examining him, I could not see what had caused his death.

I went into the house but it had already been ransacked of food, and someone had defecated on the armchair that struck me as particularly

---

[58] Somewhere between May 23rd and 25th 1940.

ghastly. On his wall was a small crucifix, and on instinct I took it down, and put it in my tunic; as I write these very words I am looking at it on my desk. On returning towards the front door I was grateful that caution had made me look first as some Germans were rolling a huge gun[59] into place, so sneaking out through the kitchen I hid in some brambles until it was nearly dark and continued on my way. I had several near escapes like this, saw first-hand the tragedy of war upon civilians, I learned what it was like to be alone and terrified, and was nearly shot by my own side as I crossed over what might loosely be called the front line.

I had to report to a Captain Morris or someone, and he directed me with three others onto Dunkirk where, I gather, we were being off-loaded and returned home. We almost sprinted. As you can imagine I have read a great deal about the stories relating to Dunkirk. It always makes me smile that our history books almost paint it as a victory, like the later battle of Arnhem; history when written by people with vested interests is always focused and slanted in a certain direction. Dunkirk was the end result of an appalling disaster. We had been thoroughly beaten and chased out of Europe by a highly trained and professional German army. Our equipment and dead comrades were spread across the countryside like so much unpleasant detritus.[60] Looking back I realise that Churchill[61] and those who cared, had to make a defeat look like a victory, and the evacuation was brilliantly organised[62] from some hole in the cliffs I used to climb a few years before as a boy. I saw cowardice, bravery, treachery, terror, criminality, and compassion.

Man's character was open to display in Dunkirk. I parted from my companions in the town because they found some of their mates who were drinking themselves silly in a café, and also robbing the place as if they owned it. I felt disgusted and moved on, wondering what they could possibly gain by being legless, as we used to say. The place was alive with British and French soldiers, and planes kept attacking the town and the beaches so crowds and groups would suddenly disappear. I gathered that French and British soldiers were holding the perimeter of the area so the evacuation could take place, I watched army chaplains holding the lines on the beaches and encouraging the men not to scramble past one

---

[59] Probably the (in)famous 88.

[60] The BEF lost 68,00 soldiers, dead, wounded or captured from may 10th until 22nd June; 2,472 guns left in France, 20,000 motorbikes, 65,000 other vehicles, thousands of tons of food, ammunition, and well over 400 tanks.

[61] Churchill presented Dunkirk as a miracle, but knew the prognosis was gloomy pointing out to Parliament that 'wars are not won by evacuations.' He needed the public to pull together.

[62] Admiral Ramsay organised this from beneath Dover Castle in the famous White Cliffs.

another. I gather a number of chaplains were taken prisoner because they stayed to the last and with the wounded.

Not many history books comment on this. Nor do they tend to comment on the gathering hostility between the French and British. Long after the war when I started to read about what had happened I realised the *entente cordiale* was strained at the highest levels. A group of French soldiers[63] looking for the evacuation points were directed straight towards the enemy lines, and an hour later I watched an English soldier trying to help a wounded Frenchman; I offered some bandages I had found, and I noted that the English soldier had tears in his eyes. He explained to me they had become good friends. Every aspect of human life, good and bad could be found in that French port.

This was highlighted for me when I survived thanks to someone else who saved me. I have to this day no idea who it was even though I tried to find out. All I can remember is standing on the pier when some Stukas appeared. There was a shattering explosion, and I could feel myself being lifted high into the air, and then I was trying to swim in cold water with heavy army boots on, when another attack started.

When I opened my eyes next I was in a hospital bed in England. Someone had bothered to pull me out of the water, drag me on ship, and brought me home. I was incredibly lucky, with so much death and dying someone had bothered to help me. I thank him whoever he was. I was in a bed somewhere near Derby of all places, no one knew my name, and I had been unconscious for a long period of time with a fractured skull. The doctor said that the nature of the damage was not bomb blast, but probably my unconscious body had been badly handled when they dragged me aboard. I had to stay there for nearly six weeks before they would consider it was healed. I was told it was not a serious fracture but it had to knit together, but once fused that part of my head would be quite solid. I dropped a card to my Dad and to Edna, I was surprised when they did not reply, but for some reason neither received my cards. As I now know Edna thought I was dead, Dad and Father H were hoping I was a prisoner about to escape, and I was relaxed reading Charles Dickens in clean sheets somewhere in Derby.

MD's NOTE

It was at this juncture that Horace, Wolfgang and Harry met with me again to discuss their intentions. I was struck by Harry whom I felt to be the driving force behind the project. They liked the fact that their shared

---

[63] In the end over 100,000 French soldiers were evacuated, 3,000 stayed to fight with De Gaulle, most opted to return.

notes had proved revealing and interesting; Wolfgang's grasp of English made it easy for them to understand the German expressions he frequently used.

It was Wolfgang who highlighted the main issue of their goal, who originally suggested that writing about their experiences would be cathartic. He thought that if he put it on paper the intense guilt he continued to feel, the spiritual depression he experienced might in a confessional way help him come to terms with the past. Instead the nightmare of the girl who smiled remained with greater intensity, and as he dredged up his past during the war years other dark memories returned.

He also felt tortured by the possibility of his position being exposed; he said he trusted me 'to cover tracks,' to use his expression, but he simply did not trust journalists as they would dig and dig. He felt he had the most shame to bear that would make headlines, and Harry pointed out that he and his family were in a difficult situation. Horace said very little, because what had happened in his life had taught him to keep a low profile, so low the finest radar would never find him. The fact was that of the three men one was a wanted war criminal, one was technically a wanted man, and the third had sound reasons to keep his name out of the headlines.

Wolfgang was also worried about a German soldier called Erich Priebke who had taken part in the Ardeatine massacre in Rome,[64] and had felt confident enough to go public, but there was now the possibility of a trial.[65] This Priebke was about the same age as Wolfgang, and for some reason haunted Wolfgang despite Horace and Harry claiming he was not in the same category. The girl who smiled was a constantly reminded Wolfgang that he was not that much different from Priebke. I recalled thinking of the thousands of old men who had fought in that war and were burdened with memory; when children and wives said 'he never spoke of the war'

I was beginning to realise why there was so much silence. The history of the war can be gleaned from professional historians, self-justifying memoirs of generals and the occasional biography of everyday soldiers. I thought that these three men who were prepared to share their experiences in this unique way should be more widely read and said so. They agreed, but stated categorically that I was only to seek publication after they were all dead.

---

[64] Infamous Ardeatine Cave/Catacomb massacres 1944.

[65] He had been convicted in 1996 having talked about the incident in 1994. When he died in Rome 11th October 2013 aged 100 there were riots and no one wanted the body.

CHAPTER FOUR

Middle War Years

HORACE 1940 – 1942

I tried to find out how Harry had died but it was generally believed he was killed in the retreat or taken prisoner; nobody seemed to know. I assumed he was dead because of what I had been told, and hearing no more from Edna went back to my duties with a heavy heart. I considered going to see my parents but my father's attitudes, and even my mother's I found disturbing, and I decided to take what limited leave there was in London. I did write to my mother later, but I never received a reply.

I was back on duty in early September 1940 and spent most of the time on patrol duty along the coast as there was frantic talk of a German invasion. We had to train much more now,[1] which certainly helped my wound to heal and stop aching. It was boring apart from the time we were sent to guard a downed Dornier near Rye until the boffins arrived. A quick inspection of the plane revealed that the crew had obviously parachuted out, and within a day the RAF boffins had extracted everything of interest and the plane was removed. I suspect they were collecting as many parts as possible with a view to rebuilding one. I was surprised what good condition it was in, and was questioned closely by my senior officer and an RAF chap who said that they suspected that the pilot had landed the craft and had we searched the vicinity?

I was confident that we had arrived about three hours after the report of the downed plane, and I was grateful that I asked my men to spread out and search and question people. A month later I heard that the pilot had landed the craft, and had been caught speaking English with an appalling German accent; it was not raised with me again. They were nerve racking days in so far that most of us had neck ache as the end of what we now call the Battle of Britain which raged far above our heads. On one of my short leaves I confess I was leaving a dive in Soho when an air-raid started. It was nowhere nearby but the noise and fire from the East End was palpable, I decided to go underground, but found the underground railway system was closed. This struck me as silly, because even if the trains had stopped running the deep shelter would have been useful to those exposed above ground.[2] At this stage the bombing seemed confined to the docks but bombs could fall anywhere, and I decided my visits to

---

[1] Montgomery had overview at this time and was stickler for keeping men fit.

[2] Eventually, after petitioning, the tube system was opened, and on September 27th 1940 as many as an estimated 177,000 Londoners sheltered there during a raid.

London should be taken with care.[3] I did not get much leave, and feeling Edna had turned me down, despite our passionate evening, and not wanting to go near my parents I relaxed with my reading books and various duties. I did go with a chap called Tom to spend a few days at his home in Manchester, but as we drew into the station a serious bombing raid started,[4] and we had to seek shelter in the station itself.

The sense of a potential German invasion remained fairly dominant in our minds, but I was beginning to think that the enemy was not that interested in us, especially since they did not have total control of the skies, and the Royal Navy remained a formidable foe. There was also, in the New Year, some good news coming out of North Africa that seemed to many of my friends a signal that we might hold our own.[5] I was more uncertain; I had witnessed the ease with which the highly professional Wehrmacht, back by the ruthless Luftwaffe had cut a swathe through the Low Countries and deep into France. I will never understand why they did not cross the channel in the June/July of 1940.

The French had the largest army, and they simply crumbled as did their politicians, and we were not much better. I would never have dared express this during or after the war, but I believe the British Army was not up to standard. It had acted as a policeman in the interwar years in various parts of our so-called empire, but the officers were weak and I never thought much of the leadership, even long after the war when I started reading the various official and unofficial histories. I think we survived because of the Royal Navy, the RAF and Hitler obligating the USA to come to our rescue; and that was all we did, survive. I have jumped somewhat ahead of myself, but the views I held in 1941 to 1945 I feel have been justified by some of the more solid historical appraisals of recent years. I was later to land up under the much vaunted Montgomery, who won the battle of El Alamein which had been largely planned by his predecessor, took his time pursuing Rommel along the North African coast allowing more resistance, played his silly egotistical game with Patton in Sicily allowing the Germans to escape over the Messina Straits, once again wandered through Italy at a snail's pace towards suffering Salerno, promised to take Caen in three to four days in Normandy but had to wait for months until it was bombed to rubble, then turned Arnhem, a massive defeat and loss of our best fighting men, into what he called a 90% victory.

---

[3] Contrary to popular myth early German bombing was tactical under the guidance of Luftflotte II leader Albert Kesselring, but lack of precise bomb aiming apparatus meant even tactical bombing was largely indiscriminate.

[4] That must have been December 22nd 1940 when Manchester was badly hit.

[5] February 6th, 1941 – Wavell's desert army occupies Benghazi, Libya and on March 7th British invaded Italian-held Ethiopia from Somaliland.

I remember once seeing Alexander and was deeply unimpressed; no doubt a gentleman, but he would have been better off holding forth in the Athenaeum club or a similar club that he no doubt frequented. I had tasted the professionalism of the Wehrmacht, and soon the papers were talking of Rommel as if he were a hero. This was nonsense, despite the eulogies written about him, he was to start with an ardent Nazi and our incompetent leadership was up against German professional arms, not some demi-god called the desert fox. The Germans were professionals and we were amateurs, so although I kept this to myself, I am glad to have had an opportunity to express it now; that bit, to use Wolfgang's phrase, was cathartic. My point is I was not an enthusiastic soldier, and like the vast majority my main aim was to keep my head below the parapet and be alive when the war ended. I had developed a serious hatred for the Germans; they had thrown our life into disarray and, as far as I could see, were bombing innocent civilians. I am not an intellectual like Harry, and I know that we bombed them later in the war with a vengeance that made their efforts look puny, but I have always felt that they allowed themselves to fall under Hitler's guidance and they started the whole messy business.

Thus, in 1941 I did not volunteer to join commandoes and did not volunteer for anything that looked potentially dangerous. I knew the world was changing, especially when the House of Commons[6] was destroyed, but I intended to be alive when it had stopped changing. Food was becoming a depressing matter; even buying clothes was not easy,[7] and when I heard the Hood had been sunk[8] I felt that times were indeed serious. Even I knew that if we did not control the Atlantic we would be in danger of starving to death. I noted that in some pubs the beer was being watered down and generally life off duty was no better than being on duty. I suppose having expressed my views here, and on reflection looking back at this last page, I now realise this was when I suffered my first degree of depression; it has dogged me all my life on an on off basis. Perhaps putting it into writing may help.

I spent a good deal of time organising patrols, which were mainly for practice in mid-Kent, sometimes near Canterbury and Ashford, other times more concentrated patrols down on the coastline. Keeping fit was the order of the day, but despite all the training, and the reappearance of new weapons I could not fathom how we could possibly beat the enemy. No one said this out loud, but I suspect many of us who had fled the Wehrmacht from Dunkirk felt the same. I think we were all cheered up

---

[6] May 10th 1941 in a 550-bomber raid.

[7] June 1st 1941 clothes rationing introduced.

[8] May 24th 1941 sunk off Iceland; interesting that Horace never mentions the immediate retaliatory sinking of the Bismarck.

when Hitler suddenly attacked Russia, if only because it took some of the pressure away from British shores. When one of my senior officers claimed that Hitler had lost the war with this move I failed to believe him because the news indicated the Germans were virtually opening Moscow's front door. In the Far East the Japanese had invaded Hong Kong and Malaya and bombed the American fleet all on the same day.[9] As far as the Far East was concerned I was once again a heretic in so far that I saw no reason to try and defend so-called colonies the other side of the world. I never expressed any opinions at the time, and I suppose I may appear somewhat fatuous even now, but we promised to write down our thinking however embarrassing, trite and guilty it may make us. I was pleased when Pearl Harbour brought America into the war; at least we were not on our own.

It made me think of the time when I had been called to the Headmaster's office to be caned, and I felt nervous until another more senior culprit arrived; having company in distress makes it easier to cope. The news reached us that the 2nd Division would be rounded up from our various duties and local exploits, and we were going to be shipped to Egypt. I have never forgotten how many of my fellow officers and many of the men felt excited at the prospect. I pretended I did, but in fact the prospect of dying in some North African desert felt appalling and not exhilarating in any sense of the word.

We first picked up the rumour sometime in late January just after we heard that Rommel had launched yet another offensive.[10] I decided the time had come to try and make contact with my parents; I ought to say goodbye to them, even though I was uncomfortable with them both; father with his sense of social snobbery and Mum caring for nothing but her garden and local status. I had heard that Dover had suffered, and was already called Hell Fire Corner,[11] but I was really surprised at the damaged town. It reminded me of my father's work as a dentist because there would be a row of houses, and five or more would be missing like a row of teeth with several extractions. It caused me to think how stupid war was. By destroying Mrs Smith's house or Mr Green's grocery shop what good could this possibly achieve apart from a lifelong hatred of everything German?

It was no longer possible to take a short cut to my home because the back roads had been cut off since they passed through the radar site, a small airfield and many gun emplacements; the area was the front line,

---

[9] Dec 7th 1941.

[10] 1942 January 21st, Rommel launches offensive in Libyan desert.

[11] Much of the Battle of Britain revolved over South-East Kent, the harbour and ships in the channel were bomber targets, and the Germans were able to fire shells over the channel; this was a frightening prospect for Dovorians because there was no warning.

but thanks to Hitler's attack on Russia reasonably quiet for the moment. When I did arrive at the familiar front door it was clear the place was closed up; even my key that I had kept did not work because the locks had been changed. I actually felt quite stunned. As I walked into the garden that overlooked the channel I thought my mother was attending a small privet hedge, but it was the neighbour. She looked at me suspiciously, not recognising me in my uniform. Once we established we were both *bone fide* I discovered that my parents had decided St Margaret's was too dangerous and a likely place for an invasion. Father had closed his business and moved, if I recall rightly, to a town outside Cardiff called Penarth. The neighbour told me she was sure my Mum had written to me, and she thought that they were living in a Hickman Road, but she was uncertain because she had received no letters.

The neighbour was determined not to move, and tended my mother's garden simply for something to keep her mind off the war. Her husband, who I think he was called Tooke, was serving overseas and she was determined to keep their home in one piece. I know late postwar Harry did some digging and knew more about Major Tooke, but it was many years before I heard what had happened. Apart from breaking and entering I had nowhere to sleep. Mrs Tooke offered me a bed but I refused politely, and cold as it was slept a few hours on a deckchair in the garden shed. I took the old 350cc BSA army bike I had borrowed for three pints, and in the early hours drove back towards Canterbury, first pausing outside Edna's home for a brief minute. I had to pick my way cautiously because there were army blockades everywhere and the dimmed lights on the BSA were not very good. I was stopped by the Home Guard three times but my uniform meant I was only stopped, not questioned.

As I drove through Lydden, a small village outside Dover I nearly fell off the bike with a huge explosion that seemed to come from nowhere; I stopped and looked around and could see nothing, so I continued up Lydden Hill only to be met by another roar and this time I saw a flash. There were some troops standing by a barrier and I paused to ask them what was happening. They saw my officer's tabs and with a degree of caution said the railway guns were firing at shipping. I never realised we had such guns and drove of wondering whether we were shelling the French coast in retaliation.[12]

---

[12] Horace's note on this is interesting; it never occurred to him that, given his estimate of timing he was probably passing the hidden huge guns trying to sink the German warships *Scharnhorst, Gneisenau* and *Prinz Eugen* as they made their dash from Brest to the safety of Wilhelmshaven. It is tempting to note that Horace often never queried what was going on.

I thought about writing to my parents under the address somewhere in Hickman Road, Penarth,[13] but life soon became too hectic. The news from North Africa was discouraging, just as we were packing up to board we heard that Rommel had captured Tobruk,[14] and later was within sixty miles of Alexander.[15] Everyone seemed in awe of Rommel and even in the *Times* newspaper they mentioned his name with a degree of reverence. I have never understood, even to this day, why we elevated this German general so much; I thought even then that the advertised brilliance of enemy command was a way of excusing the weakness of our own leadership. If the enemy is deified then our failures may become more acceptable. Again I never voiced such opinions, my life would not have been worth living, but since the war I have read that some historians are now coming to the same conclusion. To have mentioned this doubt in 1942 would have been an act of treachery, and as I have already noted, I am not one for putting my head in the firing line, especially my own side.

The journey to Egypt was appalling. As an officer I could walk the decks when I chose, even so it was packed and the old liner stank from top to bottom of human sweat. The soldiers below decks were given time on deck in small groups and at limited times. We appeared to travel out deep into the Atlantic[16] before heading towards Gibraltar where we had all hoped for a call in port, but we scurried through the straits in the darkness of the night. No lights, no smoking on deck, it was an uncanny feeling to know that had it been daylight we would have seen Europe on our left and North Africa on our right. Instead the few of us up and about spoke in whispers as if a U-Boat might hear us. On the port side some chap nonchalantly lit his pipe and there was uproar; although he was a Captain, not one of the Buffs I might add, a military policeman threw his pipe into the sea and he was marched off for not too friendly chat with a senior naval officer. Keeping fit was not easy, but we drilled the men and ourselves when we could, but the weather was becoming unbearably hot, and I was relieved to be given the order to change into new gear, which meant khaki shorts making it feel like being back at school again. I played draughts, chess and read; I avoided card games because too much money was coming and going, and without my father's assistance I was always strapped for cash; it would have been more serious as an officer in peacetime, but not so bad in war.

---

[13] I could find no reference to Horace's parents anywhere in Penarth, and certainly not in Hickman Rd where, extraordinarily, I lived for a few years in the 1970s.
[14] June 20th 1942.
[15] June 30th 1942 Rommel was held up at El Alamein.
[16] Probably to avoid the Bay of Biscay with lurking German U-Boats as well as aircraft.

We had a terrible fright at one time; I think we must have been close to Malta because several German planes dive bombed us, but from nowhere some spitfires or hurricanes appeared and shot two of them down with loud cheers from us all. That evening most of the ships in the convoy disappeared and that, along with the appearance of spitfires made us think Malta was close by; we were never kept informed, or I missed it. As the German planes came down I was surprised at how suddenly they grew in size and noise, but their bombs, fell wide. The destroyers opened up and dodged around like sea terriers, but having been sea sick three times I remained satisfied I had joined the army, as bad as it was.

We landed in Egypt in July [17] with the 44th Division and it struck me as total chaos. The heat was overwhelming, there were flies everywhere, Arab traders trying to sell anything from tea bags to the pyramids, and offering us their daughters, sisters and mothers for our pleasure. As the men were organised into groups I found I had an hour or two just to wander around the edges of the port, but found the place depressing and the idea I had developed of investigating ancient Egypt was soon put aside as military policeman after military policeman redirected me away from where I was wandering.

There was a real fear of spies, and I may have been a junior officer but no one was taking any chances; I wondered why there were so many Arab traders around, any of them could be in German employment. We slept in filthy and hot bivouacs that night, an early morning call and we were on our way towards El Alamein. Today the name has a familiar and famous ring to it, but in July 1942 it was a ghastly three building railway post in the middle of nowhere, and seemingly busy with every variety of khaki battledress. I saw a group of men who were completely unshaven; one huge man with a black beard seemed to stir a vague memory from my past. I wandered towards them and I was not made welcome, but although I recognised the big fellow it was probably because he was famous. Later in the day when I was having a quiet smoke with the rest of the platoon brewing some welcome tea, it occurred to me that I had seen him play rugby on several occasions, but I have never been able to pinpoint the name.[18]

It set me wondering about the different types of people war brought together; scholars, business men, lawyers, sportsmen along with plumbers, bricklayers, road sweepers and civilian life was now irrelevant, all one needed to know was the chap standing next to you was trustworthy and in support. I remember Harry's father saying the world

---

[17] The 2nd Buffs reached Egypt in July 1942 with the 44th Division.

[18] This was undoubtedly Blair Mayne who was in the SAS (which would account for the beard) and in North Africa in 1942; an Irish player who toured South Africa in 1938 with the British Lions.

was in a mess because all the best men and potential leaders had died in Flanders, and I was now sure history was repeating itself. Corporal Aitkens and Harry had saved my life, and they were both working class as my father would have noted. In the desert I could already understand that what personified a man was his character, his personality, not which school he went to or his social standing. As I reflected on this I watched the men of my platoon organise the tea and one brought me a mug; I confess I almost felt affectionate towards them. Suddenly I felt they were my family and I had to look after them. For this reason the next day I chose to avoid the offer of a seat in the cab, letting the sergeant take it while I joined the men in the back.

We were put down, as far as I could see in the middle of nowhere. That evening, once our tents were up, I attended the officer's briefing and saw the maps. They did little to inform or enliven me, a close scrutiny of the map clearly indicated I was correct, we were in the middle of nowhere. Just bits of sand in a desert so vast it was beyond my comprehension. One of my men asked me why we were fighting here in the first place, looking back he swept his arm towards the flat grey horizon and said "if the bloody Germans want it, let them 'ave it. It's no good to God or man." That we were defending Egypt held little water with them, or the oil-fields, these ordinary men were preparing to fight, for their families in Kent or Sussex, which was a long way away. That night I experienced the strange phenomenon of the desert, during the day I was so hot I felt I would expire, but at night I nearly froze to death. We had all been warned about the climate, the scorpions and insects on board ship, but like children we all had to experience it to understand.

I gathered that Rommel had already attacked the El Alamein position as we were disembarking and being transported,[19] and us new arrivals were being sent south of Alamein because those at the top anticipated Rommel would try a southern flanking movement. As we moved on most of us hoped the big wigs had miscalculated, like they usually did, and that Rommel would do another head on; after all El Alamein was near the coast and a direct route into Egypt. What we did not know was not so much the tactical genius of the generals, but that they were always able to read Rommel's messages through Ultra.[20] In fact Montgomery, I now know, knew the exact spot where Rommel was intending to attack, and troops fresh from our Mediterranean cruise were about to become the

---

[19] July 1st-27th First battle of Alamein; Rommel attacked but was repulsed.
[20] The name for code-breaking the famous Enigma machine that was the highly sophisticated way the Germans transmitted their messages. It remained a secret until the 1970s.

front line at a place behind the lines called Alam el Halfa.[21] Because we were behind the line I thought we were reasonably safe, but was a little alarmed at the number of tanks, mainly Vals[22] that were being positioned for immediate use.[23]

We knew the battle had started by activity above us in the sky; in fact I am not sure whether Rommel may well have won had he had the same air of superiority. I think before I describe what happened to me I ought to point out that this was not the great battle of El Alamein, it was a sort of preparation in which eventually Rommel was forced to withdraw; not that I knew any of this at the time.[24] We had the company of Indians and Kiwis,[25] but the noise and shelling deprived us of any comfort or hope of survival. I could see nothing around me because it was dark, but the horizon, which was alight with bright flashes and sudden explosions appeared to be drawing us in.

As day dawned it was the sand, smoke and perspiration which stopped me having any clear vision. It was a typical war scene; one had to hope the chap next to you knew what was going on because it was all total confusion and sheer fear. I jerked into a sharper reality when the Bren gun crew on my left suddenly opened up. Looming up ahead I could see what looked like a group of approaching soldiers. They dropped very quickly and I remember thinking that I hope the Bren gun had not hit our own men who may have been retreating; I found it very difficult to see clearly, but comforted myself with the fact the Bren gunners may have had binoculars because I had lost mine. My own men were in slit trenches we had hastily dug, and behind us the tanks were now firing at a steady rate. It may seem ludicrous now, but I can recall thinking that if I survived this I would probably be deaf. There are few moments in war for heroism, only fear and the desire to stay alive. Films that portray war as a heroic exercise do their viewers great harm.

Sometimes men do brave things because they are scared, some because they are angry; sometimes it is because of Dutch courage when a cache of beer or wine has been discovered. However, I had a sergeant who said that in battle he considered himself dead anyway, and only

---

[21] In an Operation called *Brandung*, Rommel tried to break the Eight Army before it built itself up.

[22] Probably Valentine tanks of the 46 Royal Tank regiment.

[23] Montgomery used the tanks in an anti-tank/artillery role, stationary in the first instance.

[24] Montgomery has frequently been criticised because it was believed that had he released all his armour Rommel's *Afrika Korps* would have been destroyed. Montgomery always argued he was building up the Army so there could be no mistakes.

[25] In Auckinleck's plan the ridge was held by the 21st Indian Infantry Brigade under the command of the 2nd New Zealand Division.

hoped his wound would be fatal when it came. As a dead man walking he was actually brave, and on that dirty ridge I watched with amazement as he ran out in all that hail of bullets and shells to drag back into his own slit trench one of our chaps who was fleeing and had been hit in the legs. I was not brave, and, furthermore, apart from looking over the top occasionally and shouting to my chaps to keep looking ahead there was little I could do. The last thing I recall was the sound of shells exploding in a long straight line;[26] to this day I have never been able to discover whether they were ours or the Germans.[27]

When I came to I was in the back of a truck and feeling not only sick and hot but in immense pain. I knew I was hurt, but was grateful I was obviously being taken to a medical facility; I recall hoping that the local doctors were good. I looked sideways and saw another Buff insignia; I could not recognise the person because his face was swathed in bandages. I tried to raise myself against the bumping of the lorry, but I had a terrible pain in my legs and my arms seemed useless. I just collapsed back and for a moment I think I drifted in and out of consciousness. This was the second time I had been wounded and I was beginning to think that this might be what they used to call a *blighty* wound.[28] Some chap climbed out of the cab while it was still moving and offered me a drink of water which although warm was most welcome; he looked at me as if wondering whether I was alive so I smiled and was grateful to him when he offered me a lit cigarette. I know today the whole world is against smoking, but that soldier's gift to me at that moment was better than a chunk of gold. It was a powerful cigarette but I waved my thanks to my benefactor who cheerfully waved back as he climbed into the cab.

After an hour of constant driving I tried to look around the truck again. To my astonishment there were eight of us crammed in and I appeared to be the only conscious one that made sense of me being the only one to drink his water. There were at least four or five Germans with us, although by the looks of two of them they were already dead. The exertion merely looking round sent me back into my own world of confused dreams, and when I came to again I realised I was on a stretcher and being carried to a tent in the middle of the night. I looked up at the chaps carrying me and realised they were using prisoners to do the lifting

---

[26] Probably a creeping barrage.

[27] During the Alam el Halfa battle the Allies suffered 1,750 casualties, the Buffs approximately 100; the Valentine crews close on another 100; total of 700 +/- English casualties of which over 200 were listed as missing or prisoner.

[28] Blighty is slang for Britain; used first in Boer war, common in the Great War, less common after 1918. It referred to a wound serious enough to take you out of the line but not serious enough to make life too miserable.

because they were two *Afrika Còrps* men. I think I must have passed out again because the pain was now overwhelming. I was semi-conscious that I was being looked at under a bright light, conscious that I was being attended to, and then the next time I was aware of what was going on it was bright daylight. Both my arms were in stiff bandages and my right leg also.

A chap walked by and offered me a drink and placed, once again, a lit cigarette in my mouth. When he saw I was having trouble holding it he put it to my lips, he held it for me, and then withdrew it as I inhaled and expelled the smoke. I spoke to him about what was wrong with me, but he just shook his head. I thought this was strange until the doctor came to me and spoke in German. It was only then that it dawned on me that I was a POW, had been saved by a German recovery truck, operated on by a German surgeon, and helped to drink, and given cigarettes by the very people I had started to hate. I lay on the stretcher dazed with disbelief; silly as it sounds, even then I reflected on my father, and heaven only knew where he was now extracting teeth, and his views on Aitkens the working class man who saved my life, and now he could learn that the enemy had also saved me. Whether he ever did know I was a POW I never discovered.

WOLFGANG 1940-1942

I have just read Horace's account and was relieved that at least he received decent medical treatment from my Wehrmacht colleagues. This would not have happened in the Eastern war or the Balkans, little mercy was shown if you came from East of the German borders, especially if one were Russian. Sometimes we were ordered not to take prisoners, other times they might be collected up for either work parties or starved to death to save ammunition and expenditure. Our treatment of fellow human beings in the East and even in the West, if they were partisans, was simply appalling. It took me sometime to realise this, but I shall write about this later. They used to say the North African war was fought cleanly. I was not there, but I am not sure there is any truth in this view.

There were no great centres of civilians, there were next to no partisans, the enemy could hardly use the detested sniper in the desert surroundings, and there was a grim anonymity about minefields, artillery and tanks. The desert was not personal but it was not a tennis match. I think that while we were taught to see anyone from the east as subhuman, we regarded those in the west as more like us, especially the English.

They had our royal family, although they had changed their names,[29] and we had always had a healthy respect for the immense power hidden in their colonies, and in their Royal Navy. We had often been taught that the English were migrant Germans and it was only in this century we were at odds with our distant cousins. Today I do not believe any of this nonsense, the Russians are not subhuman any more than Jewish people are, and even if the English were distant cousins it is long lost in a racially complex DNA strand; in the war racial bigotry was instilled into us in such a way we rarely questioned the evidence.

No one knew who Harry was when he was in hospital, Horace's father disappeared, and despite so-called German efficiency I was in the latter part of 1940 believed to be dead. War, even amongst us efficient Germans is always chaos, confusion, a waste of life, and achieves nothing apart from creating sadness and hatred. I found myself being repaired, as the medic put it, in a hospital somewhere near Potsdam, and discovered that I had to have what I can only call scaffolding constructed around my skull. Apparently the bullet missed killing me by an unbelievable margin, and the bayonet wound in my shoulder had not healed because it had developed an infection.

The surgeon explained to me that I was in danger from the infection that they kept as surgically clean as they could by dressing and redressing it, causing me some pain. The bullet had, they feared, cut a swathe through that part of the skull which I can only describe as somewhere between my cheekbone and the temple. It would heal but I had to keep still as they hoped the parted bone would eventually fuse. It was for this reason I had the scaffolding attached to my head; the infection in my shoulder caused me to have a fever sometimes and I became restless which was a problem with my facial mask, so I was often drugged to keep me still. Sometimes the drugs were very effective, and I would descend into that deep sleep as if I were under an anaesthetic that is like a timeless black hole making me think it was like a temporary death. Other times I would dream of being at home with Hugo in happier times, but somewhere in these moments of mental agitation and restlessness, the girl who smiled would be there, once I was convinced she was sitting next to me as I lay immobile in my bed. Eventually the shoulder stopped being painful, but the right side of my face was a continuous throb.

They had sewn my ear into one piece, but it looked quite ugly, and I lived off pureed vegetables and thin soup since the injury stopped me from chewing anything of any substance. During this time I lost a lot of weight, and when they removed the scaffolding and I was allowed to

---

[29] This happened during the Great War with the adoption of the name Windsor, and also Mountbatten.

walk, nearly two months after sustaining the injury, I felt unbelievably weak. I had another month in a recuperation ward and then the surgeon who had operated on me in the first place told me he had authorised a few months off, that I could return home, but to look after my skull until it was properly fused.

I never felt much joy or happiness in those bleak days, but the thought of returning to my mother in Marktsteft gave me that sense of boyhood excitement; I could hardly wait for my travel permits. My head was carefully bandaged from top to bottom and I set off with my permits. My bandaged head and uniform ensured I was given a seat, room, and sometimes the occasional drink. There were one or two who did not seem to appreciate my uniform, but generally I felt something of a hero during the journey back home. The public mood was ebullient; it appeared that everything the Führer had promised was coming to fruition and that England would soon ask for peace or be invaded. I cannot recall correctly, but I think it was late October that I arrived home, I do recall that the news which was full of information about the Italians invading Greece.[30]

My mother was over-joyed to see me, and I found it slightly embarrassing that she cried when she saw my bandaged face. I explained that the bandage could come off and it had been placed there for travelling purposes and to remind me to give it time to heal. One of my comrades had sent a card to me wishing me well, and I gathered that most of the regiment was close by the Moselle River and growing in number.[31] I heard from no official or senior rank or even a note from HQ. My mother took the bandage of my head and gasped; looking in the mirror I could see why. The scar ran across my right cheek and was a florid purple, and it was self-evident that my ear had once been in two parts and a significant section was missing. I was no picture for a poster or a photograph, but at least I was alive and feeling better. I reflected on the medic who said we were being repaired. We were not being healed but like machine tools or weapons of war being repaired to be 'used' again. I spent the first month indoors reading and watching the world pass by; I took the surgeon seriously and made sure I kept my head well away from bumps and knocks to give myself a chance. At least by December the scar was less purple, but still very obvious.

Neither Mum nor I had heard a word about Hugo, but I persuaded her that Hugo and I were not great letter writers. When I look back my heart now bleeds for the way we failed to keep in touch with her, took her for

---

[30] Which happened on October 28th 1940.

[31] The LSSAH spent 6 months in Metz where it was expanded to Brigade size of some 6,500 but still retained its designation as regiment.

granted and simply expected her to be always there waiting for us, to pick us up, kiss us and make us better. I had suspected for a long time that Mum had a greater fondness for Hugo, but I was not aware of it so much on this extended leave. However, I could not but note that despite the local world being full of confidence, Mum appeared unsettled. At first I thought it was because of the lack of news from Hugo compounded by my scarred face, but it ran deeper than us boys. Mum had friends in Hamburg and they had told her how British planes had dropped bombs which set houses on fire,[32] and then there was news that there had been a serious raid on Mannheim, which all reminded my Mum that Dad had always claimed the British will never stop until they win, that they were cold blooded and ruthless. I tried to persuade her that in France the British had run faster than the French, but she pointed at my face and asked 'and who did that to you?' She had a point, but I concluded it was not the British who seemed to be depressing her. Eventually I sat down one evening determined to find out what was making her feel so unhappy.

'I'm not sure, in fact I am certain the government is making mistakes and being unduly cruel to some people. I used the think the Führer was our answer, but I am beginning to think he's out of control and wicked.'

I can recall to this day how stunned I felt; I even looked around our living room to see if there was a spy listening in to hear her outrageous words. Mum would not let me answer or protest, but told me how she had a month before I arrived home visited Bayreuth when some Jews had been expelled from their home.

'It was appalling. I only wandered over the street to see what the crowd were jeering at, and an old lady, must have been in her eighties, a woman of about forty and a teenage girl had been stripped of their clothes and were being forced to crawl on all fours. If they hesitated two elderly men were beaten with truncheons, the older one had blood pouring out of his mouth, probably from a broken jaw. I had to walk away. They had degraded them in a way we would not do to animals. This 'beat the Jew out of town' has become a macabre game for those with deprived minds.'

'But they are sub-human,' I argued, 'and are our enemies.'

'What sort of enemy is an eighty year old woman, or her daughter and granddaughter, and I gather their two men were both doctors. When they capture the British pilots who drop bombs on our cities they are fed and watered. We don't treat them like that.'

I could see it was worthless arguing and I knew my mother was beginning to see I was not convinced. She argued that the Jews the Führer had criticised were the bankers and capitalists, and there was no differential between the physical Jewish body and mine. I was going to

---

[32] 1940 November 16th first use of incendiaries with Hamburg as the target.

mention circumcision but held my tongue; I had heard this point of view before and could not contest its validity. I think that evening my mother sowed some seeds of doubt in my mind, which, with the girl who smiled, would not go away. My mother also mentioned our neighbour Heinrich who we had loved as boys. He had been overheard criticising the government and had been sent to Dachau Concentration camp for six months. When he returned he was less than half his weight, his thick black hair had gone, his left arm would not work and he would not speak. He went to bed and died. His wife was broken hearted, and being a close friend of my mother had not spared the detail. He had stayed alive only to defy the authorities, making it home simply to die in his own bed with his wife near him. Even I had liked Heinrich, he had always been kind to us boys, and it now made sense that when I saw his wife a few days later she turned away from me; she knew I was in the SS, and I was too proud and embarrassed to say I was in the Waffen-SS.

I stopped probing my mother, but tried to warn her that unlike Heinrich she had to be careful to whom she spoke about such matters. I read the newspapers with interest, noting that our Allies the Italians were having a poor time in Greece.[33] I continued with an old text book to read some English, and a friend of my Mum gave me some help. Although as a country we appeared to be militarily untouchable we still had poor food rations, and once, sitting in a small café I overheard some women complaining that the 'big wigs' always seemed to fare well, fancy cars and plenty of food, but for all 'the conquering' as they called it, they had not reaped many benefits. German society was a strange mix; there was a sense of triumphalism, a growing fear of not breaking new laws, almost inducing a fear of one's neighbours, astonishment that food supplies and the promised standards of living seemed no better, if not worse, and my Mum caused me to detect a slight sense of unease about what the Führer was doing to people. By the time we reached January 1941 I was unsettled at being at home, I was convinced my head was healed and yet I had not received the promised call-back letter to my regiment. I decided to pursue the matter for myself.

Eventually I received a call from a policeman who gave me travel documents to take me to Potsdam where I reported a week later, had my wounds examined and declared fit. I often wonder how long I would have got away with being at home had I said nothing; the hospital had forgotten me, and so had the regiment. When I hear people today talking of German efficiency it makes me smile.

---

[33] 1940 November 4th the Greeks counter-attacked expelled the Italians pursuing them into Albania.

It is at this juncture that I stopped writing for a couple of weeks. I have to confess it has started to depress me, and I really do not want to write a sub-standard badly researched military history. When the three of us discussed putting our experiences together as an act of contrition, or a cathartic cleansing it was to the purpose of sharing with one another what went through our minds. Harry and Horace have been clever the way they have given some background and then written about the things that mattered. I am somewhat pedantic, and want to write a complete background of what happened and where, but I suspect that not only will my failing memory make mistakes, but it would be a tedious exercise.

To put it briefly I was reattached to my regiment but there were so many new faces I recognised no one. My scarred face indicated to newcomers I was already a veteran as we would say these days, and my rank, which had not changed gave me a small degree of respect from the many bright-eyed youngsters ready to do battle for the Fatherland. The only study or reading in the mess bars and barracks was *Der Stürmer*[34] and the occasional but rare newspaper. I recall feeling angry for being so keen to sign on again since the company back in the regiment was just as tedious as I had found at home. I found the training easy; I had managed, despite the necessary recuperation to have stayed fit, and I was grateful that the grapevine indicated we were going to be on the move to what they called sunny places.

By late March we had moved south to the old Macedonia and set ourselves up in the ancient town of Prilep; there were rocky outcrops and mountains and we trained in them for several weeks. It was clear that we would be fighting the Greeks, having been obliged to come to the assistance of the Italians who had failed miserably. The Italians were a source of humour at the time, but that was mainly unfair, they were under equipped with weapons and ammunition, badly led and inadequately clothed for Greek mountain weather conditions. Our task was to follow a Panzer-Division[35] deep into Greek territory securing it and putting down any resistance. I was attached to some armoured cars that penetrated deep into the Balkans. Later when I looked back my group was side tracked as a flanking movement, and in the months' fighting I never saw any regular troops.

We were fighting what was going to be a major phenomenon of the war, first in the Balkans, then Russia and also in Northern Italy. I am not talking about the resistance often mentioned in regard to the French; this

---

[34] A violently anti-Semitic and near pornographic Nazi broadsheet by the infamous Julius Streicher.

[35] This probably refers to an operation launched on 6th April 1941 when the LSSAH followed the route of the 9th Panzer Division, which was all part of *General der Panzertruppen* Georg Stumme's XL Panzer Corps.

was a very different war. The French were almost civilised, at least to start with, their resistance was writing pamphlets, letting down tyres, daubing walls, putting up posters; they did nothing serious until the war was virtually over. Partisans in the east loathed us with a venomous abhorrence the French could not muster. We came upon them in Albania within a few days. One of our detachments had halted where a tree had fallen across the road and got out to investigate only to be shot down. To our horror the bodies had been stripped and nailed to trees lining the road; two had been tortured and had experienced castration, and one had his skin flayed while alive, and died from the pain of having acid and boiling water poured over him. I have often tried to determine where we found this place of hell; I know in Greece we had turned west at the town of Florina and were heading towards the Albanian town of Korçë leading to Yugoslavia, but it was a hilly forested area and ideal for partisans.

We never stopped for fallen trees after that incident, a scout car or bike would return with the information and we would fan out. The partisans had gone, and we buried our comrades and motored on with extreme caution. It was a strange feeling in the armoured troop carrier, we said little, but there was that extreme mix of hatred and fear. At the time we thought this was not only illegal but immoral, and we genuinely felt we held the moral high ground. We were soldiers making the place safe, and were being opposed by ruthless and heartless medieval criminals, who defied the description of human. Later the moral high ground theory collapsed for me, and for most Germans it did at the end of the war when we had time, and were also obliged by the enemy to understand what had happened.

My mother had sown doubts in my mind, but they were only doubts and as I sat there with my comrades I knew I would not hesitate to kill the first partisan we came upon. There was what I can only describe as an atmosphere of blood lust amongst us all, and after two miles we came upon a small cluster of houses, not large enough to be a village, more like a hamlet. We paused, and our commander pointed out that the trap we had just left was only two miles away, and these people must have known about it, but even if they did not their deaths would be seen by the perpetrators as a reprisal warning. He may have been right because we forced the people out of their homes, and there were no men at all, just women and children. It was probably their men who had tortured and killed our friends.

There was no use speaking to them as there was no commonality of language. They were herded together and taken towards the road where our vehicles were stationed. My group searched the houses for anyone hiding. They were not homes as I understood homes, they were more like huts, and the poverty was self-evident. There was no food or drink worth keeping, no books, a few agricultural implements, and it appeared that they ran a smallholding between the ten or twelve homes. In one house a large mongrel dog started to come towards me but I took no risks and shot it. We then torched the houses, hearing some gunfire in the background we guessed a few more dogs had appeared. Not one man, not even an old one ever showed up. When we got back to the vehicles one of my comrades laughed and said that would teach them. I thought he meant the burning down of their homes, but he was looking up the road. I stopped in my tracks spellbound. The eight or nine children had been nailed to the trees lining the road, and the women had received the same treatment as well as having their breasts cut off. In the April sunlight the flies were already swarming over the blood as the women cried and wept.

I want to record as I write this now, that at the time, not later, I felt disgusted at the sight of what we had done. I felt we were justified in burning down the homes, but killing women and children in such a way I had not anticipated, I thought that making them homeless was sufficient. That night we slept under canvas in a guarded grove. I recalled the time I had helped kill the Jews on the understanding they were sub-human, I reflected on my mother's challenge that of course they were human, and that night, when I did snatch a moment's sleep I dreamt of the girl who smiled, but behind her was my mother nailed by her arms to a tree and blood was pouring down the length of her body as flies swarmed around her. I could say nothing about my doubts to anyone as there was a sense of self-righteous justification that we had revenged our comrades. I think I could quite easily have nailed a perpetrator to the tree, but not his wife or child; furthermore we had no proof that it was their menfolk who had done the deed.

As we set off in the early hours, now with several other contingents in line, I wondered if I were the only one who found the torture of the women and children wrong, and whether other were plagued by the occasional nightmares. The others talked about *Kriegsbrauch*,[36] explaining it as an excuse for the excesses of the massacre, arguing that a violent and extreme reprisal will soon bring the war to a halt and that makes the method humane. I recall even at the time wondering how one could call such an action humane, but I am quite serious that many of my number were convinced by doing something terrible like that incident would shorten the war. The men would not join the partisans and would stop fighting, so our brutal response was better for everyone in the long run; the greater good. Today I am embarrassed to admit we could possibly think like this, but as a group it held great sway, and if there was

---

[36] requirements of war...

anyone like me who had doubts I shall never know, we were too nervous to share such heresies.

We were very quickly advancing from Albania up the Dalmatian coast[37]and met occasional resistance, but by the end of the month we seemed to be in control.[38]The fighting was fierce but we had superior weapons and it seemed as if we had pacified the area very quickly. There were many who supported us, fascists like ourselves or at least sympathetic, but they were all divided, especially the Serbs and Croats. It did not take long before we realised that the Balkans may have technically capitulated, their royalty fled and government, for what it was, surrendered and collapsed, but not the people, especially the Serbs who quickly formed themselves into well organised and very brutal partisan groups. Looking back from half a century I have a nerve calling them brutal, but they were because it was the only language we understood, and heaven knows we were brutal enough. I know of little realistic literature relating to the Balkans war, which has recently been overshadowed by the atrocities that took place there following the death of Tito.[39] I know we slaughtered entire communities, took few prisoners and tortured people to track down partisans.

On the other hand I had always promised myself that I would rather save one bullet for my own head than be caught alive by them. I have already described the massacre I witnessed, and there were many more but I am reluctant to go into detail. In fact after writing about the way the women and children were killed I stopped writing this for a month; I felt so sick in my heart at the memories I have provoked. I look back and wonder how I did the things I did. I was pursued in my dreams by the girl who smiled, when I saw children and women hiding from us my mind travelled back to the massacre near Korçë, and once when I saw a pile of dead Jews about to be ignited with old tyres and wooden rafters I remembered, as I looked at the corpses my mother telling me they were just as human as we were. There was the body of a beautiful young woman clutching her dead baby; she had looks similar to a girl I knew in Marktsteft. I did reflect on what was happening but life was hectic, we were always on the move and constantly having to fight, and so life seemed to pass very quickly.

It was near Sarajevo I nearly came unstuck for the third time. I do not recall the names of the various places, they were alien to me but I have looked at a map and can recall the location where I nearly met my maker.

---

[37] During mid-April 1941; there was no mention in the archives or histories of this specific massacre, but such brutality was very common.
[38] April 13th Germans take Belgrade, April 17th Prince Peter flown to London and Yugoslavia capitulated, British troops evacuate Greece that surrendered on April 23rd.
[39] Fought throughout the 1990s.

We had been travelling towards Sarajevo along a wide and twisting River called Neretra, and were gathering in force at a place called Glogosnica, characterised by its poverty and surrounded by beautiful mountains, but spoilt by the presence of partisan bands. We were working alongside a Wehrmacht mountain troop and had paused to relax by a lake called Graboričko; some men were having a dip in the lake just to remove the grime and dirt of the journey, it was far too cold for me and I wandered along the side of the shore towards what I took to be a small boating house.

Sitting around a table was a group of very senior Wehrmacht officers looking over a map, but totally relaxed with bottles of wine and that glorious smell of cigars that I still hanker after. Naturally I kept my distance and stopped to light a cigarette and look at the scene. My attention was caught by a slight movement in the bushes behind the boathouse; at first I thought it was some children, but I caught the glint of metal and experience taught me it was probably a weapon. The first thought that crossed my mind as I put my cigarette out was that the officers had not placed some of their men as guards in the bushes, a strange habit. I walked towards the officers gripping my machine pistol carefully, and I was just on time. I shouted to the officers to drop to the floor, they looked at me with total astonishment as if I were the threat, but three of the four dived down towards the hut the fourth stood as if to confront me. I fired past him at the three men who were attacking; they were not well armed, shot guns and old rifles as it appeared to me, and my aim was good bringing two down immediately, the third shot the standing Wehrmacht officer and turned on his heels. Suddenly the whole scene came alight with small arms fire.

There were others firing at me from all around the bushes and small trees. I rushed up to the wounded Wehrmacht officer and dragged him to the cover of the building. I can recall thinking that these senior officers had no immediate guards and only fancy luger pistols to fight back with. The racket was drawing our own troops to the scene but they had to approach with caution; we had walked into a hornet's nest. It seemed that these men were intent on capturing an officer because while heavy fire sprayed the approaching troops three more men appeared from nowhere close by the three crouching officers, but I managed to shoot one and the other two withdrew. To do this I had to come out from the cover of the tree, and I felt as if my legs and lower part of my body was being thumped by stinging bees. I collapsed, having been heavily shot in both of my legs and a nasty pain in my stomach. As I rolled over I thought that this was the beginning of the end.

It was not as we all know. To cut a long story short I was the darling of those Wehrmacht officers who, when the fighting was over pulled out every stop to make sure I was not only given immediate medical attention, and it was painkillers I needed; I was flown back to Bavaria to a small hospital in Bayreuth. I was going to be out of action for several months, but was for a time the hero of the moment. I already had a bronze Infantry Assault Badge, which was upgraded to silver, along with a gold Close Combat Clasp and an Anti-Partisan Guerrilla Warfare Badge, but there was talk of the coveted Iron Cross 2nd Class, which depended on the recommendation of the officers whom I had saved. It never happened because the same lack of precaution that they had shown at Glogosnica from which I had saved them, they repeated closer to Sarajevo where all but one was killed.

I was in hospital for weeks as I had twelve different bullet wounds, eleven in my leg and one passed across the centre of my tummy just a centimetre below by umbilicus. The stomach wound was painful but repaired itself very quickly, unlike my face it was a hidden scar. My legs were a different matter, apart from the fact that I would never wear shorts in public or swimming trunks, bones in both legs had been damaged. I had five operations and some careful therapy afterwards; thanks to the Wehrmacht officer whose life I saved, I was in a first class setting and being looked after. The company was fun; we played a great deal of *skat*[40] and chess, and talked about the staff, the nurses and doctors, none of us mentioned where we had been or any specifics about the war. It was apparent from the number of wounded that the fighting was increasing, and total victory was not round the corner. When I left for home I hoped that they would forget me again, and this time I would not remind them.

HARRY 1940-43

It is a slow process recalling these memories so many decades after they occurred, and sometimes painful. When looking at Horace I can now fully understand why he thought I was dead, even my own father was uncertain, and it took Father H eventually to track me down. Reading how Wolfgang was shot I wonder how he survived; in fact all three of us were lucky to have survived as long as we did, and with later events which brought the three of us together it is simply unbelievable we are writing this account today. Wolfgang has, if I read his German notes correctly, hidden a message between the lines of his last letter. I think he needs Horace and me to reply more swiftly with our sections because I suspect he believes his time is running out. He has much on his

---

[40] Popular card game.

conscience, but today I see the man he became, not the ill-led boy he once was.

Because of my head wound I was stuck in convalescence for what seemed months. The doctor looking after my case explained that once the wound was healed my skull would probably be back to normal, but time was the answer. Whether he was telling me the truth or giving me encouragement I have no idea, I just took it for granted. I can recall having problems with memory to start with, but that was probably due to the severe blow to my head. I took a book of verse from the trolley, Gerard Manley Hopkin was one of the poets, and I was fascinated by the line 'mind, mind has mountains,' as I lay back wondering what life was all about. The doctor was curious that I found this work absorbing and asked about my background; when he heard I had been accepted at Cambridge he asked why I was not an officer.

Later I was visited by a Captain in some other regiment who had obviously been speaking to the doctor. He questioned me at length about my background; I told him how I had received a basic education at Dover County School, but how Father H had spent years preparing me for entry into Cambridge. He took the questions further testing me on my knowledge of history, and was curious about my knowledge of Latin, but more especially my German. Before I knew it I was talking to another officer who was not English; I suspected he was a German though I thought it rude to ask directly. I was asked if I were interested in becoming an officer, but I declined. My heart was never in the military, I had only signed on for the duration as far as I was concerned; I wanted another crack at Cambridge that now seemed so distant. I was persuaded to leave the Buffs and was talked into the Royal Signals Corps.[41]   To begin with I objected because I gathered an enlistment for eight years was the norm, but was assured that I could sign on just for the duration. The other extraordinary mandate was their height requirement; I was six foot, which was taller than their usual demand![42] There was an absolute demand for the Corps as the war increased, and they were especially interested in recruits with an aptitude for languages.[43]

It took most of 1940 to recover, but in the winter of 1941 I found myself undergoing training at Catterick Camp.[44] Before I arrived at what I can describe as the most boring of camps I spent much time improving

---

[41] It started life as part of the Royal Engineers Signal Service, but on 28th June, 1920, the Secretary of State, none other than Winston Churchill, signed a Royal Warrant creating the Corps of Signals and six weeks later George V conferred the title Royal Corps of Signals.

[42] Royal Signal Recruits had to be at least 5 feet 2 inches tall.

[43] By 1945 the strength pf the Corps was 8,518 officers and 142,472 men.

[44] Signal Training Centre at Catterick.

my German, and because of a hint by the interviewing officer started some basic Italian. I have to confess I had discovered a real enjoyment in studying languages.

Catterick was, as far as I was concerned in the middle of nowhere, but I was not being fired at or bombed and soon became interested in the technology of telephone systems, laying wires, wireless apparatus, signals and the use of codes. Because of my language skills I was also part of the group that was trained in what I can best describe as scanning the airways listening for enemy reports and information. We were trained in driving lorries, cars, and what I loved most motorcycles, especially my favourite the old BSA 350. After the war I was able to purchase one, and was quite certain that they had re-sprayed a khaki one red! There was little time off, indeed there was a sense of panic as the authorities seemed desperate to train up as many men as possible. Someone asked why women were not being trained, and we were told they were for home use, but the Signal Corps would always be close to the front, and some units may be behind enemy lines; that closed that conversation.

I went fishing with a chap called Simon on the nearby River Swale, we caught nothing, were frozen and I was bored; that put me off fishing for life. I went into Darlington and nearby Middlesbrough but there was nothing there of interest, so I took to occasionally walking on the Yorkshire Dales, a thing I still enjoy doing to this day. Catterick was a deadly place for bored young men, and only a shortage of spare-time and money, as well as watered down beer stopped a good deal of trouble in the local pubs. I liked the occasional beer, but I had moved away from wanting to go out simply to drink as much as possible and indulge in trivial and inane conversations. I honestly do not believe I had become a snob, but Father H had made me aware there were more interesting things in life than the barmaid's bosoms, and I also felt a high degree of loyalty towards Edna, despite the fact that my letters were never answered. The facilities at Catterick were limited, but I was allowed to develop my German and made some real inroads into Italian. I found the exercises in running telephone lines tedious, but enjoyed the wireless, telegraphs, Morse and other codes very interesting, and, not meaning to be boastful, emerged with some excellent marks. I was getting near the end of the course and was admiring some new motorcycles that had just been delivered when my friend Simon said I had a letter.

I nearly broke my neck getting back to the barracks, I was simply dying to hear from Edna or Dad; I had written so many times and had heard nothing. In those days phones could only be found in well to do professional homes and the lack of communication had become a concern. As soon as I saw the letter I knew it was from Father H, he had very distinctive handwriting. I still have the letter to this day, and I attach its contents here.

My Dear Harry, Thank the Lord you are safe. We have all been under the delusion that you were either killed or a POW. I believe your friend Horace was convinced you had been killed. I tried to contact him but he too has disappeared. I used some of my old connections to find out what had happened to you. In all of the confusion following the miraculous retreat at Dunkirk nobody seemed to know of you or where you were. War creates terrible confusion. Even your own regiment was uncertain, thinking you had been taken prisoner. Eventually an old friend of mine tracked you to Catterick, where, I gather you have been your usual stubborn self in refusing to become an officer.

Your father left Dover thinking you were dead or a seriously wounded prisoner; he has very courageously decided to leave his work in Dover to become a merchant seaman. It was very brave of him at his age, but as he said to me, if the army have lost then our only chance of survival depends on bringing food and equipment into the country. I have always admired your Father's incisive thinking. I have written to him in the hope he hears the good news that all is well with you. Dover has become something of a front line, the battle in the skies, which they are now dubbing the Battle of Britain seemed to take place above our heads. German bombers are attacking ships just off the Goodwin Sands, attacking the pens,[45] and, as you will have heard they are now shelling us across the channel.

The terrible thing is one does not get any warning, no sounds of planes just a 'whoosh' followed by an explosion. Poor old St James's Church near Castle Street was recently blown to pieces. Do you remember the service we all attended there a few years ago? Times have changed. Dover has changed and so will you. Your experiences to date and whatever happens in the future are going to have a dramatic effect on the way you view life and other human beings. I know this because of my own experience in the last war.

The Germans are a militaristic bunch; they are good soldiers but can be cruel. Occasionally you may come upon a civilised German, they do exist. You will travel through some pretty miserable times, some dangerous times, you will suffer from boredom, fear, anxiety, restlessness and you will question both God and man. What I am trying to say, Harry, is that this war had nothing to do with God. God gave us free will and evil men have caused this war abusing God's gift. Harry, keep the faith,

---

[45] This probably refers to heavy cement shelters built for Motor Torpedo Boats (MTBs).

and come home safe. God's Blessing on you, Father Harold. P.S. I hope
you are keeping your academic studies and prayers alive.

I always kept that letter because it expressed eminent common sense. Whenever I came upon man's inhumanity, and I was still to see a great deal of pain and suffering inflicted by man on man I recalled Father H's words that this was the work of man abusing the gift of free will. We made the choices not God. Without free will we would be mere automatons, free will makes us human and evil arises from us when we abuse our freedom. I know that Wolfgang was to come to the same conclusion the hard way. I had no idea how to contact my Dad, I had written to family in Dover but Father H's letter was the only one I received. I replied that evening, but even as I was putting the letter in a post box I gathered that our new postings were being put up on a notice board.

The men were gathered around the notice boards and there was a good deal of excited chatter and some degree of moaning. I found it difficult to get to the front but managed only to find my name was missing. As people drifted away I stood there with five others who also appeared mystified by not finding their names. One was my friend Simon who looked at me and shrugged his shoulders. The mystery disappeared an hour later when we five were called to the senior officer's rooms and marched in as if on report. To cut a long story short we had been held back for a variety of reasons, we all spoke a foreign language, we had done well in codes and wireless and we had been selected to be given the opportunity to volunteer for special duties.

When they referred to special duties or special services they were not a term we were familiar with, and nor was it the term it has become today. They wanted us to train alongside the commandos that had that year started to come into existence. We were not to become commandos but to train with them so we could act as a support corps to their projected activities. We had heard rumours of commandos but not a great deal more. It was a clever way of getting us to volunteer because it was presented to us as an opportunity we had brought on ourselves by doing well; how could we refuse? We were to go for further training in Scotland after one day's leave; quite what one was supposed to do with one day's leave in Catterick none of us resolved.[46]

I regretted volunteering from the moment we arrived in Spean Bridge Railway station. It was a long over-crowded and extremely uncomfortable journey. We hoped when we arrived to be given a decent

---

[46] In February 1942 the commando training depot was established at Achnacarry in the Highlands by Brigadier Charles Haydon.

meal and taken by bus or at least lorry to the training grounds. Spean Bridge was the beginning of the training ground. Our kit was checked and we were given more to carry, and were force-marched what I believe was ten miles to the commando depot.[47] I always felt I was reasonably fit but the speed of this march indicated we were not as fit as the sergeant and his men who marched with us; they treated the march as if it were a Sunday afternoon stroll. It was instilled in us from the very start that worse than death was to have RTU[48] appended to our reports, and, the surly looking officer looked at us with studied interest, stating that no signallers had made it yet.

Later I discovered none had made it because we were the first. Our physical fitness was tested to the limit, and just when I thought I could be no fitter harder tests were concocted. We forded rivers, manoeuvred small boats, climbed mountain ranges and rock faces, and, as we coped with this we were given the added torture of handling live ammunition and explosives. In my short time there I was aware of many men giving up and having RTU appended to their files, one man was killed on a rock face, and another injured by a grenade. They were building Nissan huts, but my entire time was under canvas. Despite these ghastly conditions we were expected to stay clean, salute officers and polish what brass we had. We did not have a going away party but finished with night exercise landing from boats and using live ammunition, and we were only a support unit.

Several times I considered throwing in the towel arguing with myself that not only was life unpleasant, but I was going into a job that had a high prospect of an untimely death. I was shouted at, abused, threatened, bullied and physically exhausted all for the prospect of an early death. It struck me that it would be easier to have RTU attached to my file, but I was a proud young man, and a little older than most of them, so I stayed to the bitter end. Simon and I stayed as a team and found to our astonishment that we were a support crew for a Commando unit consisting mainly of Germans, German-Jews, and a few Austrians.[49] It was small and obviously the intention was to build it up in size. We practised with them for what seemed like years; in fact it was less than five months. My German improved no end, and I was astonished at how well they spoke English, especially given that some of them had only started a year ago.

Some of the other units resented their presence, and I have to be honest and state that I found it extremely odd to be training alongside

---

[47] This happened to all recruits and although the distance may have felt like ten but it was closer to eight.

[48] Returned to Unit.

[49] This was No 3 (X) Troop officially named the Miscellaneous Troop in 1944.

Germans, even if they spoke English. One of our exercises was to scale an icy covered mountain ridge, climb up a small rock face and then set up the wireless and send some coded messages. Near the top I slipped and caught my leg in a small crevice. Try as I could there was no way I could extricate myself. It was both embarrassing and dangerous because I could not see how I could free myself, and I was beginning to suffer from extreme cold with the possibility of hypothermia.

A young German called Siegfried climbed down to me and taking off his own battledress wrapped it around me to keep the cold at bay. He could not shift my leg, and scurried up to the top quickly returning with a spade. He eventually freed me but we were late sending the signal. In the post-mortem I was getting such a dressing down that I thought I was going to be court-martialled, but this young Siegfried stepped forward and in perfect public school English defended me claiming that I had not so much got my leg stuck as that a rock had shifted and trapped me. The officer looked coldly at Siegfried who returned the look with clear disdain. I later learned that Siegfried hated the Nazis and had at one time been in the Wehrmacht, so some junior officer was not going to frighten him. I would have loved to have had time to get to know Siegfried, but that same day we all parted company.

One lesson Siegfried taught me was not to assume all Germans were evil. I had thought we were going to be attached to No 3 (X) troop, but as signals men we were needed urgently elsewhere, and we parted company. To this day I am never sure as to why we were put through this arduous task, as signallers we never received any recognition, but it must have been on our files because, as I was yet to discover, I was never given any safe jobs in HQ situations where many of my old friends spent the rest of the war.

A small group of us were given train tickets to take us across country to Cardiff on a route so circuitous we thought it must be some form of aptitude test. It was one of the most exhausting journeys I ever experienced. It took four days with endless stops, overcrowded and overheated carriages, hardly any sustenance and that was best kept to a minimum because the facilities simply stank and were foul. I have often read that during war we became more efficient, but this was simply not true. Those who planned ahead for troop movements must have had the intellectual capacity and ability of a legless centipede. We were numbers, sometimes with names, who were simply part of a transport programme that seemed to have no overall plan, or even idea of what was needed and what was happening.

In Cardiff we spilled out into what was called Tiger Bay, an area that I was to discover was infamous for its prostitution and crime rates. I have never been a prude, and I really try not to be a snob. My Dad was a dockworker and I had worked in salvage, but I found Tiger Bay appalling. It was not the prostitutes that caught my attention so much as the number of spivs[50] who lurked around the area. I wondered at their audacity given that the main customers in the area were young men in uniform travelling through the port to fight overseas, while they made their grubby money in the safety of home ports. As I had wondered during the dreadful journey down from Scotland as to who could organise a trip so badly, now I wondered how these men, mainly young men like me could evade war duties; being a spiv was hardly an essential duty. I know that today history tends to look more kindly on the spiv, even in the television programme *Dad's Army* there is a pleasant young spiv, but in reality they were petty criminals evading their duty when other people were dying. I am beginning to sound pompous, but I was not the only serving soldier who found spivs despicable. Military police patrolled Tiger Bay, but they had no authority over civilians, but I was grateful when they shovelled us all towards some makeshift barracks near Penarth awaiting departure.

For all my groaning about the lack of organisation and the apparent stupidity of those responsible for administration, you can imagine my incredulity when we arrived at the campsite to find not only that we were expected, but I had a letter waiting for me. I have always had that silly habit of examining an envelope first to see if I could recognise the handwriting, and this one seemed vaguely familiar, but remained a mystery until I had the sense to open it and discover it was from my Dad. I had little reason to see my Dad's handwriting at home, and I can recall how neat it was and what a surprise to hear from him. It transpired that he had been told I was dead and it was only Father H's indefatigable efforts to find him on his ship that gave him the news I was still alive. He knew my brother Eddie had been killed, and when he heard I also had died he went to sea as his way of 'seeking revenge' as he put it in his letter. This war, as with so many others, was tearing our family apart.

The letter had been written three months before, re-establishing my distrust of administration, and all I could gather about his whereabouts was the fact that the letter had been posted in Liverpool. He asked me to write to my sisters; I had already done that and had heard nothing. His reminding me of Eddie threw me into black doldrums, and I did not go out that evening with my mates for fear I might want to punch the nearest spiv on the nose; Eddie had died whilst they made money.

---

[50] Spiv was a word which grew in currency during the Second World War; it referred to smartly if not over-dressed 'suited' men who dealt in the Black Market and other criminal activities.

I have no intention of trying to write my biography, we all agreed that we would write what crossed our minds, what we thought influenced us most, what stood out in our memories and not pull any punches. By the end of 1942 I was sick to death of just hanging around, and being bossed about by idiots who were easing their boredom by imposing their orders on lesser mortals. Ever since those days I have had an automatic distrust of minor bureaucracy and its officers, a distrust of petty officials, and an intense dislike of the faceless officialdom behind the myriads of forms we human beings have to deal with in our lifetime. To this day I deeply resent filling out tax forms and driving licence renewal forms, and become irritated when I encounter any bossy receptionist at the surgery or dentists; places I inhabit more and more as I age.

From Cardiff we were shipped to North Africa in a vessel where the conditions were just as disgusting as the train journey from Scotland. We were locked in holds which were boiling hot, had little to no exercise, the ship swayed and rocked continuously and we were all aware that if we were torpedoed or bombed those of us below decks had no chance of survival. Christmas Day 1942 was celebrated with a couple of extra sausages, some luke-warm watered down beer and the occasional song. Someone produced some paper hats and a chaplain appeared for a moment, but looked positively horrified at the sight and smell of us. I was allowed on deck with a hundred others for half an hour on a badly organised rota; it is a memory I shall never forget because it has influenced my politics to this day.

We looked up to the upper decks where officers and some nurses were having drinks and looking out to sea as if it were a holiday cruise. Some looked down at us as if we were animals in the zoo being let out in the pasture for a brief moment, some even pointing at us because a few did some exercises in the fresh air. We could hear them talking, and one rather loud junior officer said the smell arising from our hold clearly indicated the working class never washed. I looked at him with a feeling of animosity that I normally reserved for the enemy; his round cherubic face imprinted itself on my memory and in one of those strange coincidences I was to meet him face to face later in life. I recall with some interest that Horace was an officer, who at least had the decency to be aware of the dreadful class division.

We arrived in North Africa after the battle of El Alamein, and as a signaller I found myself attached to a small tank unit that was trying to probe the way ahead into Tunis. Montgomery may have won the battle, but his pursuit of Rommel along the North African coast was ponderously slow. It has been commented on by historians, but it was also observed at the time. Most of us were happy to go slow, especially us new arrivals; none of us were in a rush to get killed. I always believe Montgomery's reputation has been inflated beyond reality, and, as Horace noted, Rommel's repute was also highly exalted and often used as an excuse for our failures. The slow chasing of the retreating Germans and Italians along that long coast gave men such as Kesselring time to bolster their defences on what was called the Mareth line,[51] and bring in reinforcements. As most people know the Americans had now landed along the coast and I was attached to a probing unit to try and penetrate part of the Atlas Mountains[52] in west to central Tunisia. The going for the tanks was difficult, which made life difficult because as a signals group we were expected to reach a particular observation point and report back. Eventually, with a machine gun crew and a mortar team we worked our way up a sharp ridge and found some shelter in some shallow caves near the top.

We were well supplied with everything but water which we rationed with care. We were told to expect a breakthrough of American armour at any time and had to report on any air activity, or any German signals we picked up. Despite being North Africa it was extremely cold at the top of our ridge, especially at night, and the only air activity was our own North African Air Force and the air waves were silent. I played cards, chess and read Thomas Hardy. It seems strange, but Trollope and Hardy were popular amongst many, mainly I suspect because it was nostalgic for an idyllic England. Apart from the lack of water and the cold at night we might have been on a camping holiday. During the latter part of February all hell seemed to break loose, below us were German and Italian soldiers, tanks and guns in great numbers, and our only hope was that they would not climb our ridge or spot us through their precision Zeiss binoculars. I managed to hear some wireless messages, they were intermittent and crackly but I gathered they had delivered a crushing defeat on the American forces. There were twelve us on the ridge and we were out of water but could not move for fear of being seen.

Two nights later the enemy moved off as swiftly as they arrived and we managed, with extreme caution, to find our way back to the HQ from which we had set out. The news was not good, the American troops had been unprepared and their first encounter with the highly professional army Wehrmacht had been a sobering encounter. Later in life I read that Eisenhower admitted his troops were unprepared, even finding engineers ordered to dig into rock to give cover for senior officers; 'it was the only time, during the war, that I saw a divisional or higher headquarters so

---

[51] Old French defence; not a continuous line but a series of small forts and gun emplacements.

[52] The Grand Dorsal Chain of the Atlas Mountains through which the Americans intended to pass.

concerned over its own safety that it dug itself underground shelters.'[53] Eisenhower, amongst the reasons I later read, listed for failure 'greenness, particularly among commanders,' as well as the failure to comprehend the capability of the enemy.[54] Many were killed and thousands were taken prisoner.[55] As I moved around I realised how lucky I was to be in the Signals; I had been uncomfortably close to the enemy but was not expected to be engaged. Later, when we moved into Tunis and the Germans had capitulated, I had yet more spare time on my hands. I assisted with getting the wounded on board some hospital ships. Many of the wounds were horrific, and I was sure that many would die long before they neared the British coastline.

I reflected on the spivs in Cardiff for a moment, but decided there was no point in seeking a moral high ground; in this war morality had long disappeared. I walked along the edges of cages set up for German prisoners; we were told not to speak to them, but my German was helped by listening to their conversations. I was surprised at their ages; most of the chaps I worked with were in their twenties, the men in the Afrika Korps ranged from teenagers up to middle-age and some older. They looked drab in their cages but as in all humanity there was a total mix. Some looked scornfully at their guards and onlookers; others smiled but most avoided eye contact. I overheard many who believed they would win the war and be freed within the year, such confidence astonished me. I heard another stating he was pleased to be a prisoner because they would be better fed, and the British were decent like them. The vast majority sat around staring at the sand or the sky.

One thing I recall from my time in Tunis was the sheer boredom of hanging around wondering what was going to happen next. If anyone claims war is exciting and romantic that would be a downright lie. The amputees I shifted onto the hospital ships knew there was no romance, and the German prisoners, and their guards did not feel any excitement, they were grateful to be alive, although suffering from extreme boredom and a nagging anticipation as to what would happen next. Tedium eats into the soul and fear follows the same route.

---

[53] Eisenhower Dwight, *Crusade in Europe* (London: Heinemann, 1948)p.157.
[54] Ibid, p.163.
[55] It led to the humiliating spectacle of some 4,000 Allied POWs being marched through Rome.

CHAPTER FIVE

FINAL WAR YEARS IN ITALY

HORACE 1942-44

Being in a German military medical station in the middle of nowhere was one of the stranger experiences in my life. I felt very much alone in the tent as most of the other patients were Germans with a few Italians. I managed to gather that the three other British prisoners who arrived with me had gone to another transit camp because they were mobile. I had shrapnel in both arms and my right leg, and I was trussed up like a turkey at Christmas in bandages that felt like plaster casts.

Both my arms were straight and I could not bend them to feed myself or drink. An elderly German gave me a little piece of pipe that I used as a straw so I could drink without help, but he fed me twice a day and, most embarrassingly had to assist me with the lavatory. I was glad the food and drink was limited because I certainly hated using the hastily prepared and hot stinking toilets. He never spoke and his face showed no emotion, although I nodded my thanks to him he made a point of not catching my eye; it was as if I never existed. The chap in the bed on my left was an Italian and he tried out his English on me. I gathered we were somewhere near Tunis and lucky to be out on the coast away from the constant bombing raids.

The man on my right was German, his English was excellent, and he chatted away as if we had just finished a tennis match. I detected some animosity from some of the other wounded, and on one occasion the German on my right shouted at someone who had spoken to me in an aggressive fashion. I suppose on reflection it was not German, Italian or English, but all very human. There is no doubt that some in that tent had good reason to hate the tatters of my uniform, some managed to stand apart from the politics of conflict and saw a wounded comrade from another planet, and, I have to make this observation, many showed compassion because I was wounded. The concept of the enemy, especially the German Nazi having compassion seemed unbelievable, but I did experience that in the medical tent, and I am now glad to have the opportunity to say so. As Wolfgang knows, I later developed a real hatred for the German war machine, but I always tried to remember the genuine depth of feeling I felt in that hospital tent.

My neighbour, Hans, came from Munich and had lived with his parents in Norwich for two years, thus his good English. His father had been a music specialist or something, and Hans was very keen to tell me all about Norwich and his love of the cathedral there. They had rented a house in the precincts of the cathedral, although Hans called it the cathedral close,[1] where he had often played cricket on the green. He was a rare German expressing an interest in cricket. Men came and went from the tent, but Hans was there for the three weeks I stayed. His injuries were also shrapnel, but it has been suggested he was put there to befriend me for information. I think that this was not the case because we talked very little about the war. I often wonder what happened to him; I liked him very much even if he was a German soldier. In some ways I was confused, having being taught to hate Germans I found myself being cared for by them. Even the senior Doctor smiled and looked like the sort of chap one expected in an English hospital.

He seemed to take a genuine interest in my wounds and apologised once when I winced with pain as he looked at my leg. I gathered later that I was fortunate to have such expertise in a remote place; I also was told that it may well have been amputation if I had not had such expert care. As you know from my earlier life I am not a gifted person academically, but my Italian and German made a degree of progress, especially my Italian, more out of necessity than anything else.

There was one stage when I was nearly lynched. The hospital base had Red Crosses painted on the tent tops, but one afternoon a lone hurricane came out of the cloudless sky and strafed the hospital killing about ten people and wounding many others. I have Hans to thank for the fact that others wanted me hung up or at least shot. I was not best pleased with that pilot, but after the war I gathered all sides too often ignored the Red Cross; that is no excuse, but war really does bring out the worst characteristics of the human race. Eventually I was given a couple of homemade crutches and sent down to a POW cage in Tunis port. It was an open cage which also contained quite a few Americans; I never realised they were fighting in North Africa. They seemed pleasant enough individuals, and one of them gave me a packet of cigarettes which, does not sound much now, but was like a bar of gold in those circumstances. We were guarded by some particularly unpleasant Italians who seemed to take a degree of delight in making us wait for water, which in that climate and weather was brutal behaviour.

I saw several sides of the Italian character, and it took me time to understand why. Some of the guards were the image of brutality, others were friendly, and some wanted to keep their distance. I have no doubt that this is true of all nations, but there, in North Africa, I was quite struck by the differences in attitudes by the Italian soldiery. The Germans

---

[1] Hans was correct; it was and is still known as The Close.

seemed more unified, not friendly, but I had the feeling they were all correct, tough, but reasonable. I would change my mind later but, I recall, it was the first time I had met Italians properly, and in my vulnerable state I was very aware of them. As the years passed by I gradually grew to understand why there were so many mixed reactions amongst the Italians. Some of them were diehard fascists and brutal in their behaviour. Others were not fascists and were conscripts who had no interest in the war, and some had relations in both England and America and were opposed to the war but had little choice but to fight. I was to have first-hand experience of this split in Italian culture in the years ahead. I was to discover that Italy may have been unified politically under Garibaldi, but those in Rome considered themselves Roman more than Italian, and the same was with the Florentines, the Venetians, the Piedmonts, those who lived in Calabria were different from those in the North and those in the Abruzzi, they lived in their own world.

Politically there was considerable division; between the extremes of Mussolini's fascism and the communists, who seemed to be growing in power, there were other parties, some moderate, some left of centre, or right of centre, some associated with the Church, some royalists, some pro-German and some anti-German. In short the Italian was so divided it demanded extreme caution and deep knowledge to know who was who. These divisions were to lead to the spilling of much blood both during and after the war, which led to a country where stability was only a dream.

One thing I quickly ascertained was that the Italian was no coward. I know that then and now, and too many jokes abound about the Italians running away and changing sides. Even in that prison pen I can recall someone saying they had looked inside a captured Italian tank and saw it had two forward gears and six reverse. The Italians may have had poor officers and political leadership, their equipment lacked German efficiency and American numbers, but I shall state categorically the Italian was no coward. Many surrendered because of weak leadership; many had no animosity towards the British and Americans, and in some cases were in danger of fighting against their own relatives. The nation which gave birth to the Mafia and which I grew to know and love were not cowardly; some of the toughest, hardest bravest men I have ever known were Italians. You may have gathered that I have an axe to grind, but, at the time I was in the transit pen, I was not fond of Italians. I think we spent a month with hardly any food, the water was minimal and brackish, and as our numbers grew we were only told we would be going to a *Campo* or a *PG*. I later realised they meant the same thing, a *PG*[2].

---

[2] *Prigione di Guerra*, a Prison of War camp.

We were all shunted onto a very dubious looking steamer one late afternoon without any warning. Crammed into several holds which had hitherto carried tanks and weapons there were no beds, no facilities, no water and hardly room to sit down. I have to say I was scared stiff, and despite some shouting up the hold in anger I think everyone of us felt terrified. We knew that the Allies virtually controlled the skies and that the Royal Navy and its submarines were at work in the Mediterranean. Suddenly we realised that our own side, our own companions were very likely going to kill us by drowning. The heat was unbearable, and despite our shouting for some water none appeared. My hold had two doors but both were firmly locked from the other side, and after two hours most of us had claimed a space on which we could sit or lie. I had feet at my head, companions tight on my left and right, and someone's head at my feet.

A senior officer tried to sort us into some semblance of order; he was not heeded, but had the effect of making us sort ourselves out. He did prove useful when some water was lowered by buckets so there was no scrambling and accidents, and it was monitored and some set aside for later. As it grew dark the holds were closed over but not entirely; someone had the good sense to leave gaps for air to penetrate what was already a stinking hole. Men had to relieve themselves in a designated corner and the stench was simply over-powering. An hour later we were nearly all sick as the steamship-bucket rolled and turned and cork-screwed its way to Italy, and even though I thought death was preferable to feeling sick, we still felt terrified by the possibility of a torpedo attack; none of us would survive such an incident. To this day if I feel fed-up or depressed by anything, I give time to reflect on that journey of three days and am grateful it is now a distant memory.

After seeing so many killed, some horrific injuries, having been injured myself, and now living in a black hole with vomit and excreta everywhere, I realised that war was the opposite of romantic. War is a purgatory with the hope of heaven and hell as a means of escape, and which made me wish I could be home again bird-nesting with dear old Harry; life was a nightmare from which there seemed no hope of escape. I think there were more than a few us who would have willingly shot ourselves had we a handgun handy.

We were, it transpired very fortunate, suffering no attacks by submarine or aircraft. It was an extraordinary feeling in that hold when first we became aware that the engines had stopped and we had berthed. When they opened the hatches I could see the Italian guards and seaman stand back from the stench arising from our pit. All of us, and I think there must have been at least two hundred in my hold, had suffered from vomiting and diarrhoea, we were hungry, thirsty and many could not stand up and had to be helped climb out of the ship to the darkened quayside, of what we later discovered to be the port of Bari. Having been lined up on the dockside, and aware that different groups of people had come to look at us, we then witnessed another side of the Italian character. A senior looking officer started to shout at the guards in an almost hysterical fashion; I could hear from my basic Italian that he was unhappy about the condition we were all in. Behind me a fluent Italian speaker informed us that this officer had seen us a week before in Africa, and was ashamed at the way we had been transported. We were, as a result of this dramatic interlude put into some railway shed and allowed access to water, toilets and showers.

We were allowed to wash our clothes and given some blankets in order to keep warm while our clothes dried. Some had lost their boots, and sandals were provided, and, to our utter relief some hot soup and unbelievably tasty Italian bread was supplied, and there was enough to go around. I tried, later, to find out who that officer was but never succeeded, he was a reminder that some men kept their humanity even in the midst of war. He was a very tall man and I may be wrong, but he was my image of an aristocrat; I hope he survived the war. We were in the sheds for two days recuperating from the sea journey and then, in smaller batches we started to be shipped out, some by train and some in lorries.

I went with a train group, mainly officers and some NCOs. We were herded onto carriages but which had their seats removed. It was better than the ship, we were crowded but not as cramped as in the ship's hold; we were given food to take, there were some limited toilets, but above all we could look out of the windows. The train moved slowly and I have to confess I felt like a little boy on an outing; I had never seen Italy before and I found the sights fascinating. We passed Foggia where we watched German planes landing, and then along the coast heading north; at times we saw the most fantastic scenery as well as the sea. It struck me and my companions that Italy had not tasted war yet. Life seemed all very normal, especially in a place called Pescara where our journey finished.

I never realised as I stood on that platform in Pescara that I was in the heart of the Abruzzo region; I had never heard the name before, but it was to become my home for the rest of my life. I shall explain later how this came about. We were put onto lorries and started to move west; the fact that we were heading in that direction was given by a bomber pilot sitting next to me who knew Italy as a holiday maker. We eventually arrived in a beautiful town called Chieti;[3] it was like a town built amongst protruding rocks and small mountains, and its medieval architecture reflected the geography, the churches and municipal building all had tall strong looking square towers. There was a lake of sorts, and people were going about their business as if the war were on another planet. To our amazement our *campo* was an old convent, and although crowded it was not unpleasant.

Two weeks later I realised we were not on holiday. Food was scarce again and we had no senior aristocratic looking Italian officer to make sure we were looked after. Water was given out as if it were expensive wine, and the guards, although not guilty of brutality were a surly bunch, and to this day I blame them for keeping some of the food we should have been given. I have often wondered what makes men the type of person they become. There were two guards who appeared more decent than the others; the one had been a young linguist student at Naples University, and the other a quarry worker. Both these men were kinder and showed a degree of compassion, so it had nothing to do with education.

I will not mention any names at this stage but the British camp commander was the epitome of Colonel Blimp. Had it not been for a danger of a revolt he would have had us square bashing, as it was he organised us into work parties to bring our new home up to what he called 'British standards.' We could not turn an Italian convent into a suburban house on the edge of his golf course, but he made us try. There was talk of escape, but unbelievably Colonel Blimp absolutely forbade such attempts on the grounds that those left behind would have to pay. I know that several were determined to ignore him, but I never discovered if any succeeded because I was part of a small party the authorities had decided to send elsewhere. I heard about this Colonel Blimp later, and his addiction for rules was to cause a good deal of unhappiness, but I shall touch upon this matter further on in the account.

Along with a group of some fifty I was walked down the hill to the station, but no train came. We waited all day; trains came and went but not the one to take us. By evening I thought we would be marched back to our convent, but instead we were locked in a couple of what I best describe as sheds with one Italian guard watching both sheds at the same time. There was considerable chatter about escape; it would be easy enough to overcome the one tired looking Italian soldier sitting on a stool looking as if he shared the same fate as we did. We had just about come

---

[3] Chieti, like Rome was eventually declared an open city and was not bombed; it was liberated on June 9th 1944 one day after the German occupying forces left. It was a crowded town as it acted as a refugee centre.

up with an agreement and an idea when, to our miserable astonishment, about a hundred German soldiers appeared also waiting for a train. Some of them wandered over to look at us; some sneered, some grinned and one or two just gave friendly nods. In a sense I was relieved because I was uncertain about what we would do once we had launched out into the countryside.

The area was remote and mountainous, we were hungry and not as fit as should be; we settled down to sleep. I woke at dawn, frozen and hungry and, to our astonishment two German soldiers appeared at the door with some black looking bread and hot soup. It all looked ghastly, but to us it was a feast; our single Italian guard had the same as us and looked equally as grateful. Had the German troops not turned up I doubt if we would have been fed at all. The Germans had embarked on a train before we had finished, but we were soon herded back up the road and found that we were being crammed onto some lorries and a rickety looking bus. We began a journey that was appalling. We bumped over unmade roads, crowded together, no sustenance, not even water, and our protests were ignored. In my part of the lorry I could not even see out because it was covered in canvas, even the rear end had a large flap of canvas covering the exit, and when it did blow open all we could see was the bus trundling along behind us. In the early evening we stopped at a place overlooking a port and a small town that we gathered was called Ancona.

One of our number had also gleaned the fact that although we had travelled over two hundred kilometres we were only half way to wherever we were going. Those in the bus had worked out we were heading north, and they had seen the most stunning views as we travelled north up the east coast of Italy. That night was spent, again cold and hungry, in a derelict building and a barn. There were more guards this time, no food, and it also appeared the guards had little themselves. It suddenly struck me that the Italians were simply disorganised. Someone gave orders about what do with us, but not how to do it; a common expression today I gather is 'logistics,' and it was certainly missing in Italian military administration. One relief was a Major, I think he was from the Royal Artillery, insisted those on the bus travel on the lorries and we drew lots for a coach seat. I was lucky, and despite the fact that the bus had benches and no cushions and the springs were worse than the lorries, at least I started to enjoy the view.

After we had travelled the next hundred or so kilometres we turned inland and headed towards the west. I shall not keep on about the journey, but it was backbreaking and quite a few of my fellow travellers took time to recuperate. No food no water, next to no sleep, but having read about the experiences of others, especially in Eastern Europe I should say no more.

We eventually arrived at the small town of Fontanellato which was a place marked by its magnificent buildings. The Italians may have been our enemies and their disregard for our safety and comfort was mind boggling, but they knew, or their ancestors did, how to build towns. The English towns of comparable size would not have had buildings of such majesty; even the best English parish churches would look dull in a place like Fontanellato.[4] We were to be imprisoned in *Campo 49* and again it was not the image of a prison camp in the popular mind. There were no barbed wire fences with towers containing searchlights and machine guns. It was a huge brick building with what I can best describe as neo-classical features built onto it and right next door to the sanctuary of *Beata Vergine del Santo Maria*.[5] It had been built as an intended orphanage[6] I learned much later, now it was a POW camp but we all felt like orphans.

The place was not ready but at least I had the immediate impression that the Italians seemed better organised here. We were lined up and the commandant, a Colonel Eugenio Vicedomini spoke to us in better English than my Italian about the rules and orders. He threatened death to anyone caught escaping, but most of us had the distinct impression that he was simply saying what he was obliged. There was always discussion about whether it was better to be in the hands of the Germans or the Italians. I was pro-German, they had healed by wounds, and fed us and I was, at that point totally unaware of the barbarity that they were committing elsewhere. My experience of Italians had hitherto been lack of food and water, a sea journey that nearly killed me, and a lorry journey that still makes me shudder. However, I had no reason to complain. We were fed, not well, but food was regular, so was water, the sanitation left much to be desired, but it was workable and we kept it in good shape.

The senior Italian officers were correct and not unpleasant, and when a naval prisoner escaped and was captured a day later he was not shot. From what I could make of it he was only reprimanded by a day without food; he did not miss much. The long boring hours were ghastly, my Italian improved no end, as did my chess and I even became something of a card sharp. We were commanded by our own senior officers to keep fit, but we were not governed as we had been in Chieti by some Colonel Blimp: I had nothing to complain about compared to how others POWs fared elsewhere, which I have since read about.

---

[4] Fontanellato is a small town in the province of Parma on the plains of the River Po and is about twelves miles west of Parma.

[5] This is a mistake, Horace means the sanctuary *Beate Vergine del Santo Rosario.*

[6] After the war it became a centre for neurological disorders.

During the long interminable months of the summer of 1943 I befriended a guard who was as keen to learn English as I was Italian. He was a huge fellow called Mario, and I would walk around with him and as we tried out our language skills; I also started to hear from Mario the news of the war. This made me, for a brief time, an invaluable source of interest in the camp. Mario had made it clear to me that he did not trust the Germans, thought Mussolini was wrong going to war, and wanted to return to his farm. For Mario the war was a dreadful error, and with relatives in America and England he was terrified he might meet them in a battle situation. I gathered Mario was not the only Italian who thought like this; he trusted me, but could not trust all Italians, some of them were very pro-Mussolini and pro-fascist. He told me how the Allies were fighting their way across Sicily, and there were rumours that once Sicily had fallen, Italy would collapse at once, and the Americans and British would land near Rome.

It is difficult now to describe the sheer excitement and speculation within *Campo 49*; generally speaking most believed this rumour, but some who had spent more time on the front line felt that the Germans would simply take over. Others believed the Germans would vacate and block the narrow mountainous passes into central Europe.[7] In addition to my gleaned information we had managed to secrete a wireless into the camp and soon we felt quite well informed. It became clear that the guards also wanted to know what was happening and there were occasions we shared with them the news. I was only small fry amongst the officers, but I knew that our commander was having long talks with Colonel Eugenio Vicedomini, but I was not in the circle of high-ups who had the best information.

At the end of August our balloon went up, I thought I was at death's door. Somehow I had picked up a dose of malaria that was going to dog me for years. I was suffering the most dreadful fevers, hallucinations, and was never sure whether I was in bed or floating in the air. I was not conscious of what happened over the next few days; in fact I was hardly conscious, and when I did come round it took me a long time to understand what I was doing in the loft of a farmhouse being cared for by Mario. He had carried me over his shoulders, at times in a wheelbarrow, and then a ride on a horse drawn cart; it was no wonder my hallucinations made me think I was at sea.

I gathered, after a time, that the Italians had capitulated[8] and the Italian commandant, whom we nick-named as *Comando Supremo* had agreed

---

[7] Rommel wanted to fight from the north, but Kesselring prevailed and fought the Allies from the south leading to a bitter warfare which continued to the very end of the war.

[8] Italian Armistice declared on 8th September 1943.

with our senior officers that the prisoners, some five or six-hundred of us were free to leave. This was a remarkably brave gesture on his part since the Germans were continuing to fight and with greater intensity.[9] I was left in Italian care because of my state, but when it became clear that Colonel Eugenio's decision was not welcomed by everyone, Mario, my Italian friend, removed me in the middle of the night and with a few others took me to relative safety. I learned later that an order had arrived at most *Campos* from Britain instructing senior commanders to hold men in their prisons so they would be safe until the Allies arrived.

Our commander ignored this, but I later gathered that in my first *Campo* in Chieti, Colonel Blimp following orders stopped men from leaving camp, so the poor devils were rounded up by the Germans and sent to German camps. I know that lots of escaping prisoners never made it home, many were caught, many became involved in the resistance movement, but why we should wait to be sent to German prison camps defied all belief. I was told that it was because Montgomery wanted order, and believed the Germans would walk out. I do not know whether there was any truth in this, even to this day.[10] In war sometimes our lives are ruined by the most stupid orders; I have never found any reference to this order in history books I have read, but it happened.

As regards my situation I was now on my own, totally dependent on an enemy soldier called Mario who had become my friend, and for food and shelter on Italian people who were also supposed to be my enemy. As I lay there in the hay of an old barn, eating some pie, none of this made sense, but it had happened.

WOLFGANG 1942-1944

I was told that I would need a long period for recuperation not just because of my legs, but my stomach needed time to recover. I was given exercises to do and every day I walked and walked. It was not that I was keen to return to the fighting, the very thought of it was beginning to make me feel nauseous. I was not suffering from what is now called post-traumatic stress despite my wounds, but I was beginning to wonder how many more barbarities I could witness. The massacre at Korçë and the girl who smiled were becoming in my mind a daily horror I was not enjoying; a memory that would not go away, and which at nights malformed into nightmares.

---

[9] On 6-9th September 2013 a conference was held in the Rocca on POWs to celebrate the 70th anniversary of this event.

[10] The little known Order P/W87190 issued by M19 on Montgomery's Orders.

As I read Horace and Harry's accounts I realise that we had all been injured in many ways, but we were the lucky ones where the injuries had not been fatal, and had not rendered us permanently disabled. We carried physical scars, but the real injuries were in the mind, either from what we had witnessed or from what we had done ourselves. I know Horace has had his moments of self-inflicted pain, and I know they have caused him great turmoil in recent years; Harry seems to have coped best, but then he has not had the perpetual guilt of the girl who smiled. Like me Harry and Horace witnessed massacres and unnecessarily cruel and barbaric deaths, but neither of them have my guilt for killing the girl who smiled, putting her down with less consideration than shooting a wounded dog.

I was at home reading a newspaper about the disaster in Sicily and capitulation of Italy when Mum received a letter about Hugo. I guessed at once that it had to be serious; it arrived in a buff envelope we all associated with official correspondence. My only hope was that as it was a letter, and not a telegram, the content would not be too serious. Mum burst into tears and collapsed on the kitchen floor as her legs had given way, obviously consumed by grief. I rushed over to her, but she could not speak for sobbing. I took the letter from her hands and read that Hugo had died while working in a Punishment Battalion. Mum was not concerned that he had been working in a punishment battalion; she was understandably destroyed by Hugo's death. I made her a hot drink of ersatz coffee and tried to comfort her, but to little avail.

I walked along the river for the next hour or so feeling sorry for Mum, and sad as Hugo and I had not been so close after my atrocious behaviour over his apparent weakness in upholding the party line, but I was also curious about the punishment battalion. I was a member of the SS, who was on leave because of serious injury, probably forgotten by the powers that be, and had no contact with Hugo's Wehrmacht officers, not even his friends. We had fought on the same side, in different parts of the world, but with different command structures.

It was a week later, Mum was still seriously depressed, and so I decided to travel to Munich to meet the officer, whose life I had saved as he had written to me from his home, telling me I was always welcome. He was not my cup of tea in those days, he was aristocratic, aloof, clever and far too charming, but I went to his home and found him there with his elderly parents. His arm had been amputated and he told me that at least his war was finished. I told him about Hugo and asked whether he could find out the circumstances through any of his contacts. He said it might take a day or two, and despite my protests he insisted I stayed with them in a spare room. The house was luxurious and he and his parents turned out to be lovely people. He was aloof, but it was simply their way of life, they were very kind to me and to my surprise, they invited me to Church with them that evening: I had not even realised it was Sunday. Naturally I was in uniform, and I could not help noticing that it caused more glances than those in Wehrmacht or Luftwaffe gear: to this day I have never been able to fathom out the nature of those glances, admiration, fear or distaste: probably a mixture. My Wehrmacht friend, he was called Otto, and later died in a bombing raid, made several phone calls and came to see me in their kitchen where I was making some real coffee. I could see that the news was not good. Hugo had been killed by a mine at some place called Donetz[11] on Feb 28th.[12] The reason he had been in a Punishment Battalion was that he had struck an officer for shooting an old Jewish woman. He had refused to take part in execution squads and was on an unofficial black list as politically suspect, but striking an officer had been the last straw.

I said nothing simply because I did not know what to think. I had shot Jews, I had shot the girl who smiled, but I was feeling guilty about these incidents, and the policy, and I had beaten my own brother over party issues; now he was dead because he stuck to his principles. I could feel Otto was also stuck for words, and his sharp blue eyes seemed to be scrutinizing my face. "We get some things wrong" he said. I thought he meant Hugo had got things wrong, but he meant the killing of Jews. That was a brave thing to say to a member of the SS; I did not reply but nodded my head and shook his hand to thank him for his help.

At home I told my mother everything, it brought the tears back, but I could detect she was proud of Hugo for standing up for what he believed to be right. I was at home another three months and still had a slight limp. I really think that my unit had forgotten I existed. During this time I became much closer to Mum, and shared with her my agony over Hugo and the beating up incident. I could not bring myself to mention the girl who smiled.

We did speak about the Jewish situation because there was a genuine hatred for Jews and it was frequently brought to our attention by the various bits and pieces of propaganda. However, Mum's original distaste for Jews had been the wealthy bankers, politicians who had signed the Versailles Treaty, and the well-to-do Jewish professional classes; she disliked what was happening to the Jews who lived down the street. There had not been many in Marktsteft, but we knew most of them, and they had all gone, and Mum had witnessed some brutal behaviour. A shop keeper called Walter Doll, who also did plumbing, had a Jewish wife, and he was told to divorce her; he refused and Mum witnessed the way they were treated by people who had once been their friends. Frau Doll was

---

[11] Near Izyum.
[12] 1943.

found dead in a side road; she had been badly beaten up, and a day later Walter Doll had walked in front of a Wehrmacht truck and killed himself.

My Mum had fallen out with some neighbours who had implied it was good riddance to rubbish; Mum was astonished the way we had turned against our own neighbours. Years later I pondered my Mum's reactions. I believe she was an uncluttered normal German woman who had been taken in by the propaganda that the Jews were the cause of the defeat in the Great War, they were therefore the enemy. She was one of the few, and I do not think anyone has any evidence to say how many thought like my Mum, who changed her mind when the Nazi policy became clear that all Jews were the enemy, even the plumber's wife. I suspect most people were not like my Mum, because they perhaps did not have Jewish friends, or were scared, or believed the Nazi propaganda, or did not have a son killed for protesting over Jewish deaths. No one questioned my mother because I was a wounded SS man and part of the mechanism.

Looking back it must have been early 1944 that I started to come to terms with the fact that I had got things wrong. I can recall sitting in our yard despite the fact it was freezing cold, wondering whether to announce to the authorities that I still existed. The Russians were beginning to make significant advances, the Allies had landed near Rome,[13] and some of our cities were being systematically destroyed by British and American bombers. Strangely it was not the self-evident failure of Germany to resist the military might of the enemy that made me question myself, it was my continuing discussions with Mum about the bestiality of German behaviour to Jews and non-Germans, and the continuous reflective stirrings of Hugo's memory and his bravery, to say nothing of my ongoing nightmares of the girl who smiled. I decided the time had come when I had to stop lurking about in backyard in Marktsteft and for better or worse announce I was alive. I wrote to my old HQs and heard nothing for several weeks; a letter eventually arrived with a ticket to take me to Berlin, or rather Potsdam.

The letter made it clear that they had thought I had been so badly wounded I was no longer of service, so as I entered the barracks I encouraged my limp to look more serious than it was. I travelled through Berlin and could hardly comprehend the amount of damage caused by the bombing raids. I think, as I travelled out of Berlin towards Potsdam I felt so seriously depressed I wondered whether life was worth living.

To my utter astonishment I was treated like a returning war hero. I gather that they believed, despite all my pain and limping, which I had exaggerated, I had volunteered to return from the dead because of the

---

[13] Anzio landings by Allies on January 22nd 1944.

shortage of man power. I was checked over by a doctor and winced when he touched my old scars, and limped around the room; I did this because I did not want to be considered a malingerer. It worked and I was called before a senior commanding officer who after the *Heil Hitler* came round his desk and shook my hand. I almost felt important. He explained to me my old unit was all over the place and that, given my condition, he was recommending that I act as a messenger, a courier for staff HQ. At times, he explained, the code machines[14] and the wireless were unsuitable for larger documents and maps, and although the code machines were totally reliable they were cumbersome for longer material. I was given quarters in some barracks nearby and was given a cubby hole with a chair and desk and along with two others to be on continuous standby to go anywhere at any time. I think the term is sinecure, but that is what my job was for a couple of months; I had nothing to do but sit by a phone and chat with the other two, play chess, brush up on my English and read. There were a few jobs rushing documents to and fro from *8 Prinz-Albrecht Straße*,[15] in Berlin, but the others had girlfriends there and always grabbed these jobs.

I do not have a precise recollection of dates but one morning my sinecure came to an abrupt end. There had been a major bombing raid on the city and some of the bombs had fallen on Potsdam, and I also know we had just occupied Hungary as a safety factor.[16] I was instructed to go with Karl, not the one I would have chosen to go with. He was so fanatical despite having lost an eye and his left hand, wanted to drive despite his disabilities to SS HQ in *Prinz-Albrecht Straße*. I insisted on driving the *Kubelwagen*[17] even though Karl had a grip on his left arm. We waited in the entrance hall and there was a sense of efficiency in the comings and goings, but I also detected a sense of urgency. Karl was hoping to catch sight of some of the big wigs, having once seen Himmler himself stride through the main entrance. He was to be disappointed because we were summoned into an office with a man in a smart brown suit, and to this day I had no idea who he was or what he was, but he was obviously high up in the chain of authority.

He sat while we stood to attention. He gave me a substantial brief case which he insisted I should then and there chain to my arm, having

---

[14] Undoubtedly a reference to the Enigma Machines.

[15] The Notorious number 8 was the location the Reich Main Security Office, SD, Gestapo, and the SS. It is now the site of the Topography of Terror memorial and museum. The street is now called Niederkirchnerstraße.

[16] The last major raid on Berlin by RAF was March 24/5th 1944; it was becoming too expensive in life and materials. It also makes sense of the Hungarian occupation which was March 19th. Wolfgang was probably at the near end of March 1944.

[17] Like a small jeep…probably a type 82 which was in regular use.

noted that Karl had a hand missing. He gave me the key and the other one to Karl; when I asked what the second key was for he told me that it opened the brief case, and would stop the small bomb detonating. I looked at him with an apparent look of puzzlement, and in a cold matter of fact way he told me that if any unauthorised person tried to open the brief case it would explode, and "you would lose more than your hand," he added. I know Karl was not amused, and I certainly was not, but we could see he was not trying to be amusing, just coldly unpleasant. We were to fly from *Flughafen Berlin-Tempelhof*[18] straight to Munich, there a flight would be waiting to fly us to Rome. We were to deliver the brief case directly to *SS-Obergruppenführer* Wolff[19] who would accept it from us knowing about the explosive briefcase and the high security level of its contents.

I have to confess we were pleased to leave that office and suddenly felt very important when we discovered that our Kubelwagen had been taken, and we were chauffeured to Tempelhof. It was as if everyone knew we were doing something important, but we had no idea what it was all about; we were just carrier-pigeons. We flew in a Junkers 252[20] along with some cargo and a few Wehrmacht officers who kept well away from us. It was a bumpy and uncomfortable flight and we could see nothing; any romance of travelling by air was dispelled for me then, and has remained even to this day. I had hoped for a break in Munich but we were escorted from the plane directly to another version of the Junkers, which looked like a corrugated shed.[21] This time we were the only passengers, no cargo; a flight just for us; it made us both wonder what we were carrying in the brief case. We were able to sit up behind the pilot and his navigator and I was now feeling air-sick, and not even the view of crossing the snow covered mountains could endear me to this way of travel.

As we dropped down over these huge geological barriers that divide Italy from central Europe the plane flew very low indeed. The pilot explained that we would soon be approaching an area around Rome where Allied fighter aircraft lurked, and they might have trouble seeing

---

[18] Tempelhof airport was one of the pre-war iconic airports for developing European passenger services. Despite protests it was closed in 2008 as part of the process of establishing Brandenburg Airport.

[19] Karl Friedrich Otto Wolff (May 13th-1900 – 17th July 1984: General of the Waffen-SS; he had been Chief of Personal Staff to Himmler and SS Liaison Officer to Hitler; was supreme commander of all SS-Forces in Italy; negotiated surrender with Dulles at end of war.

[20] Junkers 252 was a cargo aircraft and appeared in late October 1941; strangely only a few were built for the Luftwaffe.

[21] Undoubtedly the Junkers 52 made at Dessau and covered by the unusual corrugated duralumin metal skin to strengthen the whole structure.

us is we were just above ground level. This certainly did the trick as far as I was concerned; the thought of being attacked by British or American fighters stopped me feeling air sick, but fortunately we saw nothing but clouds. We had been on the go since the early hours and it was nearly dark as we landed. All we had eaten that day was a few biscuits washed down with some disgusting warm water; being a carrier-pigeon was not so much fun; even Karl had lost all his sense of excitement. I was glad to get my feet onto *terra firma* but not for long, we were almost bundled into a kubelwagen and driven through a series of road checks and into Rome's darkened streets. I had been told that Rome was a city unaffected by the heat of war, but now the Anzio Beach invasion was so close by Rome was in black-out, but there were still crowds of people around [22] and, to our amazement, no sign of any bomb damage.

Everywhere in Germany there were signs of aerial bombardment, some parts of some cities simply were piles of rubble, but here in Rome I never saw a single bomb site.[23] We were taken to a hotel and sat in the foyer and at last given some bread and cheese and even a glass of wine. Surrounding us, both in and out of the hotel was a substantial number of armed Wehrmacht guards; we were obviously at the centre of the command. I know that General Wolff was our boss, but the command in Italy fell to Field Marshal Kesselring, so it was to our astonishment that we saw him walk across the foyer with several others and head out to some waiting cars. I knew it was Kesselring because he was often photographed and always looking cheerful.[24] Karl spotted another General whom he recognised as General von Senger who Karl muttered, should have been a priest. How Karl knew this I have no idea, but years after the war I discovered that not only was this General a Lay-Benedictine Tertiary, but was a Rhodes Scholar who went to Oxford University.[25] As he walked towards the door, I was struck by his huge protruding ears and the fact that he saw the pair of us with our mouths full of cheese staring at him; I shall never forget the way he smiled. We were nothing to him, but the fact he could bother to smile in our direction was something I have never forgotten.

---

[22] During this period Rome became a centre for many refugees fleeing from the conflict moving south to north.

[23] Wolfgang must have travelled on route free of damage; there were several bombing raids on Rome in 1943 and 1944. Pope Pius XII had tried unsuccessfully to have Rome declared and open city which eventuated on August 14th 1943 either through Hitler's or Kesselring's agreement.

[24] The Allies knew Kesselring as 'Smiling Albert,' a sobriquet given to him because he always smiled for the camera, and was known for his charm; he was also highly professional and ruthless.

[25] Frido von Senger und Etterlin, aristocratic Roman Catholic family, (1891-1963) and father of Ferdinand von Senger famous Bundeswehr general and author.

We waited an hour, tired but alert as we watched people coming and going; in that hotel foyer we saw more important people than we had in Berlin. Eventually we were ushered into the presence of General Wolff who was standing alone behind a small desk. He was a tall handsome man who seemed quite genial and gave the impression of being a very pleasant person, who even joked about the fact we had carried a small bomb.[26] I undid the chain from my very red and sore wrist, and Karl gave the general the key; he opened the brief case, opened the door and gave a square box to someone telling us he did not need the bomb in his office. To be quite honest, I know that years later there were dark issues surrounding General Wolff, but he struck me as a decent man, and he made no fuss about removing the bomb; there were many senior commanders who would have given it to a junior to do in another room. Before dismissing us, he told us to find a room in the same hotel, either in the attics or the cellars where there were plenty of beds, and to be prepared for a further courier's task the next day.

We eventually settled down with some SS comrades in the attic, sharing a room with four others. They wanted to hear the news from home, but apart from the bombing raids and the Russians moving west there was little we could share. We learned that in Italy, just down the road from us the Anzio beachhead had become a bitter fight, and at a place, just south of Anzio, called Monte Cassino the fighting was hand to hand and continuous.[27] More to the point the Italians had betrayed us by changing sides, and there were some illegal and dangerous partisans trying to shoot us in the back. The general word was that these partisans not only had the total support of the wider Italian community, but were being supplied by the Allies with modern and sophisticated weapons.

We were therefore astonished when we returned to the foyer to see some Italian officers standing and waiting. I shuffled over to a comrade at the desk whom we had met the night before, and he explained that Mussolini still had some fascist troops ready, but, he said, 'they were all spaghetti.' We did not see General Wolff that morning, but were told to take some of the documents in the same briefcase, without the bomb, to a place called Teramo. An officer showed us on a map where it was, but

---

[26] From the Eichmann trial it started to become clear that Wolff had been involved in the Holocaust and photos from the *Bundesarchiv* show him with Himmler visiting concentration camps. He had a degree of protection from the Americans and remained a controversial figure until his death in 1984.

[27] The Anzio landing and Monte Cassino battles are well documented; both areas were held by the Germans much longer than anticipated, not only because of German military efficiency and fighting power, but a degree of inexperience and ineptness by Allied commanders. It was about this time that the sheer weight of Allied forces started to win and move the battle lines further north.

assured us we would be conveyed by a small SS-troop and have some Italian officers with us who were also heading in that direction. It was not until we were in our familiar kubelwagens that it dawned on me that neither Karl nor I was properly armed, but I felt there was a general feeling that all would be well, that it was going to be a day out.

As we moved out of Rome I saw more of that wonderful city, even glimpsed the Vatican which I noted was guarded by what looked like our paratroopers; this surprised me because I thought they were all fighting at Monte Cassino. The city was still crowded even though it was early morning, and we headed out into the countryside that looked battle free. We took cover at one point when an enemy fighter was spotted, but we were soon on the move, and this time I was thoroughly enjoying the view. It was much better than aeroplanes. We seem to pass through the most beautiful mountain ranges I had ever seen,[28] the weather was perfect, if only it had been a picnic.

We had just passed through a place called L'Aquila and heading, according to my map to Assergi when some instinct warned me to look up. I suppose I had developed a sixth sense because I felt something was wrong, but there was open landscape and the world looked tranquil. I even wondered if my nerves were too shot through for my own good, and so started to look around with care because I simply felt things were not right. We were in a convoy of five Kubelwagens, and ours was at the back, the Italian officers immediately in the car in front, and three SS leading the way, the one in front armed with a mounted machine gun. It may have been the leading car that gave us a sense of security which, as we rounded a corner suddenly exploded. From an overhanging rock a group of men were throwing down the small hand grenades so favoured by the British,[29] as well as raking the front cars with machine guns from several vantage points. Our driver swerved off the road to avoid some rifle fire and I was thrown out into a ditch. The Italian car stopped more sensibly and they sought cover below the rocky outcrop, I had no serious weapon to hand and felt vulnerable.

The firing continued for at least five minutes, the machine guns paused as if to reload, but from my angle I could see that the first three cars had no survivors; there were SS uniforms and bodies at every conceivable angle. Overhead a plane swooped low firing its guns, a lone German fighter had appeared from nowhere, the first one I had seen since I had been in Italy. The partisans on the rock face simply disappeared back into some trees and after a few moments I started to look at the

---

[28] Wolfgang was taking the road to Teramo via the famous National Park with its three distinctive mountain ranges.

[29] Mills Bomb.

damage. As I suspected no one had survived the grenades and machine guns, they were all dead to a man. Karl was alive but was badly bruised and probably had some broken ribs from rolling over stones. Our driver was dead, the kubelwagen had rolled over while he stayed in it; his neck was self-evidently broken as I could see his head was in an impossible position. To my astonishment two of the Italians had been killed; I thought they were safe, but another told me, the one who spoke some German, the fighter had caught them on its second run.

At least their kubel was in reasonable condition so I took Karl and placed him in the back seat and sat with him as the two Italians drove around the carnage and drove off at an alarming rate. This time I had equipped myself with a machine pistol and plenty of ammunition. Suddenly the Italian turned off the road towards a small farmhouse. I demanded to know why and he said that they would have supported the partisans; no one else was in the area. I remonstrated that it was more important to clear out of the area and return with back up. They refused and I could see they needed some sort of satisfaction, some revenge. I checked my machine pistol just in case as the two Italians unprofessionally rushed through the door. I heard some shouting and a shot, and thought they might have been right; with their hands up a large man came out with the tatters of an Italian uniform, another who looked like a farmhand, and old man and old woman, who reminded me of my mother and two little boys, and finally, a man who appeared to have a British tunic on. The Italian officers gestured towards him as if to say they had been right. They lined them up against the front of the house and while one stood guard the other went searching. I was fed up with the war so I just stood there and lit a cigarette, looking at the man in a British tunic. In my schoolbook English I asked him if he were English and was pleased I understood his reply; he was a POW.

Eventually the other Italian returned and before I could put my cigarette back in my mouth he pointed his gun at the elderly couple; when I said they were Italian like him he retorted they were traitors to Mussolini and shot the women and the old man in one short burst, the two boys dropped to their knees. Without thinking I reacted, the cigarette dropped from my hand, I shot the Italian with my machine pistol, and his companion as he swung round with his pistol. I looked round at the kubel to see Karl was in the driving seat and was moving away from me as fast as possible. He may have had broken ribs and a missing hand, but he was not risking me turning on him. Even as the kubel disappeared round the corner I knew I was now a traitor. I put my gun down on the ground and wondered what I had done. I sat down in a state of shock, wondering whether I had reacted because the woman had reminded me of my mother, or whether I was just sick and tired of massacres. The man with the tatty Italian uniform walked forward picked up the gun and pointed it at me. I did not care whether he pulled the trigger or not. The English POW walked over, took the gun from his hands and sat down opposite me just looking. I knew from his face that he recognised a man sick of war like himself. It was the first time I met Horace.

MD'S NOTE

Wolfgang struggled writing this last section mainly because he believed looking at the events he described, that he had suffered some form of mental breakdown. He was aware that Horace had stopped his one-time Italian guard, Mario, from killing him, but for many months after this event he did not care whether he lived or died. Looking back he confirmed for himself what he had already considered in the immediate postwar years, that the girl who smiled, the witnessing of massacres, his mother's revelation that Jewish people were human, and the Italian woman gunned down by the Italian officers and who looked so much like his mother, all this transpired to be the straw which broke the camel's back; it was all too much. Wolfgang actually came to see me at this juncture with his notes that I sent by mail to Horace (who was not into computers, which were not so popular at that time) and digitally to Harry, who was attending some conference.

The three agreed however difficult the memories they should be told as they happened. The problem was that from late 1944 to the late spring of 1945 Horace and Wolfgang, and soon Harry would, for this period of time, as in the summer of 1980, be writing about the same events because the three of them were together. Wolfgang had a proposal which Horace was very keen to support; Harry was more reluctant to write the account for all of them during this period of time, but agreed to do so as long as their notes reflected what they felt, and that he would quote them directly using italics as with this incursion. It was agreed, and the next chapter was accepted by all three as a sound account.

1944-45 HARRY, FOR HORACE AND WOLFGANG

I read once that Charles Dickens was criticised for having too many coincidences in his novels, but this joint autobiography also has many and reflects life in a very real way as I have long experienced in my seventy plus years. Wolfgang has described with total honesty how he turned against his own side, and virtually suffered a serious nervous collapse because of the sheer brutality of war. Horace stopped him being shot by a furious Mario, and within three days of this incident I was with them. How this extraordinary meeting happened I have yet to unravel, but first I shall describe what brought me to that part of Italy. I do not want to spend much time on my own life at this stage because it was tedious and the recounting of it will reflect that all too easily.

I was shipped with a command group to Sicily where my job was to receive radio messages from forward units. I was safely behind the lines, and I confess that I found it somewhat distressing to hear the demands, requests and in between the sound of anguish of those up front. Perhaps the worse aspect was hearing about disasters that I knew about at the time, but were either kept secret for years or played down. The Operation against Sicily[30] was supposed to start with American and British paratroopers, but many were lost and killed because the planes were flying off-course and facing turbulent winds; I heard the pilots were inexperienced and only fifty-four ever landed on Sicily, many disappeared in the sea. Since then I have read more of the disaster in modern histories, but it was hardly mentioned postwar, and in his self-serving memoirs Eisenhower claimed they feared a great loss of life, but in his weak postwar apologia claimed 'though statistics later showed that casualties were less than we feared, it was still a tragic incident.'[31]

Another airborne lift was repeated on July 11th when Patton ordered up 144 C-47s carrying 2,008 soldiers to be dropped inland. One USA naval gunner mistook them as the enemy and most others opened fire. In all, twenty-three planes were lost and thirty-seven badly damaged. The airborne force suffered 318 casualties; 88 dead, 162 wounded, 68 missing. On July 13th a third airborne left Tunisia with 1,900 members of the British 1st Parachute Brigade and disaster was repeated, of the 1,900 paratroopers … only about 200 reached their objective, and that was too few to do the job properly. I gleaned much of this information long after the war, but even in those days I knew that the preparation for such an exercise was poorly carried out; I was reliably informed that not only was

---

[30] Called Husky.
[31] Eisenhower, *Crusade in Europe, published by Heinemann, London: 1948*, p.191.

there inadequate training, but there was considerable inexperience and I believe, and I know I will be unpopular in saying this, the inept command was responsible for the loss of too many lives. Later, when various generals wrote their autobiographies they frequently wrote of the importance for the west of the sanctity of life, but I think they paid more regard to their personal grandness and success than they did for *Tommy*. Because for a few months I was at various HQ I was able to see men like Montgomery, Patton and especially Mark Clark[32] who had in common the need to be photographed as men of action. I was struck by the size of their egos.

However, this is not supposed to be an account of how I regarded the men who commanded, although we agreed to write what we felt at the time. When the invasion of Sicily was completed and the Germans had regrouped in Italy[33] it soon became apparent that the Italians were a divided nation. In Sicily many had decided it was not their war and simply surrendered. I led a peaceful life for a time, left on Sicily and hoped I had been forgotten, but someone knew where I was because I received a letter from Father H that brought me down with a blow. My dear old Dad had been serving on an oil tanker that had been torpedoed in the mid-Atlantic with no survivors. Both Eddie and Dad had been killed by this war that I was beginning to detest more and more.

Eventually I was sent to the recently captured Foggia airfields and had barely settled in when I was transferred to Bari, an important port on the south eastern leg of the Italian peninsular. Salerno was done and dusted, just, and now our armies were bogged down at Monte Cassino and at Anzio. The general belief had been that once we landed in Italy we would march straight to Rome. Quite why our commanders always underestimated the skill of German soldiers I do not know, not least when it was apparent, even to me, that the Italian mountains were easier to defend than attack. Bari was in a serious state of disrepair; I was told that the Luftwaffe had hit the port not long ago with a major raid sinking many of the ships in the harbour. It was so devastating that it was known as 'little Pearl Harbour.'[34] I was attached to the dock authority which was run by the navy but with army help. One evening in the bar I was told by a drunken compatriot that during the raid one of our ships had been carrying gas-bombs which had exploded and killed hundreds of soldiers

---

[32] Mark Clark had his own press corps and was insistent that he should always be photographed 'from his best side.'

[33] The Germans managed to get all their men and equipment over the Messina Straits; sometimes known as the mini-Dunkirk the Allies appeared to make little effort in stopping them.

[34] Dec 2nd 1943, sinking 17 ships.

and sailors to say nothing of Italian civilians, but no one was supposed to mention this ghastly fact; I could see why he was drunk.

Apparently the authorities had been so complacent they were unloading at night under the full glare of spotlights; the Luftwaffe had no trouble identifying their target. Whatever we were doing with a ship full of gas bombs[35] is still beyond me. To avoid my drunken compatriot getting into trouble I kept my mouth shut, but I could see the signs of the devastation, and although after the war I could never find out any information, it started to be verified around the mid-1960s; it transpired my drunken friend was right, we had taken internationally illegal gas bombs into a brightly lit-up port and suffered the consequences. The ones who suffered most were the Italians because the authorities never disclosed what had caused the damage, so the hospitals had no idea what they were treating.

I was in Bari a mere few weeks when my life changed. My small unit were called to Bari HQ where planes were coming and going and the nights in our tents were cold, noisy and generally unpleasant. I can recall it was early April but the weather was wintry and the news worse. Because I had taken part in Commando training I and two others had been selected to make a parachute drop. I protested I had never jumped out of a plane, and the other two were in the same position. That had little effect on the two officers who were organising us; we were sent to a corner of the airfield, and there we were given hasty instructions about landing, we jumped from six foot and twelve foot ledges, and then swung down by a hoist from a tower. We were not actually given a practice jump, but simply told what to do.

Our gear would be thrown out of the plane at the same time. Having heard what happened to the parachutists in Sicily I was convinced my end was in sight. Even if we landed safely our task was formidable. We were not told anything, I suppose in case we were captured, but I surmised that a breakthrough was being anticipated on the Gustav line[36] because our mission was to remain hidden in order to send back information on German movements. We were teamed up with a bomber aircrew of an odd plane, and I may have this wrong, but I think it was called a Baltimore. I thought about protesting, no parachute experience, we would be living of the land, and we had not volunteered to be landed behind enemy lines. I did not and we were informed that there was no real risk because they anticipated our position would be secured by our own troops

---

[35] Liberty ship called the John Harvey.

[36] The Gustav Line was a series of defences south of Rome with the high Monte Cassino as its pivotal point. The landing at Anzio jus north west had been carried out to cut the Germans off, but the delays in a breakthrough were a long time coming, a military and political embarrassment.

soon. I remember the pilot of the plane, he was called Philip, smiling at me as if he knew it was the last time I would be seen, and a tall thin young man called Joe Chilton, the navigator.

I have to say that years after the war when I was in Norwich I bumped into Joe Chilton by sheer chance; his wife was doing flowers in the cathedral and he and I went to have a beer in a small pub called the Adam and Eve. I met Joe twice in my life, once when he helped me on and off the plane and then fifty years later! We were part of a bombing flight and we were to be dropped somewhere near the east of Rome and hide in some hilly olive groves. We never jumped because of navigational problems and Joe Chilton was convinced that if we exited the aircraft where the points were given we would fall right into the centre of German forces fighting on the Gustav Line. We owed our lives to Joe Chilton because he was right as it transpired; no one even apologised. Two nights later we were off again but no Joe Chilton this time, and I had the unnerving feeling that this navigator did not look so proficient. It is difficult after this period of time to explain what I felt like as that plane took off in the early evening.

The roar of the engines, the bumping down the runway, and the prospect of jumping out and then landing on the ground in enemy territory caused me so much fear the previous time, I could hardly eat the day before, and the old joke about needing brown corduroys was nearly true so I kept my tummy empty second time. We were only in the air about half an hour when we were mustered in the tiny space. To this day I shall never forget the roar of the noise outside when the flap was taken up. The wireless set and some weapons were thrown out first and a gentle nudge and I was out. The parachute opened with a horrific jerk, and my instinct to try and swim stopped as soon as I opened my eyes and looked around.

The plane was nowhere to be seen, the other parachute with the equipment was below me, but as much as I scanned the area I could see no sign of my two comrades. I cast my frightened eyes down and saw the landing spot was white, I was landing in snow or so it seemed. I was not sure whether this would be safer or not, but by landing in snow I knew I had to be in the wrong place. Years later I gathered that the pilot had shouted "abort," but by that time I had gone. Unlike Joe Chilton, to whom I owe a great deal for saving me on the first drop, this navigator was less proficient; I later discovered the name of the navigator who pushed me out in the wrong zone, but I shall take that to the grave with me.

I hit the ground as I had been taught, but I was still convinced that that both my legs were broken as I lay on my back gasping for air and suffering from sheer shock. It was not dark, but the evening was settling in and I soon became aware that I seemed to be looking up at a mountain of all things; the snow was at least two foot deep, but I was in one piece. I could even see the other parachute dangling from a fir tree of some sort. There was no sign of any other parachutes and, as far as I could tell, there seemed no human life in the vicinity that was a relief. I had no idea where I was and it was not until after the war I established where I had landed. It had been in the Abruzzo region in the middle of one their famous national parks.

I had landed in the lower regions, thank goodness, of the park's highest mountain, the Corno Grande,[37] but because of the snow I thought I might be in Switzerland that illustrates the confused state of my mind at that moment.[38] The wireless set was smashed to pieces and was completely useless, so I buried it with the parachutes in a pile of loose snow. I equipped myself with a Sten-gun and slung a good old fashioned Lee-Enfield .303 over my shoulder. I carried as much ammunition as I could manage, and with extreme caution started to make my way down the hill. I had to stop during the night because I was scared of stepping over a ridge in the dark, but I was too wet and cold to sleep anywhere. In the trees the snow felt less deep, but gaining footholds proved treacherous. By the time I decided to rest up I doubt whether I had covered more than half a mile.

Two days later I had seen no sign of human life, but was nervous about bumping into Germans so I kept to the tree lines where possible, and merged amongst rocks. The weather improved, there was no shortage of water to drink, but my rations were soon gone and I was extremely hungry. Eventually I started to see the occasional homes and hunger drove me to one where some smoke was rising from a chimney. I approached with extreme caution, but there were no vehicles nearby and with my Sten-gun at the ready I opened the door and looked in. There was a whole family sitting at the table eating from a bowl of stew, the appetising smell I tasted even as I approached the house. I could see they were harmless and lowered my gun. Their faces were aghast, three women and three children, no men. One of the women pointed to my uniform and I tried to explain I was English; that did the trick. I was soon at the table eating their vegetable soup, no meat, but that was irrelevant. They had no maps and I still had no idea where I was, but they kept telling me the '*tedesco*'[39] were nearby, eventually I realised they were talking about Germans. They were worried that I was alone and self-evidently did not want me in the house if the Germans came by. At least I

---

[37] 2912 metres.

[38] On Corno Grande the snow stays on the ground through May and often into June.

[39] Italian for German.

knew I was in Italy and behind enemy lines; not that I was any good in the war now the wireless was broken and buried.

Two weeks later I had worked my way south, feeding and sleeping wherever possible, and not once encountering the *Tedesco*; I did not bother to shave or keep clean, I just moved as quietly as possible in case I walked into advancing Allied troops. I skirted towns and even villages, and was very grateful for the commando training I had undergone in Scotland; I never thought that would be the case, but it saved my skin and stopped me blundering and starving. I saw people from a distance, no troops, but I kept my distance; we had been taught that not all Italians welcomed our arrival. I was amazed at the beauty of the region, mountainous yet with small farms and impoverished looking homes strung out at the top and bottom of what would appear to be deserted valleys.

I was looking at a village on a hilltop when I saw three men moving slightly ahead of me, and they were armed. They were heading in my direction so I took cover under some foliage and made sure both my sten and rifle were ready. It soon became apparent that they were as cautious as me because it was nearly half an hour when one appeared right in front of my cover. His uniform was in tatters and he had some civilian clothes on but I could tell he was a German, I stepped out right in front of him with my sten aimed directly at him, *hände hoch oder ich schieße*,[40] I did not shoot simply because he reminded me of Father H, a scar down the side of his face and even his eyes almost transfixed me. A voice behind this strange German said 'Don't shoot, he's okay.'

I told him to drop his formidable looking schmeisser[41] which he slung round him in an uncharacteristic German fashion, and waited for the English speaker to emerge; when he did it was my time to feel dumbfounded because I was looking straight into the clumsily shaven face of Horace. However, if I felt dumbfounded, once Horace recognised me, which took several minutes, and me to call him by his first name, he almost collapsed, and was held up by the German and some Italian soldier who appeared from behind me. It was the oddest reunion we could have experienced. He thought I was long dead in France, I had heard he was a POW in Germany, and we were standing in a remote part of Italy completely and totally lost in the weirdest of company; a Waffen SS and an Italian soldier, apparently on friendly speaking terms. I thought, to use a modern expression, I was on another planet, or at any moment I might wake up. This was a coincidence we all found so improbable we almost wondered years later about sharing what had happened as we would not

---

[40] Hands up or I'll shoot.
[41] German sub-machine gun.

be believed. As it transpired we did not want to publish under our own names because of what happened, and after the second coincidence decades later we felt the same.

Two hours later the four of us sat around a small fire in the late evening eating some mutton which the Italian, called Mario, said I should not ask about. He seemed a pleasant enough chap and he had decided the war was over. He was a giant of a man, but with a gentle spirit, but, as I would find out, very brave and able. It was a war he did not want in the first place, he was not going to fight the Germans, and certainly not the Allies, and he did not want to be a partisan. Mario was more concerned about the partisans than anything else, especially the communists who were ruthless. He also explained that he had picked up in the villages, where he could wander with care, that there were fascist groups, SS and Wehrmacht all over the place who were also proving ruthless. I looked at this chap Wolfgang, who was SS, but he did not even blink, he was carefully pulling meat from a bone. We were quite a linguistic group; Mario spoke Italian and English, Wolfgang German and some English, Horace English and some Italian, and me English and rapidly improving German. If there was something we could not understand or get across, it was usually Mario who managed to sort it out for us.

As far as Mario was concerned he was going home to his small hill farm near a place called Santo Stefano di Sessarrio[42] which he felt was his right and should be safe. Horace was going with him and Wolfgang was tagging along. I heard all about how Wolfgang had saved their lives, but I could see he was feeling depressed, but, as the weeks passed by I realised the depression was caused by what he had done and witnessed. He explained to me a few days later that he did not want to fight again, that Hitler was leading his country into what he called Hades, and all he wanted to do was survive the war and go home to his *mutti*, mother. Had he been a Wehrmacht soldier I might not have been so surprised, but I have never read of SS defectors since they were trained to be totally loyal, unquestioning and fanatical. He and Horace had both become deserters. Horace was fed up with the war and told me he was going to survive and live in peace somewhere and somehow. He also confessed to me that because he thought I was dead he had tried to form a relationship with Edna, but she was unwilling. I growled a bit, but he did explain, and Father H had confirmed that everyone thought I was dead. I stopped being grumpy the next day when Horace returned with two rabbits and some stolen wine.

---

[42] A small commune and hill town in the Province of L'Aquila in the Abruzzo region. High up and remote it was almost abandoned and some magnificent medieval buildings lay in ruins with less than 100 inhabitants. Very recently it has been restored.

It was a strange combination of an English officer, an English NCO, a Waffen SS soldier and Italian guard being together, dodging others and living in the wild. We moved slowly, always with extreme caution, sometimes staying in the same place for a day or two. Our main danger was being spotted by potential enemies using binoculars from some high point, and even the occasional aircraft. I used an old blanket we had stolen and stuck small branches and grass over it, and if we were suspicious we ducked under it; Mario made another one. On one occasion we spent an entire afternoon under these blankets, aware that a group of unidentifiable men were looking down the valley we were trying to navigate. I covered my face in dirt, which was not difficult, just in time to raise it, and spot some armed men. They had to be partisans the way they were dressed, walking by less than hundred yards away. I had to shake Wolfgang who had fallen asleep and was snoring like a wild bull. That evening I told the others I had no intention of deserting, but that I would appreciate their company until I could re-join the lines. However, I pointed out that in their cases it would be best if they jettisoned their uniforms. They agreed, and had been trying to do so for some time, but it was not easy. We were not far from Mario's home, but our progress was slow as we had to move with the greatest care.

A day later Wolfgang, who had gone searching for food, was captured by a small group of partisans staying in a shepherd's hut. It came to light as we went looking for him, and found him tied to a fence post while four partisans sat nearby drinking and eating. We had not been seen and decided to approach them quietly, but then for safety reasons we decided I should hang back in case matters did not resolve themselves happily. Mario and Horace strolled towards the group who sprang to their feet. Horace was telling them that the German was their partner, and they were working with another partisan group. I could not hear the details, but there was an angry exchange going on, Horace telling me later that they were a communist group waiting for others, that the SS man would be interrogated and shot and there was no argument, and if they continued to argue the point they would shoot him now.

Mario said something in Italian that made them very angry, and one of them closed the bolt on his rifle, and walked up to Wolfgang with the obvious intention of shooting him. I was just over a hundred yards away and it was an easy shot, but there had been no time to lose because even as my bullet felled him he had pulled the trigger, the bullet going heavenwards. Wolfgang was lucky I had been ready looking through the sights. Not long ago I had nearly killed him, now I had saved him. There was a world war raging all around us, but we as a strange eclectic group had our own personal war to fight. The other three spun around to find

Horace and Mario holding guns at the ready. Uncertain as to how many others were watching from the perimeter, they put their weapons down.

Wolfgang was shaken but in one piece, and thanked me profusely; later in the week he mentioned the same irony that I was the man who had nearly shot him, and then saved him from being shot. The three remaining partisans buried their comrade fearing we would kill them. Horace was quite willing to do so, but Mario protested that they were Italians, just misdirected ones. We took their weapons and let them go, making sure they had no idea that way we were going.

A day later we wondered whether we should have shot them. We came upon a scene in the valley where one man was burying five corpses. Mario spoke to him and we discovered they had been a group loyal to the government partisans whom the communists had shot for not being communists. It struck us all, especially Mario, that not only was there a world war raging its way through Italy, but we were caught up in a complex civil war.[43] I recall spending sometime wondering what had happened to me, I had killed an Italian to save the life of an SS or rather an ex-SS soldier; life was becoming incongruous.

According to Mario we were closing in on his home district, but we could see in the valley several groups of men bearing weapons; we could tell it was not German or Allied troops, they were not organised and they were dressed in varying pieces of clothing, but they were armed. Wolfgang noted that many seemed to be wearing a red scarf so we thought they might be communists. We certainly did not want to meet them. It soon became clear that we were not going to be able to cross the valley, and so Mario led us back the way we had come to find another route. We spent nearly two weeks living in the barn of one of Mario's neighbours. There were no men there, just three women, one of who turned out to be Mario's sister, called Maria. She was certainly not like Mario, petit and stunningly beautiful. It was, we gathered like Mario's family set up, keeping sheep, growing olives and living off the land. It was a really rustic place, lonely, but unbelievably peaceful. The Germans had taken nearly all the sheep, leaving a few, and all the pigs with the exception of an old sow. I found it astonishing that the Germans had paid for the sheep and pigs, but according to Maria they had just taken them without payment from her family's home.

Wolfgang looked blank, but said there were German officers and German officers, some more human than others. Maria said I was told, that the Germans behaved more correctly than the partisans who took what they wanted. She reckoned that some of the partisans were driven

---

[43] There were many partisan groups at variance with one another, and even after the war the killing continued to a massive extent.

by a variety of politics looking to a postwar period, but many had used the situation as an excuse for robbery. Horace had lost none of his public school charm and was soon spending as much time with Maria as he could, pretending to help her and improve his Italian. It looked harmless enough but I knew Horace; however, Mario did not seem to mind so I spent more time lazing in the warming sun with Wolfgang, whom I was beginning to like. Sitting there on a sunny Italian hill surrounded by olive trees eating some form of Italian bread, the war seemed not only far away but did not make sense at that moment.

*(**Editor's Note**: In the notes Wolfgang had sent he mentioned that Harry had the look of a dedicated killer, and when he had pointed the gun at him on their first meeting he was certain he was about to be killed. Later, when Wolfgang thought he was going to be shot he had not expected Harry to save him. He also recalled the times they sat together while Horace was away with Mario and Maria, and noted that "I started to feel a genuine affection for this strange Englishman.*

He was not an officer but Horace, the real officer, treated him as his senior. I found Harry to be a clever and genuine person who I started to like as a friend. I thought from his face he was going to kill me, I never thought he would kill a partisan to save me; I certainly did not deserve it. Spending hours and hours in the peace of the Italian countryside with Harry as company, speaking some English and some German we became close friends, which if you had suggested this could possibly happen a year earlier I would have hotly denied.

The war raged somewhere south of us but we all seemed to have opted out for different reasons, and had bound ourselves together for survival, but in some strange way due to the stress and danger, we became our own family. Mario, and I had deliberately opted out, I think Horace had no intention of fighting anymore, and although Harry talked of getting back to his side he never appeared to be in a hurry."

We were all aware of the constant danger. Initially we were concerned with the communist partisans because Maria had picked up the gossip that the men we set free had naturally told the others, and we were being searched for as a renegade group. I suppose if I am being honest that was an apt description. In addition to the partisans there were German patrols, some Italian fascists still searching for partisans, and we were also a little uncertain how far we could trust the local population, which, like us was haunted by fear and famine. Food was a problem and finding it was a task hampered by having to be careful.

*(**Editor's Note**: For those readers not familiar with the complex nature of the Italian Partisan movement here are some brief notes: After Mussolini's rescue the Badoglio/Royal government had fled south and Italy was fractured; as the Italian historian Claudio Pavone wrote, the 'armed resistance of 1943-1945 was, simultaneously, a national war, a civil war, and a class war.'*

As the war moved north the partisans became more active, and were made up of every nationality, a contemporary diary noting that 'a band of partisans had formed in the neighbourhood, all nationalities, Italians, Poles, Yugoslavs, a few German deserters and some escaped Russian prisoners, they roamed the mountains looting the peasants' dwindling stocks of food, stealing their beasts and raiding towns, no quarter was asked or given.' It is reckoned that by September there were some fifteen-hundred partisans of which about a thousand were in the north and the rest around Rome and Abruzzi regions, and it was to grow to a speculated 250,000.

The partisans established the Committee of National Liberation, the CNL. It was a mixture of Communists, Socialists, a Republican Liberal Party (Partito d'Azione), Christian Democrats and others. There were constant tensions, and they eventually divided into three main groups, the communist Garibaldi Brigades, the Giustizia e Libertà Brigades (associated with the Partito d'Azione) and the Matteotti Brigades (socialists). There were also many other smaller groups, some Catholic based, some Monarchists, (i.e. Di Dio and Mauri) and some Anarchists. Apart from the PdA {Partito d'Azione} all existed before Facism.

It was complex, and at times they fought and betrayed one another; on one occasion some Communist partisans had killed some German soldiers and now were 'on the run;' they were traded to a Fascist group by the Azzurri, a group of Monarchy partisans. 'Frequently the Fascists were more cruel than the Germans.' The Italian Guardia Nazionale Republicana Militia, the so-called Black Brigades, fought a savage war against the partisans. The complexity of the partisan civil war still defies any agreed historical analysis.

*This aspect of Italy's partisan war continues to this day, one of the most controversial books to have been published in Italy at the beginning of the twenty-first century was Giampaolo Pansa's **Il Sangue dei vinti**, which attacked the heroic idea of the Italian resistance movement by describing in detail the murders that they carried out during and after liberation' The book has caused outrage on the left as Pansa is seen as tapping into a new and growing right wing.*

We did not move as a group on food foraging so there were two to back us up if we walked into trouble. This had proved necessary for

Wolfgang when the partisans took him. Mario had led us into a gully where we hoped to set some snares for rabbits, instead we found, deep in the undergrowth an overturned Wehrmacht truck; it had rolled into the gully and was virtually hidden by bushes and brambles. There was one decomposing driver which made us realise the truck had been there for a few months. Shrapnel marks seemed to indicate that it had hit a landmine, and despite the stench of the driver's body we searched the lorry for any food, hoping for tins or good old German sausage. To our surprise the lorry contained some old pictures, hundreds of books and manuscripts in Latin and various bits and pieces. Mario could not read even Italian, but eventually Horace worked out that the contents of the lorry had come from the monastery of Monte Cassino, and some of the contents from Naples which had been stored in the Abbey.

They were, we thought at the time being taken to Germany as part of the looting programme. After the war we were proved wrong, the Germans, under Kesselring, and a German arts team had actually been trying to save historic articles of value and had sent them to the Vatican.[44] Quite why this lorry was in the middle of the Abruzzo mountains and valleys remains a mystery. Postwar some articles had gone missing, the suspicion being that the SS were pleasing Goering who had a reputation for accruing valuable pieces of art. Horace stumbled out of the upturned lorry with a small wooden box which he hoped contained cans of food, he brought it because it rattled with the sound of tin, he found nothing else, so we crawled up to a ledge and sitting together prised the lid open. We were disappointed, there were some carefully wrapped ornaments, icons, crucifixes, and silver articles which I recognised as what Father H used to call 'the elements,' containers on the table beside the altar containing

---

[44] A Lt-Colonel Schlegel, who 'before the war had been an art historian and librarian,' was the true instigator behind saving the considerable treasures at Monte Cassino, and is still honoured there to this day. When Schlegel and a Lt Becker, members of the Herman Goering Division approached the Abbot, Dom Gregorio Diamare, suggesting they save the treasures and library, the monks were suspicious because of Goering's reputation as 'perhaps the most celebrated snapper-up of unconsidered trifles in the Second World War.' Eventually they accepted this once Weizsacker spoke with Kesselring, who, with Senger, authorised they be transported to the Vatican, a safe place. After the war Kesselring implied he was the true saviour of the Cassino treasures; he may well have signed the order, but the initiative started with men like Senger and especially Schlegel. Most of the art treasures of Naples had been placed in the monastery, and it took three weeks to pack; 'considering the precarious position of the German armies north of Naples, it was an extraordinary use of military effort.' It was suspected with some justification that not all the work arrived at the Vatican but an appeal 'was made to Kesselring himself, {and} the recalcitrant Goering Division finally agreed to return part of their holdings.' Some Italian treasures were purloined and some lost forever.

wine and water and other things such as lavabo bowls for the priest to wash his fingers over.

We had just rewrapped it all, with its sense of the holy when we heard some voices. We knew we were being tracked. Behind us on the ledge, where we had pushed the box of holy relics was a small cave, and we all managed to crawl in and find it was more extensive on the inside. As gently as possible I pulled some branches over the entrance to conceal the space and Wolfgang and I both watched out with our guns at the ready. We were right to react this way because the area was suddenly full of partisans, many wearing the red scarves. The lorry did not seem to interest them, they were, I think, looking for us. We stayed there until dark and the last voices had gone; we re-emerged, stiff and cold, and covered the entrance in case we needed it again. We split into pairs and moved out with extreme caution, but it was clear in the fading light that we had the place entirely to ourselves. We returned to our barn four hours later, still hungry and I wished at that moment I could have sausage and mash in my favourite café in Snargate Street, Dover.

Hunger was the least of our problems; Maria had picked up the fact that the Allies had asked the partisans to be as active and disruptive as possible, and it was generally reckoned that the Allies were about to make a break through.[45] Since we had not seen a single German we were unsure why the communist partisans were so busy in this area apart from looking for us. Maria said they were establishing their authority in the district so they could control Italy after the war. I had to confess that I thought she was wrong, but after the war I read that many astute people and historians thought the same. We were trying to survive in an area where any military activity would be pointless; there were no main thoroughfares and no major towns of any significance.

Our hope was that the war would pass us by. We decided after a week that Wolfgang and I would stay hidden at the barn, which belonged to his neighbour inhabited at the time by two women, and that Mario, Horace and Maria would go to Mario's; we decided this on the ground that two can conceal themselves better than five. Three glorious weeks passed with no interruptions and no dangers. I was aware of Allied aircraft above us, but apart from that and the occasional sound of artillery a long way off, we may as well have been on holiday. Wolfgang and I chatted about everything under the sun and caught hares for ourselves. It was during this period that Wolfgang trusted me sufficiently to tell me

---

[45] Given that Horace's notes indicate it was mid-May they had found the lorry this probably refers to Operation Diadem that started on the 11th May 1944 and eventually did lead to the long anticipated breakthrough.

about some of the events in his life, especially his early life, his brother
and what he had witnessed with the treatment of the Jews.

It was not until we met again long after the war and I read his notes
that I began to fathom the depth of his guilt, and his nightmares about the
girl who smiled. I started to get to know Wolfgang as he was coming to
terms with past choices, and the knowledge that his youthful enthusiasm
had enveloped him in a fanatical love for an unbelievably evil regime.
His mother's change of heart and his brother's underlying goodness had
stopped him in his tracks. In war we all did evil things, I had killed men
and would do so again, and I knew that our masters and commanders
were not guiltless, but for all their inexperience and ineptitude against the
professional German military machine, they were not Nazis intent on
eliminating a total ethnic group. After the war, having read some of the
histories, I realised how incompetent many of our acclaimed commanders
were, but they were not evil.

We survived as an oddball collection of four different men because we
had agreed on a tacit, but never expressed alliance, of looking out for
each other in a world intent on killing us for a variety of reasons. In the
middle of a sunny morning I forgot where I was and walked around a
small copse of trees armed only with my rifle, when I was suddenly
confronted by two men with British sten guns raised in my direction. I
could see that they were communist partisans, and from the triumphant
looks on their faces I knew that I was in trouble. I tried to explain I was a
British soldier trying to make my way back to the lines, but they ordered
me to put my rifle down, and bound my hands behind my back. I stood
there wondering what would happen when they made me kneel. When
one stood behind me and the other moved away a safe distance I was
suddenly aware that they were going to execute me.

I was frightened, but I also felt really angry that I had assumed there
was no one around. I was angry that I had lost my sense of caution, and I
felt, and this is strange, that I was letting my family, Father H and Edna
down for dying like this. As we know I did not die, Wolfgang returned
the favour and two single very fast shots and both partisans were dead;
one was immediately lifeless, and the other kicked out for a moment or
two then died. I only relate this because it underlined the way we had all
become so dependent on one another. I had feared that Wolfgang was too
far behind, but his military prowess saved my life. None of us could have
survived without the others. We took a pair of binoculars from one of the
men, they were German, Zeiss if I recall rightly, and they became very
useful as we continued to eke out a living in such hostile territory.

Mario and Horace returned to us a week after this incident with news
that the Germans were moving north in a controlled retreat, not that we
had seen anything but partisans. Mario had been right in telling Horace

when they escaped the POW camp that his area would be safer, telling him it went nowhere and nobody went there. We were sitting together up on a shaded incline, having set some snares discussing the future when we saw movement below us, heading towards the house and barn. Horace looked through the binoculars and said he did not recognise the uniforms; they seemed to be wearing French type helmets but striped pyjamas. I had a look at them and saw they were just as Horace described. They were, we thought French Colonial troops, and as it transpired we were correct. I for one breathed a sigh of relief but not for long. There was some screaming and it must have been loud because we were a fair distance away, and it did not take long to realise that two women were in trouble.

There must be other French Colonials on the way but we felt we had to go down and try and stop what we guessed was happening. We were some distance and we had to move with caution because two of the four were standing outside smoking. Before we reached them one of the women who had given us the barn ran out of the house in a state of undress only to be shot dead. We all stopped with horror. Suddenly others appeared, there was much laughing and we realised short of a suicide attack there was nothing we could do. The major group moved off after half an hour and we crept forward again. Soon we were in the olive trees, less than a hundred yards and the four were standing outside smoking and laughing. There was a shout from up the valley and they picked up their gear and started to move out, except one who went back into the house. Mario crept forward and followed him in while we watched for others.

The remaining woman, I think she was called Lisa had been raped and then brutally killed. The fourth perpetrator was slumped across the doorway, Mario had slit his throat right through to the bone, nearly decapitating him. We all quickly left the site to return as a group to Mario's to ensure Maria was safe. Mario later heard in the local gossip that these strange soldiers were called Goums,[46] and it transpired the Italians were more frightened of them than the Germans. Mario's place that was larger than where Wolfgang and I had been hiding was almost palatial in its rustic character, and had not been visited by any troops, German or French. I was certainly wondering what we were going to do. Horace and I would have to re-join our units when we could, though I detected Horace was uneasy about this prospect. Mario was home and dry, but we were unsure about Wolfgang; his SS serial number[47] was enough to betray him as a member of the SS. We were now, albeit after a short time, good friends, and we had all heard rumours that some SS men

---

[46] Gourmiers, French Colonial Troops from North Africa. Fierce mountain troops, but they were lacking discipline, and infamous for the rape and pillage of local areas. One French general said "they only lived for brigandage and war."

[47] SS had their serial numbers boldly tattooed on their arms.

were often shot on the spot. Even if I pretended he was my prisoner I could not guarantee his safety and although I had saved his life, I was more than conscious that he had kept me alive. His English was good but he was very German, and the wretched tattoo would stop him pretending to be Wehrmacht. We split again, this time Wolfgang and I going to a small shepherd's hut about a mile away, all of us wondering how we were going to cope when the battle line was north of us.

(*Editor's Note*: *Again, amongst Wolfgang's notes was a reference to this moment of time when the four split up for safety reasons. He had written 'that I knew that Harry was concerned for me, perhaps more so than Horace who was, I suspect madly in love with Maria. Mario was a good friend but I was a little unsure about how he viewed this ex-SS monster; it had only been Horace who had stopped him killing me when we first met.*

Harry was concerned that if I fell into the hands of the French colonial troops from Algiers, or the Poles, or even some British troops my chances of survival would be limited. It was certainly no good me trying to find my own side; I was undoubtedly a wanted man there as much as we were amongst the communist partisans. I have to confess the future appeared bleak. I treasured the fact that I had found such a good friend in Harry, albeit English, but I did not want to cause him too many headaches.

I even considered just wandering off and trying to live a solitary life until there was some sense of safety and order, but in Italy, as in Germany, this was going to be unlikely. It was Mario who eventually came up with a solution.)

As it was, Mario appeared one day with news. Rome had fallen to the Allies and had been declared an open city, free from fighting, and that Allied troops had crossed the English Channel and were invading France through the area of Normandy. This news was music to my ears. He had also heard that Allied units were now in the area and we had to arrive at a solution as to how the four of us had come into existence. It could take a good deal of unpleasant and risky explaining, and we had better split up; the communist partisans would be seeking revenge on us, and moving individually might make us more difficult to spot. Mario had made contact with a Father Benito, who, on hearing about Wolfgang was willing to hide and care for him until the anticipated frenzy had calmed down.

We sat and talked, because three of us were facing a conundrum of being seen as deserters, and Mario was not entirely safe given the volatility of Italy at this time. I had no intention of deserting, but if I am honest it was constantly in the back of my mind, and the longer I delayed returning to duty the more trouble I anticipated. Wolfgang had lost his sense of 'selfhood' and did not really want to recover the original version, but was concerned not so much about his physical self, but as to what sort of person he would become if he survived the war. He never expressed it this way, but I felt it at the time, and years later Wolfgang said I was not far off the mark. I was now convinced that Horace had no intention of going back to war, but I knew I could not cope with the ethics of desertion and the disgrace that would ensue. It was never mentioned for years, but I read in a recent serious study of the Italian campaign that in the spring of 1944, where we were at that time, on average ten British soldiers were convicted of desertion each day, and that an estimated 30,000 were 'on the trot' in Italy.

The Americans convicted 21,000 deserters during the war, many of them in the Mediterranean, and there were a considerable number of self-inflicted wounds. I think there were a number of reasons, the fighting was in places bitter and personal, and Italy was a place that looked attractive to a deserter compared to a wintry Russia. Many had lost their nerve, which I have always believed the authorities do not take seriously enough, others, I suspect like Horace, had become disenchanted with war, others like Wolfgang sick of the killing, and some, like me were uncertain as to what was being achieved in Italy. The three of us had survived several theatres of war, we had all been seriously wounded and none of us knew what to do with the future.

However, in war we rarely decide what happens, events take over and we are tossed about pretending we have some control. Wolfgang and I spent a few days together, swore eternal friendship as soldiers do, and he left with a an elderly looking priest called Father Benito who brought him an old black cassock to wear; a wonderful disguise for a Waffen-SS soldier. Men rarely hugged in those days, but as we parted our handshake told us both that over the months of surviving together we had become close friends. It would however be another thirty plus years before we met again. The next two days I spent alone, tidying myself up and preparing to walk west where I hoped to find British or American troops. I heard a bell being rung which caught my attention, and some distant and spasmodic rifle shots. I took the precaution of merging into an olive grove and after a few minutes Mario, breathless and without a weapon appeared looking for me. He explained the partisans were back in force and were around the small valley we were in; he also took me by the shoulder and told me they had killed Horace.

Barely had he told me this dreadful news when right in front of my eyes his head seemed to explode at the same time as I heard the crack of a rifle. I ducked instinctively, feeling Mario's body crashing down on mine, and I can even recall the warmness of his blood on my neck. I also felt a thump in my shoulder and knew I too had been shot. I could barely move because of Mario's weight and the pain, but I was conscious of the fact that I was suddenly in the middle of some serious fighting; there was the sound of machine guns, and even some hand grenades. I passed out.

This part of my story is insignificant, but like a jigsaw I need to put it in place albeit as briefly as possible. It was the communist partisans who killed Mario and shot me, but as they were coming down towards my prostate body they were met by an onslaught of fire from some Polish soldiers who, as far as they were concerned, had just seen a British soldier shot. I was lucky that I had just cleaned up my uniform and was not wearing mufti. My wound was bad and for two days I was carried by some captured German soldiers towards medical facilities, pumped through with morphine I still felt the pain every time there was a bump or a slip. I was sorry Mario and Horace were dead, especially my old friend from boyhood Horace, and I lived with this belief for nearly forty years, saying prayers for him each week.

I was eventually seen by medics and repaired as one of them succinctly put it, but with a gamy left arm that was an excellent blighty wound, I was shipped home eventually from Naples. I was asked by a senior officer what had happened and he soon returned with the news that it was generally believed I had been dropped in the mountains by navigational error, and everyone was surprised I was alive. I need not have worried about being challenged as a deserter; I was viewed more as a heroic survivor. I was able to tell them about Horace's death, and they wanted to know a great deal about the various partisan bands, but apart from cursing the communists there was not much I could tell. When victory was declared in Europe I was knocking on the front door of my old home in Albert Road, Dover, grateful that one of my widowed sisters, Edith had moved in. I never thought in my wildest dreams I would be sleeping in my old bedroom in Dover once again.

CHAPTER SIX

IMMEDIATE POST-WAR YEARS

HORACE, ALIAS MARIO BLANCO 1945-80

I have now read Harry's account of our coincidental encounter and concur with everything he stated. I shall never forget the sense of unreality on first seeing Harry; as he faced Wolfgang on that initial meeting I was convinced he was going to kill him, he looked like a determined killer, and instinctively would have distrusted anyone he suspected of being SS.[1] Harry was unshaven and dirty, and at first I thought he looked like old Harry, then I realised it was actually Harry. A man I genuinely believed to be dead somewhere in France suddenly appeared in the middle of Italy.

If any reader finds this difficult to believe, it was more difficult for me because until Harry spoke, I thought I was hallucinating. It took a few weeks for Harry to come to terms with Wolfgang, and then both Mario and I noted they had become very close friends. On reading Harry's account it was the first time that I knew how Mario had died. When we discovered the remains of his body a week later we assumed he had been killed either by the Germans or the Italian fascist groups[2] hunting partisans; I never knew it was the communists who killed him. We could not find Harry's body, but such was the evident results of the carnage in that valley that once again I assumed Harry must be dead, but with Harry I always hoped he had got away with it. I often wondered about Wolfgang, but years later Father Benito, who never gave anything away, simply said Wolfgang was fine.

It is my turn to explain why dear Mario, to whom I owed so much, told Harry I had been killed. It was a planned subterfuge. Some partisan had taken a shot at me with a small calibre rifle, probably a .22 and hit me in the back of the head. It knocked me senseless, but Mario eventually got some old doctor to me who told me the bullet appeared to be wedged in my skull; he did not want to remove it because between the time of the incident and the doctor being dragged in it was healing. The doctor thought it may have penetrated the skull or lodged in it. He believed that trying to remove it would be more dangerous. It never hurt me, just a small lump and it is still there. It was at this time I proposed my plan.

---

[1] *British Soldiers Book*, 1944,p.13 - British soldiers were instructed that 'the SS are a more carefully selected and better drilled body of thugs.'

[2] Many massacres were done by Italian neo-fascist formations such as the *Brigata Nera*, and partisan elements some wearing German uniforms.

I had fallen in love with Maria. Harry noticed but thought it was a mere passing fascination, because we had often talked about my love of women. This was very different, I genuinely loved Mario's sister and we did not become lovers until Mario had been killed. I do not think Harry would have stopped me deserting, but I felt he wanted me to return with him, which was always paramount in his thinking. My time with Mario and Wolfgang had made me sick and tired of killing, I was not a born soldier like Harry, and I knew that Harry would find it impossible to be dishonest. Even as a boy he was always very straight, and I really did not want Harry to know that I had seduced Edna on one occasion. I asked permission of Mario to marry Maria and he agreed with pleasure, and when I explained to him about Harry probably wanting me to return I devised this plan, that the bullet had killed me. Mario would mislead Harry to this effect just before he left. I had no desire to return to England, I loved Maria, loved Italy, and terrible as it may seem really did not want to track down my parents. For me it was going to be the start of a new life.

It was not easy in the early years; I grew a beard, disguised myself as an Italian illiterate farm worker, and pretended I had fled north from the fighting around Naples. I portrayed myself as being very shy because it was at least another two years before I could pass as an Italian, and then one pretending to have come from Calabria, since the locals seemed to sense strangers by instinct. I was horrified when a British army unit stopped by and wanted to know all that had happened in the area; Maria did all the talking while I pretended to be the local idiot. I nearly lost it when two privates, thinking I did not understand English mentioned the possibility of having Maria alone for a few moments. Despite the evident risk I stayed around all the time to keep her in my sight. They were not so much interested in the Germans who had surrendered and long gone, but the partisan communists who were still a risk.[3]

I can only describe it as a sort of civil war that passed us by, returned and then went again. Even though it was 1946 and the war was finished there were still some unpleasant killings between different resistant groups, some seeking vengeance, and in some places some ex-fascists were simply dragged out strung out from the tree branches. There is nothing sweeter than revenge, but it led to some horrific and unnecessary deaths. The war had brutalised men, and it was from this I had been so happy to escape.[4] When I look back I think it was some ten years before

---

[3] After the war the ruthlessness continued, and it is estimated at a conservative level that some 30,000 may have been killed in this way, though such figures must always be suspect with the lack of records

[4] In postwar retribution ... 'for every 100,000 people in each country, Holland saw only a single suspected collaborator killed in vengeance, while Belgium had more

this imposed brutalization of young men started to fade away, but because of the frictions and factions in Italy it took its time and its toll.

Maria and I continued to work what had once been dear Mario's legacy, his small farm which he always talked about when I was his prisoner. In England we would have probably have called it a small-holding, and we were never rich but we survived. Once the invading troops had gone, the Germans and then the Allies, hunger stopped being such an issue. At least our small valley could feed us. We were well and truly isolated; our nearest town was Santo Stefano di Sessanio and that, at times seemed deserted. A great number of men never returned, and as the postwar years progressed many of the youngsters emigrated to America and England in particular. I always found it ironic that because of poverty many made their way to the very country from which I had volunteered to be a fugitive. It was many years before I was confident enough to go to any place where there might be inquisitive people.

I can truly say I was so much in love with Maria; I did not miss other people's company. Once we were married by Father Benito, who at that time refused to mention Wolfgang, I was entered on civil registers, and was accepted as the odd southerner with pale looks who had moved into Mario's home. I was lucky with my dark hair, but I think most of our neighbours treated me with a deep suspicion for four or five years. Maria taught me a whole new way of life. In the small house there was a massive Dutch oven, and once we acquired the right type of wheat or grain Maria would cook the most marvellous bread in this strange oven. It was domed-shaped with special bricks underneath, clay slabs and tons of ash, which was always warm and which when heated up cooked the most marvellous bread, crusty on the outside and quite solid inside. We used to spread our own olive oil on this instead of butter, and it tasted like nothing I had ever tasted before.

There was a large black cooking pot over the fire, and as the area returned to peace I shot deer and wild boar which Maria cooked, later Maria salted or smoked our excess meat and traded it for wheat. Soon we had chickens, three goats and shot wild rabbits. Later we acquired pigs and by 1950 our own sheep, and tended the olive trees. The olive oil in our area later became much sought after but not in my time; nevertheless it started to give us an income. Maria never ceased to surprise me and taught me so much, from how to butcher meat to curing it and even taught me how to press sheets of pasta over a wooden frame and make my favourite dish of *maccheroni all chitarra*.[5] We lived for the early

---

than three, France more than twenty-two, and Italy somewhere between twenty-six and forty four.'- Lowe, *Savage Continent*, p.150.

[5] Still a favourite Italian dish.

years like Robinson Crusoe alone in our valley, keeping our distance from the world. We had no radio and I rarely saw a newspaper, which never bothered me.

Our nearest neighbour was a chap called Silvio di Franco, a small wiry Italian who lived with his wife on a similar holding to ours in the valley over the ridge. Eventually we became friends when Maria gave birth to our one daughter Lisa, it was Silvio's wife who acted as midwife and soon we trusted one another. It must have been about 1948 I was helping Silvio with a new pigsty when two armed strangers walked towards Silvio's house. As I had hoped to shoot a boar on my way to Silvio's I had my good old Lee Enfield .303 with me which I had concealed, so when we moved towards these men, who happened to be standing very near the place where my rifle was hidden.

It was clear to me that the two strangers were American deserters and their Italian was not that good. As far as they were concerned we were ignorant Italian peasants and so spoke freely in English about their intentions to come back later, grab the food and enjoy Silvio's wife. Silvio was totally oblivious of this situation, and was taken unawares when I took out the .303 and pointed it straight at the head of the one whose weapon was most handy for use. I told him in a very business-like manner that I was undercover, and they had walked into an entrapment situation, where we were looking for Italian fascists. I could tell that they believed me at once; they had not anticipated meeting an English officer disguised as an Italian farm labourer. They looked nervous and glanced around at the area to see if there were more of us. I then told them that I knew they were deserters and their only chance was to head east rapidly and get out of the area as fast as their legs would carry them. Heading east took them away from Maria and towards the coast. They moved away at great speed, but I kept my rifle at the ready as Silvio and his wife stood there with their mouths wide open. I felt confident the two miscreants had believed me, and as soon as they had gone I explained why I had reacted the way I had. Silvio looked at me with his head tilted at an inquisitive angle, and asked how, as an ignorant Calabrian, I could speak such good 'American'.

There was no point in lying and I told the truth; Silvio was somewhat taken aback, but his wife had suspected the truth sometime before. Once I had explained the intention of the two intruders Silvio shook my hand and brought out some precious red wine. Silvio and his wife were the only ones who ever knew I had once been an English officer and they never betrayed me, because they stayed faithful to the promise we became over the years very good friends. Sadly, only a few years ago Silvio had acquired an old tractor and it rolled over and crushed him. His dear wife and daughter were so distraught they left the area, and joined some family in America. Maria stays in touch through airmail.

Throughout the 1940s and 1950s Maria and I lived a companionable life as country hermits, and people who had known me in England would have thought I had gone seriously rustic and native, but this complete change of lifestyle suited me perfectly. I rarely read about or cared about world events. I understood that the world stood on a perpetual precipice of potential disaster in the Cold War, and that Italian politics remained turbulent and unstable with local politicians not behaving much better. Maria would pick up English books for me whenever possible, and I was so grateful when she found a complete set of Dickens. We kept ourselves to ourselves and made it clear to the local communist fraternity, and all the other factions, we were ignorant of politics and wanted to stay that way.

We were desperately poor and noted that many of our neighbours were leaving the neighbourhood because the rest of the world seemed to be growing wealthier while we felt ourselves to be in perpetual decline. America and England and even Germany were becoming points of immigration for the youngsters who saw no future on our hill farms. At times even Santo Stefano di Sessanio seemed as if it had been deserted, but our life continued as it had begun in 1944. I remained fit, and lost my corpulent girth becoming wirier as a result of working for a living on our hillside that was hard labour. Maria worked with me and retained her beauty. We educated Lisa; Maria in everything Italian and I taught her English as if it was something I had taught myself. When we were obliged to send her to school she was not only top of the class but drew attention to herself by the extent of her learning, especially her English. No one would believe that a young girl from a labourer's family on an Abruzzi hill farm could be so well taught. At first I thought it might be my undoing, but by then no one questioned who I was. I do not want to write too much about my family, they deserve privacy above all things, but I am proud to note that Lisa eventually became a surgeon, married another surgeon, and after a spell in America returned to work in one of Rome's great hospitals. Maria and I are still proud of her and often reflect what Mario would have had to say at such an outcome. I now have grandchildren.

During the 1960s Silvio and I had managed to acquire some more olive groves situated between our hillsides, and although we never came to any form of formal or legal agreement we consolidated our assets. We even purchased a small fiat car between us in the mid-1960s and took turns to go out with our families, and the wives did shopping together. We now had money to spend and goods were appearing in the shops.

After Silvio's death I kept his property, as I was able to pay his wife a fair amount of money as compensation.

As you may have gathered from the first part of my story I was by nature lazy, but working in Italy changed me. I worked hard long hours, but I thoroughly enjoyed the simple life. We were left alone and that was the way I enjoyed the arrangement. During the 1970s we started to see tourists investigating the area, mainly British and French and occasional Americans. We were off the beaten track so did not see that many. I think it must have been about 1975 because I recall it was the end of the Vietnam War[6] and America's embarrassment, when three Americans and their wives stopped in our valley to picnic on the side under some of our olive trees. I was walking home when they tried to talk to me in the most appalling Italian so I relieved the situation by speaking English, but like an Italian speaks; a guise I always used. They asked me if I had lived here during the war or whether I had served in North Africa.

I explained that I had always worked here on the farm, which would have been a poor answer, but all they wanted to do was tell me how they had freed Italy from the Germans. They were embarrassingly outrageous about how they had fought their way up the peninsular despite Monty and Mussolini. I politely pointed out that it had been the Poles who had eventually taken Monte Cassino, and although we humble Italians were grateful to the Americans, we, in our valley, only saw British, French, Polish and Indian troops; the only Americans we had seen were two deserters. I knew all Americans were not like this, but as I wandered off with my pony it suddenly dawned on me that I still thought keenly about the other world outside the valley. I had now started reading the history of the war, and this strange engagement with the Americans seemed to light a fire within me to see beyond my horizons.

I know that readers may find it difficult to believe, but it was as late as 1978 when I visited Rome for the first time. We had sufficient funds by the late 1970s to travel abroad, but I was nervous about such an expedition because I did not want to apply for a passport. After the war everything was upside down and all was conflict and total confusion, I was accepted locally, and had the necessary papers, but I did not have the courage to apply for an Italian passport. Having spent years locked away in our valley, which I loved, and especially the peace, Maria and I started to enjoy travelling around Italy. I was sitting in a café in Rome smoking a small cigar and reading *Il Messaggero*[7] when I became aware that I was being watched. I glanced in the direction of the man sitting nearby, just a

---

[6] Probably May as on April 30th Saigon surrendered and the remaining Americans were evacuated.

[7] Popular Italian newspaper based in Rome and founded in 1878.

cursory glance, and hoped Maria would soon return from the hairdressers since this man's scrutiny made me feel distinctly uncomfortable. It was just after Easter 1978, and Rome was packed with tourists and pilgrims, and I thought that I should not be paranoid, it was so many years since the war, my name was Mario Blanco and nobody could know me. I was wrong. I read on but was very conscious the stranger had sat opposite me and was looking me in the face. I stared back and seeing the scarred cheek and ear knew that I was looking straight at Wolfgang. When he called me Horace I felt the disguise of many years fall away as if in that public café I had been stripped naked. I looked back and shook my head as if he had the wrong man, but he stood up and held out his hand, and I could do nothing else but respond, indeed I had become so Italian, I hugged him.

WOLFGANG 1945-1980

I lived with Father Benito for nearly a year. He told me that Mario had been killed, and that he was uncertain about the death of Horace. I now know that he took this line because he had no intention of lying. Benito's integrity was a quality I had never experienced in any other man before, apart from Harry. For Father Benito there was no nationalism; no Germans, British, Americans, Italians, no black or whites, no Jews or gentiles, just people who invariably got it wrong, or, to use his language had strayed from God their Father. He saved a village from being robbed and the women from being raped by some French Colonial troops[8] by threatening them with the wrath of Allah, or excommunication just in case they were Christians; he was well respected and loved within the community. I lived in the top part of his house dressed as a visiting brother of the Benedictine order. Although my Italian was good Benito kept me well away from the few local people because, he said, there was no disguising my German origins.

He told everyone that I had lost the power of speech through trauma, and more by example than word converted me to taking Christianity seriously; taught me to serve at the altar and to study the Christian life. After all I had seen and experienced, Benito's way of life was like a breath of fresh air and yet very human, because at the end of most days Benito would come up to my rooms, and we would smoke and drink red wine of which he appeared to have an endless supply. My only frustration was wanting to make contact with my mother, but Father Benito told me

---

[8] In Naples French Colonial troops committed over a hundred murders and over 3,000 rapes.

that as an ex-SS man I would not be treated well either by the Italians or the Allied troops. We considered burning off my tell-tail SS tattoo number, but that was a trick too easily spotted. Father Benito was only a parish priest, but he had a brother who worked in the Vatican from whom he constantly sought advice about what to do with me. Eventually Benito was able to discover that my mother was still alive, and she in turn was told that I would soon be returning. It was to be another year, but I was given fresh papers both from the state and the Church. I know that after the war the Vatican was sharply criticised for allowing so-called 'ex-Nazis' to escape, but I know that people like Father Benito were not fascists or pro-German, they wanted the restoration of peace without revenge. However, I also know that this is still a highly sensitive area and would, out of respect for the Church which kept me sane and safe, steer clear of this issue. It was a complex matter getting me back home.

The authorities found it easier to ship escapees out of ports to South America, but I needed to travel north through tightly held check points into a massive complexity of fleeing people, refugees, avoiding those seeking people like me; it was abundantly clear that SS personnel were at the top of every list. Today I deeply regret everything, especially being swallowed up in the so-called ideals of the Waffen-SS. I only have to reflect on the girl who smiled and my brother's death to feel this pain to this very day, but I was equally pleased that I was not amongst those who guarded the concentration camps; though I must add that this was only good fortune and not down to me. When I crossed into Germany disguised as a German priest on the Italian side of the border, and an Italian priest the other side, I realised the deep intensity of suspicion that pervaded every aspect of life.

I arrived in Marktsteft in ragged civilian clothes with a third set of forged papers which appeared to show that I was ex-Wehrmacht being released by the Americans. My mother simply wept for joy as I did to see her still alive, and during those early days of being together I started, for the first time, to come to terms with the sheer enormity of the inferno I had been part of. The Nuremberg trials were in process and we heard about the Holocaust in detail. Many claimed that they had no idea what was happening, and while I was, and still am cynical about this ignorance, I have to admit that I was taken aback by the sheer industrial size of the massacres. I can make no excuses for myself or my fellows, we had accepted Hitler and supported him, and now we were faced with the consequences of our involvement. I had every intention of following Father Benito's advice of restoring myself to some sense of normality and humanity, and then devoting myself to trying to help others; this was Benito's considered advice to a person whom he regarded as seriously damaged.

I noticed a tendency amongst some of our neighbours to start viewing themselves as victims of Hitler's war. For some this would be a valid claim, but the vast majority, many of my generation, had swallowed the NSDAP policies whole heartedly, and behaved according to the corrupt directions of the regime, never questioning them. There were those who had been bombed by the British at night and the Americans by day, and yes it was ruthless, but compared to the indubitable evil of the Holocaust and the massacres I had witnessed and participated on the Eastern front, it dawned on me that it was a natural reaction, not that I ever dared express this. As the postwar years evolved, this concept of Germans being victims of the aberration of Hitler in German history, and the remorseless terror bombing of cities really did make many of my acquaintances feel they were the ones who suffered. I would mutter protests, but it was a fight against a growing tide. I think, on reflection, that was how we coped with the past and the sense of shame, that we too were victims. Another excuse which came into vogue almost a month after the war was to blame all the atrocities on the SS and claim the Wehrmacht fought a clean war. Most German males had been involved in fighting, and the SS were very much a minority, and so became the necessary scapegoat for the rest.[9] I knew, as Hugo did and suffered for it, that crimes were committed by Wehrmacht and SS; the Nazi party, the NSDAP, had made the army their own tool as much as their prodigy the SS.

The threat of Stalin's communist Soviet Union played into our hands. The Allies, the Americans in particular were nothing short of being paranoid about Stalin's plans. They needed Germany on side, or at least Western Germany, so the idea that most of us had fought a clean war suited both us and them. If it were accepted that most of us were not involved in the Holocaust and other atrocities, it was easier to become acceptable allies. We seemed to develop a hidden agenda, never mentioning Jews, feeling we were the oppressed and reconstructing the past in such a way that we could either forget it, or move on with some sense of earned justification. None of this sat easily with me in my personal state of mind.

Within six months of returning I went through the process of *Entnazifizierung (*de-nazification*)* which was the eradication of the Nazi Party elements. After the process of meeting a local tribunal I was granted a certificate declaring I was clean. Many quite cynically saw it as a farce and called it *Persilscheine*; this illustrates how insipid the de-nazification tribunals had become. Imagine my astonishment when I saw

---

[9] This feature remained true well into the 1990s when a public photographic exhibition of the war years clearly placed Wehrmacht personnel participating in various atrocities.

at my own tribunal the American observer with a man I knew had been a staunch member of the SS, (and who, I think, may have recognised me) and another who had taught us in the Hitler Youth to see Jews as sub-human. The whole process was to my benefit, but it made me very cynical because I was still seeing night after night the girl who smiled. Professionals would call it a guilt complex, and so it may have been, however, it was more than that to me. It was a very real nightmare that when I awoke caused me to think and reflect spiritually on my future.

The immediate future was keeping food on the table for me and my mother. There was a serious shortage of food made more provocative when we saw how well fed the occupying troops appeared to be. I stopped smoking at this stage, not for health reasons, but I watched men trade family food for tobacco, and women offer their bodies. I am not being judgemental, it made me sad, and although I missed the tobacco I only had to reflect on my mother's hunger to halt the irritating desire. I found work as a labourer repairing roads, but one day an old friend of Hugo's found me a post as a bus driver; even in death Hugo seemed to be looking after me. I earned little more, but it was much easier, and I was not half-dead when I got home.

My mother never recovered from Hugo's death, and I am sure it was this that had a detrimental effect on her health. Certainly the remorse I felt for Hugo and the way I had treated him hung like a millstone around my neck. I looked after my Mum as best I could, but in the bitterly cold and unpleasant winter of 1949 she died. It was a great sadness for me, and for many months after her death I felt depressed that now she would know all about me and the dreadful things I had done. I had developed an inherent belief that death is not the end of everything: it came from a mixture of Father Benito's powerful faith, and the girl whose last smile never left me. I was tempted to forget it all with drink, like some I knew, but avoided this escape route. I even wondered if my mother would speak with the girl who smiled. I know this may sound strange and nonsense to some, but even waiting at bus stops I would be pondering this as passengers were asking what the holdup was all about.

By early 1950 I have to confess I was not coping, I was in a state of depression and wondering what the future held for me. I had avoided the various reunions that were beginning to take place, and did not reply to a direct invitation from the *Stahlhelms*,[10] who from the records also seemed to think I was Wehrmacht. They were, for non-German readers, a vast

---

[10] The *Stahlhelms* were originally a paramilitary organisation that supported Hitler in the early1930s. Franz Seldte, their 1933 leader, was a member of the government cabinet who had joined the Nazi Party and offered the headship to Hitler. It remained a right-wing organisation.

Veteran's Association, very political, and tended to glorify the old days. I had no inclination to attend anything which associated with the past, and if I did it would not take long for any inquisitive member to discover I had been in the Waffen-SS. Ex-SS members, as far as I could tell continued to keep a low profile. Once on a bus journey I recognised an ex-SS man getting on the bus, he looked at me with interest but I looked through him, and he took his seat thinking he was mistaken. I made sure I did not look at him as he alighted at the terminal, and I think my attitude not only worked, but was right. I needed to start a new life and depression was stopping me.

I had attended church once or twice, feeling at home within the Catholic faith because of Father Benito and, rightly or wrongly I had the impression the Catholic priests understood sinners better. My mother had attended mass frequently, and the priest after taking her funeral asked if all was well with me. I was a little sharp stating that as my mother had just died I "couldn't feel better." I apologised at once, but he smiled and said he had, given the situation, asked a stupid question. I had attended mass with my mother and had often made my communion, but there was no way I could make my confession. A few days later I was sitting in the kitchen frying some potatoes when the same Priest, Father Otto knocked on the door. I was reluctant to talk, but such was his evident kindness I started to relax. Before midnight I had told him, without specific details, how guilty and depressed I felt about the past. He was keen for me to make my confession. "In America," he said "I am told people spend hundreds of dollars sitting on a psychiatrist's couch to get rid of their past, but God through his Church will offer you an escape route from your past without charge.

The psychiatrist not only takes your money, but he cannot offer you forgiveness, absolution." I retorted that God would not be forgiving me. "He forgave the soldiers as they nailed him to the tree," he replied. My mind somersaulted to the Balkans, and the women and children I had seen nailed to trees after the partisan attack. I went white, and he saw it. "I am not stating," he continued, "that forgiveness will not come with a few Hail Marys, whoever hears your confession may give you a tougher road to hoe than you want." The conversation did not end there. He explained that a priest will never speak about the contents of a confession to anyone; that many old soldiers were finding it a way through their personal quagmire, and it did not have to be him that heard my confession. "I killed an old Polish priest" I blurted out. He did not even blink merely noting that this incident was probably just the tip of my proverbial iceberg. "Come and see me when you have thought it over." He stood up and slapped me on the back as if I were an old friend, and left me to my thoughts.

Luckily the next day was a day off because I could not sleep that night. When I did doze off I was awoken by the girl who smiled, I dreamed of Hugo, the massacres I had seen and participated in, and my mother. How could I have got it so wrong? Next morning I knew I was in a serious state of utter depression. I even thought of the old SA leader Kurt, who had gone to seed but survived. I saw other men of my own age enjoying life as if life were a funfair. Surely to God I was not the only one who was stricken by guilt; I met no others.

It was a week later that it dawned on me that I had a growing and irrepressible belief that God did exist, did care, and that was the cause of my problem. Father Otto had to be my next starting point, and because of this I listened to him with greater care this time. He was a German version of Father Benito to whom I owe my life, as he had rescued me in Italy; the Church was not national, it covered my world. I had two choices Otto explained; pretend God does not exist and get on with life as most others were doing, or take God seriously and go back to square one, by making my confession to a priest Father Otto knew who had fought in the trenches; he may know where you are coming from.

I had to travel to Munich to meet Father Friedrich and discovered to my horror that his idea of a confession was not a matter of sitting in a blanked off confessional for an hour and then receiving absolution. He gave me a small bedroom at the top of his house, and told me that he would want to speak to me for a good week before the formality of the confessional. I looked blank, felt blank, knew I would lose my driving job, but decided to do what I was told. Father Friedrich seemed a pleasant enough man, but he rarely smiled, and when he looked at me I felt as if his eyes were already penetrating my very soul. We sat in his study, his kitchen, in my bedroom, walked in his small garden, and even in a large Park which used to be called the English Park.[11] He made me start from when I was a child, my parents, my Dad dying from gas, the Hitler Youth, my beating of Hugo, and everything I did in the Waffen-SS. I stressed the girl who smiled and told him how her face never left me, the old Polish priest, the crucifixion of women and children in the Balkans, right down to my betrayal by desertion in Italy, as well as my time with Mario, Harry, Horace and Father Benito.

I spilt everything and, I have to admit, because Father Friedrich just listened and asked questions without any sense of horror, I not only felt relaxed, but felt I could tell the truth. For six days I talked and talked and then Father Friedrich announced that he would hear my confession; I had to start with what I considered the most serious and work my way down.

---

[11] Still called the English Garden; established in 1789 and called the *Englische Garten* because it resembled an English Country Park.

He would then offer an absolution given, as he said, on conditions. I will not make this account any more tedious my going through what I said, you will have worked this out by now. The conditions were tough because, as Father Friedrich said, my sins were many and deeply serious. He would not accept any consideration that I had been influenced from my youth, but did give some reflection on the grounds that I appeared to be truly contrite. I had to give five years of my life to a cause that Father Friedrich would find for me, and only on completion would I be considered absolved. I had to wait two weeks to hear what he had prepared for me but it happened, and I followed his ruling to the letter. I first worked as a gardener and handyman in a Convent running an orphanage which was finding homes for youngsters abandoned or bereft by the war. Then I was promoted to assisting a Catholic Society helping Jewish refugees find their contacts and family members. I must have been the only ex-SS man ever to do this. In my fourth year Father Friedrich had my arm carefully tattooed so my number became part of a design of a complex cross. "This is part of your absolution," he said, "you cannot jettison this number nor your past as if they did not exist, but you can transform it." By the end of the fifth year I was working in another orphanage in Bavaria, close to my origins.

I was given pocket money, shelter and food but never paid. Nor did I need money, I was becoming happier by the day, but I was never entirely content in so far that I was still haunted by memories particularly the girl who smiled; but I was coping. When Father Friedrich wrote one September it was to point out that five years had gone by, and I was released from my penance and was, in God's eyes a free man again. I recall finding that expression of being a *freeman* a little strange, but it started to make sense because I had been deeply imprisoned by my past. It was still there but I was enjoying my task of helping those with present-day problems. I did not want to stop. I had become a serious Christian, made my communion on a regular basis, went to confession for the sins of the month, and when attached to a monastery attended their morning and evening devotions. It was this monastery, which must remain anonymous, where I spent the rest of my life. I was not one of its members; I was what they called a Lay Admission.

They paid me a small salary, I had my own cell and a study, and an office from which my job was to raise funds to continue to help refugees, and later in life those damaged by alcohol, drugs, violence and most especially children in trouble. It was a gratifying but difficult task. The needs of those needing help varied immensely, and the financial demands were not easy. I worked like a beaver, meeting industrialists, charity leaders and various councils trying to convince them to find the necessary cash.

In 1964 I turned fifty and fell in love with a woman called Eva. She had once been a Nun whom I knew in a convent when I had first been the gardener and handyman. I know Eva will not mind me saying this but she was no great beauty, and with my scarred face nor was I; but we simply fell in love in 1964 when our paths crossed at a charity conference. It was her who told me that I was known as the saintly Wolfgang, which almost hurt me because I knew the truth. She also told me that rumours abounded about me making up for my past. I blinked, and she said they are only rumours because no one can fathom why you work so hard for such a pittance. She had renounced orders only in 1963, not through lack of faith, but she felt a prayer life had to be a practical prayer life, and thus she was also helping orphans and others who had lost their way. I did not propose to her, I did not feel good enough, she proposed to me, pointing out, as she looked at the ground that she was a virgin. I smiled, and confessed I was in the same boat, and was five years older than she was. The Religious Order to which I was attached welcomed Eva as another helper, and we moved into our own chalet in the grounds.

We never had children of course, but as I write this Eva is trying to understand a new computer we have purchased and we are still in love. It is a gentle and tender relationship, and I can honestly say we have never had a bad time or a moment of doubt. I have been here long enough to see many of the Brothers move to other places, leave the way of life or die, and apart from two, the others came after my arrival. The nature of my work started to change; Africa was becoming the centre of focus, due to poverty, starvation, and local wars all creating a life of misery for the children. Brothers were now travelling to that continent and needed to take necessary goods and material for schools, sanitary systems and so forth. Eva and I worked hard at raising funds and by 1977 we were just about coping. To my astonishment the Vatican wanted to offer me an award, but I turned it down despite a protest from Father Friedrich, now with just months to live. I told Eva my whole story, and although she disagreed with my turning the award down, she understood. Before Father Friedrich had married us in1964 I had forewarned her about my complex guilt, but it has only been in the last few years, as I write this down, she has felt the full enormity of my youth; she has not wavered in her love or attitude towards me.

It was in 1978 when I went to Rome to attend a meeting of Missions in Africa and Asia, that I took a morning off for a stroll into the city to have coffee. I knew it was Horace at once. For years I believed him to be dead, but his dark hair was always wavy, now it was grey, but the style, very English, was still there, and his facial features remained dominant. I saw him glance at me and immediately perceived that he was concerned, so before he disappeared into the crowd I simply went to the table and addressed him as Horace. At first I thought he was going to run away, but he smiled that gracious smile and threw his arms around me as if we were brothers. I almost felt as if Hugo were back. For two days we talked and exchanged addresses. I could hardly believe that he had become a small Italian landowner with his own olive groves, had married Maria and had a brilliant daughter. It was part of my past I could live with. On our final evening we went out for a meal, Horace, now known as Mario, and Maria where we raised a toast to our long and lovely friendship with Harry.

HARRY

Having read Wolfgang's and Horace's account I still cannot believe that it would be nearly another decade before they discovered I was still alive! I thought Horace dead, Wolfgang I reckoned must have disappeared somewhere in South America, and then in our dotage to rediscover each other by pure chance just seemed incredulous.

I am glad of the distance in time regarding Horace, because had I realised he was still alive I might have hunted him down in anger. My first morning waking up in Albert Road found me going round to see Father Harold and looking for Edna. I had written many times to Edna but not a single reply. Father H treated me like a long lost son, and I had to spend a long time with him telling him my part in the war. I told him everything, good and bad in what was a comfortable Church of England armchair confession. I had written to him and he had replied, but I seldom saw his letters because I was always on the move, and then in the latter months fell completely off any radar. I had mentioned Edna to him in several letters and he had done his best to find her. Her mother and father had moved to somewhere up in Scotland, he had no idea where, and Edna, as far as he knew was nursing in London. Dad and Eddie were dead, Edna disappeared, the joy of home-coming seemed to dissipate very quickly. I tried to track down Horace's parents but they, I gathered, had moved to Wales some five years before. Edith and her son Frank were ensconced in the family flat in Albert Road, and she had lost touch with our other sister whose husband had been killed at sea. War had taken its toll. We never knew what happened to Edith's husband; I always suspected he landed up in prison.

By 1946 I knew that I could not pick up my old place at Cambridge, despite Father H's protestations, but once again he took me under his wing and I spent more time in his Rectory than I did at home. As I put these notes together I am making a promise to myself that I shall try not to wander into boring detail; I really am not writing a self-glorifying autobiography. I am taking this line of thought on two grounds. First it would be very tedious; I had no great mind change like Wolfgang, and no incredible life style change like Horace. Secondly, and perhaps most importantly, if I state any details my anonymity will be impossible to maintain. I became ordained in the Church of England which in both senses is a parochial church and its personnel easily traceable in Crockfords;[12] this old and venerable publication makes all Anglican clergy identifiable. As it is I am concerned that some clever journalist may make various deductions and embarrass my family, or even latch onto the wrong person and cause them problems.

My son, yet to be mentioned, who trained in engineering, has promised me that these notes and those I share with Horace and Wolfgang will not see the light of day until the great Shepherd calls me home; my way of saying I am dead. I know that Horace, and especially Wolfgang feel the same. My son has always shown a great interest in my early life, but has promised me that these sentences will only see the light of day if he thinks I can remain anonymous; even in death.

I read for a Divinity degree in London and many of my companions were like me, fresh from the armed services. We rarely spoke of our experiences and even those too young to have fought respected our position, though we had to get used to the younger ones referring to us as the 'old men.' I did not suffer any nightmares, and apart from hitting the ground in the middle of London when a car backfired, to the amusement of two younger undergraduates, I rarely cast my mind back. I was too busy ensuring that my New Testament Greek and Hebrew would pass the somewhat stringent examiners.

I was in my third year, wandering down Battersea way near St Mary's Church,[13] viewing the damage and the rebuilding when I stopped in my tracks. Over the road was Edna; she had aged, it was some eight or nine years since I had last seen her. I started to shout across the road but held my breath as I saw her reach out and hold the hand of a young boy of about nine or ten years who had just been released from school. Again my joy subsided. In my absence she had married, and as I trailed behind her at a careful distance I told myself that it was hardly her fault. My letters may have been prolific, but I knew from Father H, and home, that very few ever found their destination. I further ruminated that my sorrows were nothing compared to what I had seen in France, Africa and Italy. Despite this I followed her all the way, and watched her disappear into

---

[12] Clerical Directory for the Church of England.
[13] Famous Church standing by the river now opposite what is now called Chelsea Harbour.

one of the many prefabs[14] that were being hastily erected. I returned to the rooms which I shared with a good friend fresh out from the Royal Navy, pondering. Eventually my reflective and despondent mood made him pester me enough for me to tell him what had happened that afternoon. His advice was good and sound, and the very next day I decided to knock on her door, or at least try and find her in the street to avoid any embarrassment with a husband. We had examinations a week ahead, but it was no good me wondering whether I could translate St Mark's Gospel and Corinthians with Edna fresh in my head: set texts had to wait.

I positioned myself near the school gates and waited: I was not disappointed because she was standing there waiting with two others. Her looks had not changed, her hair, unlike mine did not have grey in it as far as I could see, and although her clothes were typical of postwar Britain, she still managed to look, as always, very smart. As I stepped out of the shop porch I had secreted myself in for observation purposes, she looked over the road and saw me coming towards her; to my horror she fell down, obviously fainted. "I thought you were killed at Dunkirk" were her opening words as I helped her up, "why didn't you write?" One of the women looked at me as if I should be shot, but then sensing the urgency of the moment offered to take Simon home so we could chat. There was a cheap café near Battersea Square, (I think they call it Battersea village today!) and we sat and talked until the proprietor made it clear he needed to close.

We moved to a pub opposite and continued. It seems silly to go into immense detail, I told her my story as fast as I could and promised more details later. I knew from Father H that for many months most people thought I was undoubtedly dead, or at least seriously missing. Edna confessed to her 'one night stand' with Horace, but cried as she said "it was you I was making love to." My feelings towards Horace at that point were murderous, and I was almost glad he was dead. I asked who her husband was, and to my astonishment she was not married. We were both in our thirties now, but I felt like a childhood sweetheart again. "Who is Simon?" I asked. I have only made love once in my life, and that was Horace; it's his child." She admitted that Horace had tried to contact her but her remorse was such she never responded, and never tried to tell him she was pregnant with his child. Her parents had been furious and threw her out of their home. I could not believe that any loving parent would

---

[14] *Prefab* was short for prefabricated houses; a major part of a delivery plan to assist the UK's housing shortage. Churchill conceived the idea in 1944 and it was legally outlined in the Housing–Temporary Accommodation–Act 1944.

react like that to their daughter, but I recalled they were very socially upright people who had tried to persuade her to stay clear from a boy who lived in an Albert Road basement.

She had heard nothing of them since. Even the training hospital did not want to know, and after the birth she was asked to have the boy adopted but refused. The paucity of nursing during the war meant she could return so long as she kept silent about her 'bastard' child. She lived with a more understanding Aunt in Clapham who had also lost contact with Edna's parents, but after a stray bomb demolished their house had moved into the prefab. The Aunt was elderly, but looked after Simon while Edna toiled away in the local hospital as a Staff Nurse. It was a long complex story, as shattering as my own war experiences.

In the late 1940s I knew that Bishops did not like their curates to be married, but I was in my mid-thirties and I would talk to Father Harold about the situation. I proposed to her in that pub, somewhere, ironically in Vicarage Crescent, and she burst into tears. It raised a few looks of curiosity from the barman, but I promised her I really wanted to marry her, and made a vow that although the marriage might take a few months it would happen. She had to go because she was doing night-duty. I went back to my rooms a different person. As an addendum to this conversation I heard that her very angry father had tried to confront the army about Horace, but they were understandably more interested in the war. He had also gone to their home in St Margaret's Bay, but heard the parents had fled the area because they were Jewish, and needed to vacate what they thought would be an area soon to be occupied by the Nazis. I am sure that Horace never knew he was Jewish. Later in life I tried to contact them, but like Edna's parents, they simply disappeared. I realised how lucky I had been with my Mum and Dad.

I passed my preliminary examinations but still had six months to go before the finals, nevertheless, all my spare time was now in Battersea which occasionally took some explaining. We did not have the same sense of liberty that modern day undergraduates enjoy, but because of my age and war experience I was given more freedom than the younger ones. I went by train back to Dover and spoke at length about the situation with Father H, whom, as I anticipated was not only deeply sympathetic, but passed no judgement on Horace or Edna. He was a priest of the old school and understood human nature in a way that I wished modern priests would. He bent the old parish rules by having Edna leave a suitcase with him and noted her address as the Rectory in St Alphege Road. He busied himself with all my needs even though he was trying to orchestrate the repairs to the church.[15] He talked to Bishops, the Dean of

---

[15] The building was damaged by a shell fired from the French coast in 1944.

my College, and contacted Keble College his patrons;[16] I found myself not only married, but after my finals moving to a one year course at a theological college prepared to house an Ordinand[17] with a wife and ten year old son.

I have to add that I found Simon delightful; he took to me and the emotions were mutual. He looked so much like Horace with dark wavy hair that I even came to think more kindly about Horace wherever his soul lay. I even smiled that he had Jewish blood in his veins; Christ was Jewish. I never lost touch with Father H and we became regular correspondents and stayed with one another on many occasions. I frequently sought his counsel and when he suddenly died I was bereft. His wife asked me to speak at his funeral which was taken by the then Bishop of Dover, and I only hope I did him justice. He died in 1957, and I have always tried to model my own priesthood on what I perceived his to be. I never achieved his standards, his empathy with people, his sense of compassion, but I tried.

These notes I am writing are not the original. Simon my trusted son, who now knows all about Horace, had been through them with a toothcomb in order to stop anyone tracing me for whatever purpose. This is why I have not mentioned specific universities or theological colleges or parishes; the Church of England is too small and its personnel can be easily tracked by the smallest of hints or clues. I apologise for this, it is not just my past which I want no stranger to explore, but my current position which journalists would thoroughly enjoy, but also to protect Edna, Simon, Horace (even though I still thought him dead at that time) and especially Wolfgang. It is not the vagueness of old age, or personal vanity, but the story we are telling together we thought important in itself, not the actors, we just happened to be there. The final reason is to keep thoroughly hidden our final corporate act in our lives when we all met in the late 1980s, because that was certainly criminal albeit that the motives were humane.

So, to return to the script as they say, Edna, Simon and I found ourselves living as a family first in what was an incredibly spacious prefab, then a small house in the Theological College grounds making the other Ordinands very jealous, then parish life as a Curate. My first title, as they call it, was in the heart of a seriously bombed city where prefabs and council houses were being built almost on a daily basis. I suppose I was witnessing the growth of the modern housing estate.

---

[16] Charlton Church was a Tractarian Church and Keble College used to appoint the clergy.
[17] Person preparing for the priesthood.

My first Vicar was a lovely person but terribly shy, giving the parishioners the feeling he was aloof. They found me very different; 'a man of the people' as some noted, and it was my first lesson, never to let one's popularity go to one's head and never to give the impression that the Vicar was odd. I was also made aware of some women who see the '*Vicar*', and although I was a curate any dog-collar is seen as a '*Vicar*', as the forbidden fruit. It was not a politically correct age, but for the sake of sanity and Edna, I was especially cautious. The local church was very different from High Church Charlton with its incense and sacred vestments, but that did me good to see all sides of the Church of England. I had to visit 'x' number of parishioners each day, knock on doors where we knew nobody, set up a youth club, speak to the Mothers' Union and attend jumble sales and fetes in the summer. It was all such a contrast, but one I welcomed and enjoyed.

Even the most ferocious Church Warden was pleasant and had no intentions of killing me. My second curacy was in the same sort of setting, but my new Vicar had a very serious problem with alcohol. Several times I was obliged to cover for him because of hang-overs, and when I said he was not well I noted some knowing looks from the parishioners and the occasional undertaker. It was here I realised the importance of the occasional offices, what we sometimes called the hatching, matching and dispatching.[18] The Church of England with its parish system was obligated to attend to the needs of all parishioners whether they attended church or not. It was a great opportunity to meet people in their own homes for the happiest and saddest moments of their lives. Funerals were especially important, the doctor and nurses had gone, the relatives and friends kept an embarrassed and discreet distance, and that left the parish priest with the bereaved to bring what comfort one was able.

Many of the bereaved became regular church attenders, if the funeral visits were done well. I instigated in this parish, as Father H did, an *All Souls' Day*[19] celebration centred on the mass (as I called it) and the bereaved would light a votive candle[20] for their loved ones. I used to light one for my parents, Eddie and Horace, which turned out to be a waste of good candle-wax, as later I discovered Horace was alive and well. Some thought All Souls to be heretical and Papist, but the criticisms subsided

---

[18] Baptisms, Weddings and Funerals!

[19] Day of prayer for the dead held on Nov 2nd a day after All Saints' Day (Nov 1st). Sometimes called the Commemoration of All The faithful Departed. It was denied in the Reformation but the Anglo-Catholic wing revived this and it is quite common in many Dioceses today.

[20] Small candle used as a personal act of worship, common in Roman and Anglican Churches.

when it was noted how welcomed it was by so many; it was a physical expression of their spiritual needs. However, I must not turn this into a sermon, but quickly move on the events which bring me back to Wolfgang and Horace.

By the late 1950s Edna was back in nursing and this time rising through the ranks. She returned to nursing because Simon had gone to the local grammar school and had been offered a place in one of the new redbrick Universities[21] to study engineering. He had a local authority grant, but it was still expensive. We both felt very proud of him, even if his style of dress was somewhat outlandish, and his hair too long. At our age it was clear Simon was going to be our only off-spring and watching him grow was a delight. I was quietly pleased that he enjoyed studying more than his biological father Horace! Simon had been gone just a year when my Vicar's drinking problem became significant. He conducted a funeral in a state of total inebriation, thinking it was a marriage service, and then claiming the undertaker was having a joke by bringing a coffin into the church.

I was called to speak to the Bishop, feeling somewhat embarrassed in case he thought I should have brought the problem to him earlier. To cut a long story short my poor old Vicar was moved away, as it was gently phrased, and I found myself as the newly instituted Incumbent.[22] This was unusual, in those days, as one often served two or three curacies before being entrusted with a parish; I think it was my age which helped. Years later I heard the old Vicar died from a liver complaint; fortunately he was not married.

I stayed in that parish for eight years and was then asked to consider a new parish in the same city. This church was noted for its Anglo-Catholic leanings and I felt much more at home. The Rectory and garden was huge; our income was paltry, but at least we lived in some style. We purchased our first car, one of the new minis and felt we were liberated on our days off. I still cycled the parish on the grounds one met more people, and a bike can be easily stopped for a chat, whereas a car is just a royal hand wave.

On my 55th birthday which was in 1970 I was opening a few cards and presents from parishioners when I had a letter which changed the nature of our lives. To use a secular term I was being offered promotion, or as my Diocesan Bishop rightly called it, asked to consider a new direction in my vocation. If you find me particularly vague here please understand that it is easy to narrow the secret of precisely who a person is, if an

---

[21] A term originally used to refer to six civic universities founded in major industrial cities in England. Today tends to refer to universities founded in 19th and 20th centuries, often associated with the new faculty of engineering or civic science.
[22] The Priest in charge, usually a Vicar or Rector.

informed journalist knows the specific position I was heading towards. I have to confess I was a little reluctant. I had not sought this position and I was very happy as a parish priest in a large and happy parish. I had two curates who had become good friends and remain so to this day, and nearly all our real friends were parishioners. Some say being a parish priest is a lonely task; that is nonsense, Edna and I were surrounded by friends and during my time in that parish there was not a single moment of personal pain, regret or any bad taste. Edna and the Bishop persuaded me, and so I moved up the ecclesiastical ladder where I shall stop and move onto 1985 when I turned 70; I was physically scarred from the war but in remarkably good health and Edna likewise. Edna had retired some fifteen years earlier as one of the old fashioned Matrons; I now retired but continued to work on the side-lines.

Although an old fashioned Anglo-Catholic I was deeply interested in the ecumenical movement. I had been fascinated by the Second Vatican Council[23] but learned not to hold my breath. I was asked to attend a conference in southern Germany that was studying some of the arguments of the recently deceased theologian Edmund Schlink. He had written an important dialogue just before he died, and members of many churches had proposed to meet for a discussion.[24] It was mainly for protestant theologians, but Roman Catholic observers were invited, my ability in German, and my growing interest in German theology, found me on Lufthansa flying to Bavaria. It was my first visit to Germany.

I stayed in a small monastery guest house, and finding the conference more and more tedious spent much time in the monastery and its grounds where I was made very welcome. You will guess by now what happened. I was sitting in evening devotions following the psalms in German as carefully as possible when I noted the man opposite, a Lay-Benedictine who looked so much like Father Harold I became obsessed with studying him. He had a scar down his face, and his ear, which had been stitched, had once been in two parts. I apologised to him after the service, explaining he looked like an old friend in England. To my utter astonishment he looked at me closely, and then said "Harry?"

It was quite amusing in its own way, we were now old and both of us had to sit down. I never thought Wolfgang would land up in a Benedictine Monastery, he had not crossed my mind for years, and he was convinced I had been killed. He was looking at a ghost, and I was looking at man who belonged to a part of my life I had long put aside. That evening I joined him and Eva for a meal and a few glasses of wine.

---

[23] Formally opened under the pontificate of Pope John XXIII in Oct 1962 and closed under Pope Paul VI in 1965.
[24] Edmund Schlink's *Ökumenische Dogmatik*, published in 1983, he died in 1984.

We talked about our lives until the early hours, way beyond my normal bedtime. The greatest astonishment was not Wolfgang's total transfiguration, but the knowledge that Horace was very much alive and they were in constant contact with each other. In my old age I can say that I believe in coincidence; it was coincidence that brought Horace and I together as boys, then in France (which given we were in the same regiment was more understandable) and again in Italy that was incredible. It was coincidence that brought Wolfgang to meet Horace in Rome, me Horace in Bavaria, and me to Edna in Battersea. Later both Wolfgang and I shared a common belief that sometimes God is behind such coincidences, but Horace would not hear of it, he put it down as sheer chance. The reader, if there ever is a reader can make up his or her own mind. This brings us all to the final chapter of our shared lives which I absolutely refuse to write, not least because it is tinged with what I believe is a devious if not criminal act, albeit for good purposes.

CHAPTER SEVEN

THE FINAL ACT

As the editor of these notes I have sorted through hundreds of pages, mostly in English but also some of Wolfgang's German. I shall continue to address Mario as Horace as this makes everything less confusing. All three had agreed to write down comments and notes and leave the rest to Simon. I, not Simon eventually wrote the contents, in a style familiar to the reader since it is my style that has put this work together. Simon read them with care making sure that the facts were correct, that anonymity was safe-guarded, and no deep offence was caused.

Horace wanted his daughter kept in the dark, and if she ever reads this and asks questions, it is my promise to neither deny nor agree, but to maintain a deep silence. Horace thought it may occur to her, if she happened to read the manuscript, because her English was extremely good despite spending her childhood as the daughter of a small Italian olive grove farmer; her natural ability in English never made sense to her. She often questioned Mario as to why his English was perfect, and why his old friends sometimes inadvertently called him Horace. This may prove to be the only loophole, but I am hoping my promised silence will preclude this possibility.

The three men, now in their seventies, and all very fit, along with their wives Edna, Eva and Maria, met in Italy for a fortnight together. The most incredibly embarrassing moment was when Horace met Edna; he fell to his knees in true Italian style and begged her forgiveness, which, because she had spent so many happy years with Harry, this was no longer an issue. Horace was the one who had the serious personal issues and revelations to ponder. He discovered he had a biological son, and that Simon knew all what had happened, apart from being aware that Horace was still alive.

The second time they met, Simon joined them for a few days. There was no escaping the fact that Simon looked like Horace, but his nurture was greater than his biology because his personality was a distinct mix of Edna and Harry. Harry could see Horace sometimes studying Simon, but was pleased to note that Simon brushed it all aside as an accident of the past. There was never any question that Harry was Dad, and Horace a friend from the past. It was a breath-taking experience for all involved. Edna immediately took to Maria, and with Eva they became such friends that past-mistakes were not mentioned. It took only a week for the three women to bond and to understand the strange background of their respective husbands. In the cold light of dawn Wolfgang knew he was a war criminal not entirely off the radar, Horace knew he was technically a deserter, like Wolfgang, and although Harry suggested no one would be concerned in the new age, Horace was still unprepared to leave his adopted country Italy, and test potentially dangerous waters, as he perceived it. Although Harry was not a deserter in technical terms only his persuasive talking and character had not raised such doubts. That is when, over some wine, they decided if the manuscript had any title it should be '*Two and a Half Deserters.*'

Horace asked about his parents and received another shock when he was told that they had gone into perpetual hiding because they were Jews. Horace said they had never had anything Jewish in the house, never went near a synagogue and were hardly religious. Wolfgang explained that the Nazis had not been interested in just religious Jews, but any ethnic Jew or half Jew, *Mischlings*. He knew of a senior judge who had no idea he was Jewish at all, who barely survived Hitler's regime; he only survived by the skin of his teeth because his wife was a German Aryan and stood by him. As Wolfgang explained this, he looked at the ground and there was a momentary embarrassment until Harry caused everyone to laugh with a joke about Horace's father, the tooth puller, or local butcher.

They promised each other not to reminisce too much for the sake of their wives, but the women prodded and wanted to know more and more, and all three men relaxed as they spoke about their lives, especially their time in Italy. They raised toasts to Maria's brother Mario, to Aitkins who saved Horace, to Hugo, Wolfgangs' decent brother, and even to Father Harold whose scarred face had resembled Wolfgang, and caused Harry to hesitate when his finger was on the trigger. In some personal notes Horace noted how they had changed; Wolfgang was still tall and thin, but he now had an easy going smile, and although his face looked like the result of several terrible duelling skirmishes, he had developed an aristocratic bearing while emanating a sense of kindliness. Harry remained a big chap, but had put on some weight around the middle and his grey hair was now turning white. Wolfgang remarked to Horace that when Harry, despite his calling, looked pensive he could recall the face of the man who nearly shot him.

The thing about Harry, Wolfgang in particular noted that if he were not smiling his blue eyes were ice-cold. Wolfgang could not help express surprise that Harry was a committed Churchman on the grounds that he thought Harry, as a young soldier to be ruthless. He then admitted that the same could be said of him and more so. Harry was especially interested in the process the Catholic priests had employed through the confessional to stop Wolfgang spiralling down through his various guilt complexes to deep depression. As an Anglo-Catholic Harry had always supported the notion of the confessional, but he was now even more convinced. He knew from conversations with Wolfgang at the end of the war, before Father Benito took him in hand, that Wolfgang was a spiritually and mentally self-inflicted scarred man.

Horace had his leg pulled because apart from his wavy hair he actually looked quite Italian. Horace the public school boy looked as if he always lived in an Italian olive grove; he had become part of his adopted country. He was passionate about Italian soccer and now studied Italian cooking and history. They tried to get Horace to go to Bavaria and to England, but Horace point blank refused. Later Harry tried again to find out what had happened to Horace's parents. The rumour had been that they had set up a dentistry practice in Penarth, but there are no records of such a practice. In the end Horace and Hugo surmised they had deliberately left a false trail for fear that Britain would succumb to a Nazi invasion. Harry decided that as he was once considered dead, so Hugo's parents must have thought Horace dead. Horace simply shook his head. He knew that he had long ago emotionally parted from both his parents, and they from him; he had been an utter disappointment to them both.

Harry spent some time with Wolfgang and in turn Wolfgang also travelled to England to stay with Harry. It was, for the three of them a new friendship, founded in the horror of the war, but now given a new energy. Harry bought some photographic books of Dover for Horace, but nothing would persuade him to leave his farm.

Wolfgang's job, and he had no intention of retiring even though he was now in his late seventies, still consumed him. He was still very fit, though Eva was beginning to find coping with old age a little more difficult. She did not have the robustness of Edna and especially Maria. Wolfgang's mission sent him to Italy many times, and he always contacted Horace. When asked on their annual holiday by Harry why Italy was so important to the Benedictines he was told by Wolfgang that there was a growing problem and it manifested in Italy, or Italy was the front line. He explained that Africa was overflowing with serious problems; especially north east Africa, as well as parts of the Middle East, refugees were trying to flee to Europe, and Italy was the first port of call. Officialdom had failed to dissuade them, and Italian bureaucracy was proving, as so often, incapable.

As Father Benito had once helped the fugitive Wolfgang now the Benedictines were doing their best to help those who slipped through the net, if only providing them with living space and food. It was costing a good deal of money since it was not the sort of activity which would make a popular appeal. They needed money and plenty of it, but could not disclose the purposes. As Wolfgang explained, it was not a nationalistic problem for the Church; they were human beings in desperate need of help.

In 1990 they celebrated Wolfgang's birthday in Horace's now extended farmhouse, and decided, despite their growing years to go for a good walk through the valleys they had once hidden in. They found it exhausting, but Horace had arranged for Maria to bring the car later that evening to pick them up. In the late afternoon Horace took them up a small incline, and Wolfgang and Harry realised it was the very place where once they had hidden themselves from the communist partisans. They even looked for any remains of the over turned lorry they had discovered, but there was nothing there. About to turn away it was Harry who pointed to the ledge in which they had concealed themselves and the box they had hoped contained food. Wolfgang was the oldest, seventy six to be precise, but he climbed up and found the hole now concealed by brambles. Harry and Horace waited for him to emerge and when he did he pushed the box ahead of him. Using his belt he dragged it out and then bit by bit lowered it to his two companions.

His trousers fell down without a belt, and both Harry and Horace were thunderstruck by the scars from the time Wolfgang had been machine gunned in the legs. They felt like naughty schoolboys and looking around as if to check they were not being watched, tried to wrench the lid open. They had done that once before, and Harry recalled it was full of altar silver. The box was still difficult to reopen because its irons bars were rusted together. They stopped trying, and with a combined effort dragged it to the place Maria had promised to meet them.

They had guessed at the time that it was either treasure from Monte Cassino or Naples, or possibly goods looted by the Nazis.[1] In Horace's workshop they managed to cut through the rusted iron and looked inside. Just as Harry remembered there were silver pieces used at the mass, as well as two chalices and a ciborium plus many patens.[2] They were old if not ancient, and they laid them out on the bench for cleaning, as they had tarnished with age. The last item was in a locked box, which once again Horace had to prise open. Wrapped up in special paper they discovered a large oval shaped gold-coloured egg standing on three legs with a small clock inside. Only Wolfgang had any idea what it was, and twenty minutes later, after some rapid research, they realised they were looking at an ancient and probably very valuable Fabergé egg.

They talked and talked for hours about the various possibilities but it was Harry who proved persuasive. All the sacred vessels should find their

---

[1] Naples museum had evacuated some treasures to Monte Cassino, but as the front line drew closer to the Abbey, then known as the Gustav Line, the German command took many of the treasures for safe-keeping to the Vatican. There were also some rogue elements involved in stealing such treasure; most survived, but not all.
[2] Ciborium is a chalice shaped for holding the mass wafers, the Host; a Paten is plate shaped.

way back to the Church, probably via Wolfgang's monastery, but with no connexion to Wolfgang and his known friends Harry and Horace. None of the three of them were personally wealthy, but nor did they need money, so Harry suggested the egg be sold privately and the proceeds given to Wolfgang's charity. It was agreed, but how to do it without attracting attention was the problem.

It was resolved that Simon should be involved, and a month later Wolfgang arrived in England, via the Dover ferry where luggage was seldom searched. In the meantime Harry equipped with photographs had discovered that it was one of many eggs commissioned by Alexander III and was last seen in Moscow. What it was doing in middle Italy could not be understood, and will always remain a mystery. It was probably meant for Goering's infamous collection.[3]

To cut a long story short Simon contacted an American connoisseur who was interested enough to travel to London to view the object. He was informed that it had been stolen probably during the last World War and if he wanted to purchase, it would be on the grounds that its recent origins must remain concealed, and could not be resold until at least 2014 when Wolfgang knew he would be dead. The immediate provenance always had to be concealed. The collector was so self-evidently surprised at his good fortune he agreed instantly, and organised for nearly a million pounds to be transferred to the Monastery's Refugee fund.

Harry was always worried about the illegality of selling stolen goods, even though he had not originally stolen them. Wolfgang was less worried, claiming that some of the Nazi Regime's plunder would now do some good, and Horace roared with laughter.

Eva died a year later and Wolfgang died within two weeks of her death. Harry was the next to die, leaving his notes with Simon, and Maria and Edna died in the same year in 2000. Horace seemed to live for ever, but died in 2009 just short of his 95th birthday; Simon attended his funeral where it was clear that Horace had been a popular and much loved local. When Simon had given me these notes he showed me an article that he had read, and it is recorded here;

'It was like being Indiana Jones and finding the Lost Ark': Scrap metal dealer discovers £20million Fabergé egg at a bric-a-brac stall

- *An unidentified American man bought the golden egg at an antiques sale for $13,000 (£8,000)*
- *After researching the piece further he discovered it was a $33M (£20M) Fabergé egg*

---

[3] Goering was infamous for collecting stolen valuable works of art.

- *Ornamental egg is the third of more than 50 Imperial Easter Eggs designed by Carl Fabergé for the Russian Royal Family*
- *After the Russian Revolution all the eggs were seized by the Bolsheviks and most were sold to the West*
- *Eight of them are missing, of which only three are believed to have survived the revolution – including this one*

By Larisa Brown for the Daily Mail and Joshua Gardner

Published, 19 March 2014

Whether this was the same egg or another we do not know, it looks very much like the one as described in Harry's notes where I saw a photograph, but such a conclusion might be too hasty. Old soldier's loot keeps turning up; at least this piece did some good.

It is a strange story of a Public School boy who became an Italian farmer, of an NCO who chose a life in the Church, and a Waffen-SS soldier who spent his life trying to redeem past deeds. At one time they all had reason to hate one another, but within the twists and turns of war they had saved or rescued one another, and before they died formed a friendship worth recording. Coincidences abound in this account which makes the whole story seem at times incredulous; both Wolfgang and Harry saw it as the hand of God; Horace saw it as just part of life's rich pattern. Simon has agreed that sufficient time has elapsed to seek publication, and he and I feel our three friends are untraceable, and will remain so. "May they rest in peace."

***

Lightning Source UK Ltd.
Milton Keynes UK
UKOW06f1345130715

255100UK00001B/20/P